WOMEN'S ROLES IN SUB-SAHARAN AFRICA

Recent Titles in
Women's Roles through History

WOMEN'S ROLES IN SUB-SAHARAN AFRICA

Toyin Falola and Nana Akua Amponsah

Women's Roles through History

 GREENWOOD

AN IMPRINT OF ABC-CLIO, LLC
Santa Barbara, California • Denver, Colorado • Oxford, England

Copyright 2012 by ABC-CLIO, LLC

Library of Congress Cataloging-in-Publication Data

Falola, Toyin.
  Women's roles in sub-Saharan Africa / Toyin Falola and Nana Akua Amponsah.
    p. cm. — (Women's roles through history)
  Includes bibliographical references and index.
    ISBN 978-0-313-38544-5 (hardcopy : alk. paper) —
ISBN 978-0-313-38545-2 (ebook)   1. Women—Africa, Sub-Saharan.
2. Women—Africa, Sub-Saharan—Social conditions.   3. Women—Africa,
Sub-Saharan—Economic conditions.   4. Sex role—Africa, Sub-Saharan.
I. Amponsah, Nana Akua.   II. Title.   III. Series: Women's roles through history.
  HQ1787.F35   2012
    305.420967—dc23   2011037276

ISBN: 978-0-313-38544-5
EISBN: 978-0-313-38545-2

16   15   14   13   12   1   2   3   4   5

This book is also available on the World Wide Web as an eBook.
Visit www.abc-clio.com for details.

Greenwood
An Imprint of ABC-CLIO, LLC

ABC-CLIO, LLC
130 Cremona Drive, P.O. Box 1911
Santa Barbara, California 93116-1911

This book is printed on acid-free paper ∞

Manufactured in the United States of America

*Nana dedicates this book to her girls, Nana Kua Yaba
Nyameazea and Maame Ama Ekpoti Nyameazea.
Toyin dedicates it to his grandmother, Mama Nihinlola.*

Contents

Series Foreword

Women's history is still being reclaimed. The geographical and chronological scope of the Women's Roles through History series contributes to our understanding of the many facets of women's lives. Indeed, with this series, a content-rich survey of women's lives through history and around the world is available for the first time for high school students to the general public.

The impetus for the series came from the success of Greenwood's 1999 reference *Women's Roles in Ancient Civilizations*, edited by Bella Vivante. Librarians noted the need for new treatments of women's history, and women's roles are an important part of the history curriculum in every era. Thus, this series intensely covers women's roles in Europe and the United States, with volumes by the century or by era, and one volume each is devoted to the major populated areas of the globe—Africa, the Middle East, Asia, and Latin America and the Caribbean.

Each volume provides essay chapters on major topics such as

- Family Life
- Marriage and Childbearing
- Religion
- Public Life
- Lives of Ordinary Women
- Women and the Economy
- Political Status
- Legal Status
- Arts

Country and regional differences are discussed as necessary. Other elements include

- Introduction, providing historical context
- chronology
- glossary
- bibliography
- period illustrations

The volumes, written by historians, offer sound scholarship in an accessible manner. A wealth of disparate material is conveniently synthesized in one source. As well, the insight provided into daily life, which readers find intriguing, further helps to bring knowledge of women's struggles, duties, contributions, pleasures, and more to a wide audience.

Chronology

Some of the early dates are approximations and do not cover every female leader or event.

B.C.E.—Before the Common Era

3100–2686	Nubian Kingdom emerges
3100–2180	Old Kingdom of the Egyptian Empire
2080–1640	Middle Kingdom of the Egyptian Empire
1570–1090	New Kingdom of the Egyptian Empire
800–200	Nubian Kingdom of Kush
332	Emergence of the rule of the regnant queens of the Nubian Kingdom, known as Kandakes/Candaces of Meroë
200	Height of Nok Culture
100	Bantu People introduce the use of iron to the region south of Sudan

C.E.—Common Era

1–700	Aksum Kingdom develops in Ethiopia
800–900	Islam religion is introduced to western Sudan
900	The beginnings of the Sudanese Kingdoms
900	Rise of the Ghana Empire
900–1400s	Great Zimbabwe

1000	Height of Ghana Empire
1000–1500	Formation of states in the Great Lakes Region
1100s	Fall of the Ghana Empire; Yennenga helps found the Mossi Kingdom in Ouagadougou, Burkina Faso
1200s–1450	Rise of the Mali Empire; Hausa City-states
1200s–1600s	Height of the Trans-Saharan Trade
1240s	Reign of Kassi in Mali
1300–1450	Oyo Kingdom is founded
1460–1591	Rise of the Songhay Empire; Reign of Daca in Bunyoro-Kitara, East Africa
1479	Portuguese build the Elmina Castle on the West Coast of Africa
1497	Vasco da Gama sails to East Africa
1518	Europeans starts transporting an increased numbers of enslaved Africans into the Atlantic world
1560–1610	Reign of Aisa Kili Ngirmarmma in the Kanuri Empire of Bornu, Nigeria
1576	Queen Aminatu of Zazzau begins her rule
1630s	Senhora Philippa controls trading post at Rufisque, western Senegal
1630–1655	Reign of Nzinga in Matamba, Kongo (present-day Angola)
1652	Dutch settlement at the Cape of Good Hope in South Africa
1690s	Reign of Queen Fatuma in Zanzibar
1700	The rise of the Asante Kingdom in West Africa
1706	Kimpa Vita (Dona Beatriz) is burned in Evululu, Kongo (Angola)
1720	Awura Pokou leads some people from the Asante to form the Baule people of Cotê d'Ivoire
1730–1769	Reign of Menetewab in Ethiopia
1760–1787	Akech ascends the throne in Paroketu, East Africa; Sierra Leone founded
1780	First "Kaffir War" between the Bantus and the Boers in South Africa
1807	Britain declares the Atlantic Slave Trade illegal

1810–1815	Saartjie (Sara Baartman) is exhibited around Europe
1818–1828	Shaka builds the Zulu Kingdom
1821/22	Liberia is founded for returning enslaved Africans from the United States
1828–1861	Ileni Hagos rules as a regent in the communities of Tigrayan and Eritrea
1840–1893	Civil wars in Yoruba
1842–1878	Reign of Djoumbe Fatima in Mwali in the Comoros Islands
1840s	Reign of Njembot Mboj in the Walo Kingdom in Senegal
1847–1854	Reign of Ndate Yala Mboj in the Walo Kingdom in Senegal
1851	Reign of Mamochisane in the Kololo Kingdom in Zambia
1856–1857	Nongqawuse plays important role in the Xhosa "cattle killing"
1868–1883	Reign of Ranavalona II of the Merina Empire, Madagascar
1863–1898	Nehanda Charwe plays significant role in the first Chimurenga (liberation) war of Zimbabwe and is executed by the British
1870	Asantehemaa Yaa Akyiaa ensures the ascension of her son, Kwaku Duah III, to the Asante throne as Prempeh I
1873	Asantehemaa Afua Kobi argues against war with the British
1881	Binao ascends the throne in Bemihisatra, Sakalava, Madagascar
1884–1885	Africa is partitioned following the Berlin Conference
1885–1905	Madam Yoko rules as a chief in Kpa Mende (Sierra Leone)
1888	Emily Ruete becomes the first African woman to publish an autobiography, *Memoirs of an Arabian Princes from Zanzibar*
1900	Yaa Asantewaa exhorted Asante chiefs to fight British in the "War of the Golden Stool"
1905	Charlotte Maxeke becomes the first black South African to earn bachelor of science degree at Wilberforce University in Ohio
1913	Women's anti-pass demonstrations in the Orange Free State (South Africa)
1916–1930	Reign of Zauditu in Ethiopia

1917	East African Women's League is founded in Kenya
1922	Mary Nyanjiru is killed in an anticolonial demonstration in Nairobi
1925	Chritiana Abiodun Emmanuel founds the Seraphim Society in Ghana
1926	Adelaide Casely Hayford founds the Girls' Vocational and Industrial Training School in Freetown
1928	Siti Binti Saadi becomes the first East African woman to record her voice
1929	Aba Women's Riots in Nigeria; Female circumcision crisis in Kenya
1931	Bantu Women's League is founded in South Africa
1936	Mary Lokko becomes the head of the West African Youth League
1943	Mantse Bo becomes regent in Lesotho
1944	Nigerian Women's Party is founded
1945	Pare Women's protest in Tanzania; Constance Cummings-John becomes the first African woman to be elected to a colonial administration, Freetown Municipal Council, Sierra Leone
1946	Muslim Women's Association is founded in Kenya; Uganda Council of Women is founded
1948	The beginning of apartheid legislation in South Africa
1949	Women march on the Grand Bassam prison in Cotê d'Ivoire
1950	Annie Jiagge becomes the first female lawyer to be admitted to the bar in Ghana
1951	Sierra Leone Women's Movement is founded
1951–1954	Mabel Dove becomes the first woman to be appointed the editor of the *Accra Evening News* and the first women to be elected to the Ghanaian parliament
1952	Rebecca Njeri is imprisoned by the British colonial government in Kenya; National Council of Women of Tanganyika is founded; Union of Sudanese Women is founded
1952–1956	Emergence of the Mau Mau Revolts in Kenya

1953	Angie Brooks-Randolph becomes the first female minister in Liberia; Alice Lenshina founds the Lumpa Church in Zambia; Federation of National Federation of Gold Coast Women is founded
1955	Women's Defense of the Constitution League is founded in South Africa
1956	Women's anti-pass demonstration in Johannesburg, South Africa; Ghana market Women's Association is founded; Pumla Kisosonkole becomes the first woman elected to the Legislative Council of the Protectorate Government in Sierra Leone; Flora Nwapa becomes the first African women to publish a novel, *Efuru,* in English; Grace Ogot publishes *The Promised Land*; Women's Cameroon National Union is founded
1957	Ghana becomes the first colony in Africa to gain its independence from Britain
1958–1959	Cameroonian women rebels against colonial rule
1960s	Congo gains its independence from Belgium; several African nations become independent
1963	Organization of the African Unity is formed
1967	Union of Burundi Women is founded
1967–70	The Nigerian Civil War
1968	Folyegbe Akintunde-Ighodalo becomes the first Nigerian woman to be appointed as permanent secretary; Annie Jiagge becomes the first African woman to be elected to chair the United Nations Commission on the Status of Women
1969	United Nations General Assembly passes the Convention on the Elimination of All Forms of Discrimination Against Women (CEDAW); Colonel Gadafi captures power in Libya
1970	African Women's Association is founded in Ethiopia; Idi Amin seizes power in Uganda
1971	Margaret Kenyatta is elected mayor of Nairobi, Kenya; Wangari Maathai becomes the first female in East Africa to earn a PhD in veterinary anatomy from the University of Nairobi; Union of Women of the Democratic Party of Gabon is founded

1972	Jeanne Martin-Cissé becomes the first African woman to be elected president of the United Nations Security Council
1973	Black Women's Federation is founded in South Africa
1974	Federation des Femmes Voltaiques is founded in Burkina Faso; Emperor Hailie Selassie of Ethiopia is overthrown
1975–1976	Elisabeth Domitien becomes the first and only woman to serve as the interim president in the Central Africa Republic
1976	Cheikh Anta Diop (Senegal) publishes his influential book, *The African Origins of Civilization*
1975–1985	United Nations Decade for Women
1980	Robert Mugabe becomes the prime minister of Zimbabwe
1984	Carmen Pereira serves as the interim president of Guinea-Bissau for three days
1986	Women's Research and Documentation Center is founded in Nigeria
1988	Society for Women and AIDS in Africa is founded
1991	Nadine Gordimer is awarded the Nobel Prize for Literature
1992	Unity Dow wins her citizenship case in Botswana's High Court
1993	Silvie Kinigi becomes prime minister of Burundi; Jean Marie Ruth-Rolland becomes the first woman to run in an African presidential race in the Central African Republic; Kampala Action Plan on Women and Peace calls for gender parity in peace negotiations; The Rwanda genocide
1994	Apartheid ends in South Africa; Nelson Mandela becomes president of South Africa; Antoineta Rosa Gomes runs for president of Guinea-Bissau and loses; Agathe Uwilingiyimana, prime minister of Rwanda, is killed in the genocide
1995	Fourth World Conference on Women is held in Beijing
1996–1997	Ruth Sando Perry becomes the interim head of the Liberian Council of State
1997	Isatou Njie-Saidy becomes vice president of the Gambia; African Women's Forum is founded in Accra; Charity Ngilu becomes the first woman candidate for the presidential race in Kenya; Zaire is renamed Democratic Republic of Congo

1998   African Women's Committee for Peace and Development is founded; African Women's Anti-War Coalition is founded; Unity Dow becomes the first woman named to Botswana's High Court; Speciosa Wandira Kazibwe becomes vice president of Uganda

2001–2002   Mame Madior Boye becomes the first and only woman to serve as a prime minister of Senegal

2002   Maria das Sousa becomes the prime minister of São Tomé and Príncipe

2003   African Union passes Protocol on the Rights of African Women

2004   Gertrude Mongella is elected president of the parliament of the African Union; Wangari Maathai is awarded the Nobel Peace Prize

2004–2010   Luisa Diogo serves as the prime minister of Mozambique

2006   Ellen Johnson Sirleaf is elected president of Liberia and the first female to be elected president in Africa

2009   Rose Francine Rogombé serves as the interim president of Gabon

2010   African Union Declares 2010–2020 as the African Women's Decade to implement commitments to gender equality and women's empowerment

Introduction:
African Women in History

African women's history has a changing effect on how we perceive and understand the African past. Only a few decades ago, the field was too small to have any significant impact on mainstream African history to such an extent that researchers who explored African women's history received very little support from their colleagues and their institutions. Historians interested in women's issues persisted in their quest for the historical representation of African women and have produced important scholarly works, as well as stimulating enthusiasm in the field, which is apparent in the vast array of conferences, fellowships, journals, and book series devoted to African women's issues. Yet, in spite of the increase in the academic interest and the successes of historians, challenges remain, and African women's history continues to be secondary in mainstream African historiography where the project of historical writing has been substantially influenced by ideological interest that privilege male representations.

African women's history, particularly during the precolonial period, is comparatively unknown, and often times generalized, due to the lack of written sources. The little that is available through the writings of Arab and European travelers from the 10th and 15th centuries, respectfully, tended to portray women only as princesses, queen mothers, concubines, and slaves. As some researchers have noted, the stereotyping of women into the above categories may have resulted from the fact that "these [early] travelers mainly interacted with the ruling classes and scarcely looked at women except to use them,"[1] or when they observed women being used by the ruling class. From these early writings, African women became stereotyped as the very picture of African "barbarity" with their high sexual drive and high fertility and therefore ignored as historical actors.

With the formal onslaught of colonial rule on the continent, coupled with the colonizers' gender-based biases, African women's roles in history became even more marginalized and submerged under male representations that occasionally mentioned women in passing. The little information available on African women from the colonial period presented them as victims of Africa's social and cultural institutions and a group with no voice or agency. These portrayals extended from the colonial period to the postcolonial period; and until recently, many researchers used the idea of victimhood as their model in writing about African women. Relying on oral sources and on other unconventional materials, some researchers have been able, to some degree, "restore" women into history, and we now have histories of important queen mothers and other revolutionary women leaders from the 16th through the 20th centuries. From oral accounts and archaeological findings, we know that from the very earliest periods of organized societies on the African continent, women were as important in their roles as men were. They played significant roles in the economic organization of communities other than their agricultural contributions. For instance, women were reported to have worked in the gold mines of the Nubian Kingdom and were involved in areas such as craft production in the Kushite society.[2]

Intriguing narratives exist about female rulers and women who wielded substantial political power and influence in their societies. Among the Kush, there were female rulers most commonly and famously referred to as "Candace." Kush women leaders sometimes ruled independently or jointly with their sons. An example is that of Queen Amanitore who ruled jointly with King Notakamani during the first century C.E. There are reports of women serving in prestigious positions as deities and as priestesses of deities and even as soldiers. In the Aksum Kingdom of present-day Ethiopia, researchers have found evidence to suggest that women held high political positions in the society. While the available information is scanty and a bit inconclusive about women's roles and positions in this society, what we have now indicates of an important Aksum queen named Makeda, who is identified as Queen Sheba in the Aksumite myth of origin. Makeda reportedly decreed that only men had the right to rule.

The reason Makeda made this injunction against women is not known. However, as some researchers have pointed out, the fact that a woman had the power to make this declaration, together with the fact that there exists in Ethiopian religious language the title of "negeshta nagashtat" (queen of queens), which is also a term for God, suggests a religion that revolved around female agricultural cults. Furthermore, it suggests that at some point in time, Aksum women wielded significant political powers, which gradually eroded. Aksum women may have also participated in military campaigns. This was a tradition that survived for a long period, and it was practiced in later Ethiopian kingdoms.[3] The Kush and Aksum examples are not exceptional. Examples of women exercising significant political power and in leadership roles have been reported among different societies in Africa, south of the Sahara. In West Africa, there is the story of the legendary warrior queen, Iyennegi, among the Mossi people of present-day Burkina Faso.

According to the legend, Iyennegi, during the time of her reign, around the later part of the first millennium C.E., defended Mossi's territory and its people by leading a strong army against any invading force. Her people not only celebrate her, but her burial has become a site of historical and collective memory for the Mossi and a source of intrigue for visitors. Another account is given of a royal woman, Njinga of Ndongo, who in the mid-1660s reportedly poisoned her half-brother and took control of state power. Njinga managed to consolidate her power in the area of present-day Angola; however, the Portuguese invasion into this region during this time frame forced her to move her people to Matamba. During her rule in Matamba, Njinga not only fought the Portuguese colonizers to cement the independence of her people, but she managed to hold on to power and transfer power to her sister upon her death in 1663.[4] In contemporary times, the Angolan people still remember and celebrate Njinga as an able ruler who led her people in the struggle against Portuguese colonization.

In other places in West Africa, a number of women have been documented as female political leaders. Among the Mende of Sierra Leone, female rulers were a common occurrence dating as far back as the 16th century. Others include Queen Amina of Zazzau, a female ruler of a Hausa state, who successfully led her people in conquest and expanded the economy of Zazzau; and the examples of Ogiso Emose and Ogiso Orhorho, who ruled among the Edo people of Benin (Nigeria). These examples indicate that even though these women leaders were a select few, their positions and roles in their societies were vital for the very survival of their peoples and a reflection of how some societies held women in high esteem—some to the point of the sacred. Here, their reproductive roles and the belief in women's nurturing powers and closeness to nature played a part in some societies, establishing rituals and festivals to celebrate women in both the metaphysical and physical worlds.

Throughout Africa, bits and pieces of archaeological evidence suggest women not only played important roles in their societies, but they also worked closely with men and collaborated with them to ensure success in various activities. From the early beginnings of both state and stateless societies, women were important producers of food; but more importantly, these societies depended on women to form alliances and to seek allegiances through marital ties. As our discussions will show, women were fundamental in building and stabilizing states by marrying into different family lines and by bringing different families together to create new social systems, to collaborate, or to expand an existing system. In other words, women through marriage sealed or strengthened alliances for their societies; secured the allegiances of other groups, which was essential for trade and political security; and created a network of families that sometimes bonded together to form a larger social unit.

In fact, many researchers have attested to the fact that in Africa, south of the Sahara, many kingdoms, including the Buganda and Dahomey Kingdoms, secured their initial existence and expanded through the creation of marital ties with other important groups. It therefore makes sense that women during these early periods of state formation would be considered indispensable to any particular group. It has been argued that early Bantu speakers may have practiced a bilateral form of descent (emphasizes both sides of the family), but it was also likely that many early Iron Age societies in the Great Lakes region practiced the matrilineal kinship system. The centrality of women in kingship systems is emphasized in a Kikuyu myth, which suggests that men plotted to seize power from women by impregnating them all at once. This myth may be a symbolic indication that at some point in time, women were in control through the system of matrilineal descent before men took over and shifted the Kikuyu kinship system to that of patrilineal.[5] In addition, the myth reinforces the fact that women were not only the bedrock of these early societies, but their crucial roles as a stabilizing force caused many institutions to be created around them.

Yet some researchers have argued that this very quality of creating stability through marriage subjected African women to the control of men, and this has been a major issue in African women's subjugation in contemporary times. In other words, the need to ensure the collective good made many societies deny women the ability to have a choice in deciding with whom and when they wanted to marry. While each side of the debate holds steadfast in its views, however, what is not in doubt is that without women entering into marital arrangements that brought groups and societies together, many of the major kingdoms that emerged on the African continent probably would have disintegrated before they even started. As it has been pointed out, women who served as concubines for kings and other influential men in these early societies played crucial roles not commonly conceived of as one of the performative roles of concubines. That is, the position of these women appeared on the surface to that of defenselessness and susceptibility to abuse in the sense that they lacked the protection that family relations provided, and they had little or no legal security. However, concubines were not as vulnerable as they appeared.[6]

There were a number of opportunities for these women to be absorbed into important families and hence into state power, and they sometimes became the very essence of state political control. For example, in one study involving the Emirates of northern Nigeria, it was pointed out that during the rule of the Askias (kings) of the Songhai Empire from about the late 15th century to the late 16th century, slaves were generally allowed to marry among themselves. However, some of the female slaves became the concubines of their masters. While the women themselves may or may not have necessarily become part of the royal family, their children were considered full members of the royal family. The study suggests that with the exception of the first Askia who was not the child of a concubine, all the other Askias were the children of concubines.[7] Concubinage, which was otherwise considered a less desirable position for women looking for family stability and security, became more or less a privileged position for the mothers of the Askias. In some societies, as among the Akan of southern Ghana, queen mothers formed an important component of the political setup through their roles in helping to both enthrone and dethrone male rulers through their judicatory responsibilities. Some had control over vast state resources such as land and taxes, and their ability to distribute resources to others and to adjudicate on their behalf entrenched their powers in state affairs. Not only did the position of queen mothers provide women a mouthpiece through which to seek redress for social injustices, but by extension, the roles of queen mothers also lifted the status of women in broad terms.

Women's roles in these early societies were not restricted to cementing political alliances or even that of producing heirs. They participated in almost everything, especially those that involved the basic essentials of everyday living such as farming, trading, child rearing, social entertainment, artistic production and distribution, religion, cultural transmission, socialization, and many more. In societies that had gendered division of work, such as in the Nok society, which was located in the region of central Nigeria, women and men were responsible for particular roles, perhaps assigned because of their natural tendencies and physical strength. Women took responsibility for childcare, food production, food preparation, and other domestic responsibilities. Men were responsible for clearing the land and other strenuous activities. Collaborative efforts between women and men appear to have been a widespread feature in many societies than has been suggested.

For instance, once the early societies had succeeded in achieving some level of stability through intermarriages, they began to shift their energies toward expanding through military conquest. While academic research has generally been inclined to focus on male aspects of state militarization, women were not necessarily left behind or considered incapable of participating in military campaigns. There are numerous examples of African women playing significant roles in the military expeditions of their societies, particularly in southern and eastern Africa. In many cases, they played supportive roles, but there were instances where women actively took part in the actual combat. For example, the women warriors whose fierceness caused Europeans to refer to them as "Amazons" were elite female troops in the Dahomey Kingdom. These women warriors were a part of the royal family, possibly the king's wives whose domestic roles were modified into military roles. With time and external influences, women's military roles in the Dahomey Kingdom diminished and in many parts of Africa, south of the Sahara.

The one fundamental fact that underlines narratives in African women's history, particularly during the precolonial era, is that it overwhelmingly tells the story of prominent women. Many researchers, in their quest to write women back into mainstream African historiography, focused almost exclusively on the formal aspects of women's positions and roles and on queen mothers and female political leaders, paying little attention to the numerous informal roles that the majority of "ordinary" African women have played, and continue to play, in their societies. Indeed, what we know about women's roles in general has been mostly generic. Therefore, in situating African women's roles in mainstream African history, we are mindful of the above issues. We therefore incorporate into our discussions the complexities of women's roles in various settings as well as the different factors that have affected women's experiences. Our goal is to provide an overview of the various roles and positions of African women, factoring into our discussions the immense diversity of Africa's social and cultural arrangements and the historical forces, from European colonialism to industrialization, which have shaped the situation and experiences of African women. Indeed, the subject of African women's roles in history covers an extensive number of societies on the African continent with distinctive geographical, social, cultural, religious, and historical settings. Even in our defined focus in Africa, south of the Sahara, we encounter a vast array of social, cultural, economic, political, and historical settings unique to each society in this region.

This region is also renowned not only for the reproductive and productive capabilities of its women, but also for its diversity in its modes of marriage, family, and kinship systems. Although many researchers have noted the prevalence of separate spheres of influence for both women and men, the region is equally known for the different avenues through which women and men interact and cooperate to ensure the survival of their societies. Furthermore, the historical experiences of the Atlantic Slave Trade, coupled with European colonialism and imperialism, transformed the social, economic, and political institutions of this region and left an indelible mark on women's access and roles in education, economic, religious, legal, and political matters. Although it is not possible to represent every society and historical event concerning women in this region, our focus on regional similarities has enabled us to provide broad perspectives on women's domestic and public responsibilities from the precolonial era to the contemporary period. We synthesize the various roles African women have played and continue to play in their societies, the opportunities and resources available to them, their vulnerability to changes, and the mechanisms they have adopted to meet the challenges they face in the performance of their roles.

This volume brings together seven chapters that highlight women's roles in courtship and marriage, family, religion, work, arts and literature, government, and education. Key themes such as separate but linked spheres of influence for women and men, the individual versus the collective/group, division of labor, effects of colonialism, effects of gender notions, and women's agency recur throughout our discussions. Chapter 1 provides an overview of the institution of courtship and marriage and women's roles in it. Here, both women and men have played major roles in social, economic, and political negotiations, which tended to privilege the collective group rather than the individual. The discussion starts with a general conception of what marriage meant in the past to Africans and what it means now with emphasis on the varying degrees of courtship and love elements in marital arrangements.

For many African women, romantic love and consent was a serious consideration for marriage, and it was a good reason to accept or reject a marriage contract, even in instances where marriage was arranged. In many cases, the roles women played in marriage initiation rites ensured the continual inclusion of love and consent in marital arrangements. The effects of marriage on residential arrangements receive attention as well as how contemporary market economic structures have shaped African marriage institutions and social relationships. Social relationships are a recognizable part of every society, and in pursuit of social relationships, societies utilize a variety of descent systems: a factor related directly to women's reproductive roles and social notions about marriage and kinship. It is from this perspective that chapter 2 extends the discussion on women's roles in marriage into the realm of family and kinship structures. The chapter explores descent systems reckoned through both female and male lines and a few others that place emphasis on neither one.

With the aim of stressing areas where women played the most roles, matrilineal descent systems receive a lot more attention in our discussion, for unlike in patrilineal descent systems where inheritance and the exercise of power is based on the male line, a matrilineal society is based on an ideology that reverence women's positions and power. It is, however, important to point out that the idea of a social organization based on matrilineality sometimes gives a false sense that women's power extends into the realm of every aspect of the social system. To the contrary, in many instances, the type of social institution generally determines the roles and levels of women's influence. For example, while women may have substantial roles and power in the domestic sphere, their roles and authority in the public sphere may be limited. Indeed, it is common to find the power women exercise to be less than the power of men in shared responsibilities.

The equity of power between women and men is most noticeable in religious activities. Chapter 3 explores the nuances of power by looking at women's roles in traditional African religions and in Christianity and Islam. We also analyze the gendered and paradoxical nature of religion and its implications for women's roles, particularly as it relates to social, cultural, economic, and political institutions in Africa. It is clear that gender constructions and societal outlook toward women affects women's participation in religious activities, but more importantly, boundaries between women and men in religious activities appear to be flexible enough to allow the reversal of roles and sometimes for both sexes to complement each other's roles. In chapter 4, we examine women's work, conceiving of "work" in the sense of the roles women have played, and continue to play, in the domestic sphere, in agricultural production and distribution, in market economies, and in contemporary job careers, as well as their access to economic resources and opportunities.

We observe that the predominant role of women in agriculture and in domestic activities was, and continues to be, vital for the very survival of people and the type of social institutions that developed on the continent in chapter 4. Since the precolonial period, agriculture has been vital in state and stateless societies, in matrilineal and patrilineal societies, in the control of power, and in marital arrangements. Women's work in agricultural production and distribution is also a functional way of analyzing women's history because agriculture has been one of the areas where both internal and external changes have been most effective and most recorded over the centuries. While the majority of African women participated in some form of agricultural activity, many women, particularly West African women, were involved in trading activities; and in some cases, their control of the marketplace extended into control of trading posts, and control of political processes going back as far as the 15th century.

Colonialism changed women's economic autonomy and power with their introduction of cash cropping, which not only benefited men, but also excluded women from the global market. We show that in all the various areas where women worked, they formed associations and cooperated with one another to protect their interests. Women also entered into new careers to help provide for themselves and their families. In chapter 5, we focus on women's roles in arts and literature. Throughout Africa's history, women have used praise songs, poems, and prose to convey much about the social and cultural values, experiences, and the general histories of their peoples. Whether they worked in the domestic or public space, women controlled their artistic outputs. This chapter discusses the highly gendered nature of African arts and literature, as well as the ways in which women have used to navigate their ways in these arenas. As with all the transformations African societies have experienced since the introduction of the modern market economy, women's artworks have undergone substantial changes due to changes in market demands and opportunities. And as chapter 4 shows, women have responded by instituting strategies that keep others out of their crafts and marketing avenues.

Chapter 6 is concerned with women's roles in government and as political actors. We return to the themes of gender, power, collaboration, and resistance that have been touched on throughout the course of our discussions in the previous chapters. African women's roles have been, and continue to be, central in African societies; yet women's access to political authority, for the most part, has generally been indirect except in areas considered primarily as feminine. In precolonial societies, in particular, women advanced to leadership positions through their sons and sometimes served as checks and balances on male leadership. Colonialism eroded whatever political power women exercised through the systematic transfer of political roles to African men. The result of the political discrimination by colonial rulers encouraged many women into becoming politically active in resistance and nationalist movements, including sometimes fighting in armed combats.

In the last chapter on education, we discuss African women's roles in education in the precolonial, colonial, and postcolonial eras. While the various aspects of nonformal education that women received and gave during the precolonial era receive extended coverage in this chapter, we also give ample time to women's lack of education in the colonial and postcolonial eras, the gendered dimensions of women's education, and the negative effects of gendering education. As the chapter shows, the history of women and education in Africa has received enormous attention from scholars, government agencies, activist organizations, and nongovernmental bodies in terms of trying to understand the effects of women's lack of access to educational opportunities and how education could be made more equitable between women and men. It has been shown that both colonial and postcolonial governments, for the most part, neglected women's education. When education was given, it was either substandard or geared toward women's traditional roles in the domestic sphere.

Postcolonial governments continued the colonial trend of educating its female population in domestic-oriented subjects, resulting in a situation where the vast majority of African women with higher education have overconcentrated in the domestic sciences. This has made women less competitive in the labor market, reduced their opportunity for advancement in their careers, restricted their access to certain public roles, limited their contributions to the socioeconomic development of their societies, and increased their poverty levels as compared to those of men. Admittedly, many African governments, together with some nongovernmental organizations from the 1960s, begun to recognize the links between education and development and the important roles women play in economic development. Therefore, they started devoting efforts to bridge the gap between girls and boys in primary and secondary education and between women and men at the higher levels of education. However, as our discourses show, African women themselves have been equally active in finding ways to increase girls' access to education and pursuing higher education more vigorously in an effort to avail themselves with contemporary economic opportunities.

Throughout our discussions, it is revealed that historical narratives about African women have generally portrayed them either as victims of cultural norms or as powerful agents of social change. In the former, women have been presented as being overburdened with domestic responsibilities and agricultural labor; facing unequal access and discrimination in education and employment; bearing the highest burden of HIV/AIDS epidemic; and being the group most affected in conflicts-related violence. In the latter, women were portrayed as powerful queen mothers and important spiritual leaders. Yet the immense diversity of women's roles cannot simply be sandwiched in between the notions of victimhood and empowerment. Therefore, we bring the two together in a form reflected in the daily activities of all African women, for in the course of their history, women have suffered, endured, failed, and succeeded together as one group. Moreover, the many social, economic, and political achievements Africa enjoys today are the result of the immense roles both "powerful" and "ordinary" women rendered, and continue to render, to their societies.

NOTES

1. Catherine Coquery-Vidrovitch, *African Women: A Modern History* (Boulder, CO: Westview Press, 1997), 3.

2. Cheryl Johnson-Odium, "Women and Gender in the History of Sub-Saharan Africa," in Bonnie G. Smith (ed.), *Women in Global Perspective* Vol. 3 (Urbana: University of Illinois Press, 2005), 9–67.

3. Ibid.

4. Robert O. Collins, *Documents from the African Past* (Princeton, NJ: Markus Wiener Publishers, 2001).

5. Iris Berger, "Women in East and Southern Africa," in Iris Berger and E. Frances White (eds.), *Women in Sub-Saharan Africa: Restoring Women to History* (Bloomington: Indiana University Press, 1999), 15; Ifi Amadiume, *Reinventing Africa: Matriarchy, Religion, and Culture* (London: Zed Books, 2001), 29–51.

6. Johnson-Odium, 9–67.

7. Sidney John Hogben and Anthony H. M. Kirk-Greene, *The Emirates of Northern Nigeria: A Preliminary Survey of their Historical Traditions* (Oxford: Oxford University Press, 1966), 81.

1

Women and Courtship
and Marriage

The roles that African women play in courtship and marriage is so vast in its diversity and range that there is a risk of oversimplification when discussing it. Not only is there an immense variety in details regarding customs and traditions of different groups and localities, but it is almost impossible, without a great deal of artificiality and categorization, to trace uniformly all of the basic standards and principles. Yet in seeking to uncover and understand the institutions of courtship and marriage, we may reasonably refer to the shared characteristics of marriage transactions and relationships in the various societies in this region. A working definition in this case could be that in many African societies, marriage was, and continues to be, a transaction between two lineages that allow the lineage of a man to secure the productive and reproductive capabilities of a woman from her lineage group. While accepting the view that many African traditions regard marriage as primarily an alliance of interest between two families or kinship groups, we give more weight to the fact that many African marriage systems also have flexible aspects that allow courtship and romantic love to be considered as requirements for marriage. Many researchers overemphasize the kinship aspects of marriage; nevertheless, kinship offers a window of opportunity to understand African marriage systems when we study it as an essential aspect of kinship systems.

Kinship, for instance, entails certain traditions that assume the notion of marriage as a contract between two family groups—establishing an obligatory relationship between the two groups, which sometimes outlasts the relationship of the married couples. In other words, for the married couples, their union is usually viewed as superficial and secondary to the wishes and needs of the larger group. Therefore, even when the bond between the original couples ceases to exist, that bond of the two families may continue. This principle of a continuing relationship or alliance has serious implications for the groups involved, with both men and women playing crucial roles in negotiations to ensure that any contracted marriage will reinforce a group's social, economic, and political position and ties in the society.

Due to the kinds of social, economic, and political negotiations intended for the benefit of the group rather than that of the individual, we find the grounds from which many researchers have condemned the indigenous institution of African marriage as depraving to women. Many researchers have contended that African women play a minimal role, or perhaps no role at all, in marriage transactions; and women, regardless of marital status, are generally dominated and exploited, with little control over their daily activities. Those who hold this view argue that customs such as child betrothal, polygyny, the treatment of widows, marriage without consent, the heavy workload of African women, the expectation that women must be obedient to their husbands, and the right of a husband to discipline his wife show the wrongful nature of African marriage systems toward women.[1] The implication here is that if one finds a system where women have control in marriage transactions, that system would be a deviation from the general pattern. However, there are numerous examples in many African societies where women have exerted, and continue to exert, considerable influence over marriage.

Indeed, in many marriages while men may have complete control over their self-acquired property, women, in many instances, are equally entitled to independently control and manage any property that they may have acquired through personal earnings or inheritance. This can be found in some parts of West Africa, where women focus modestly in agricultural production and are engaged more extensively in trade. A Fulani WoDaaBe woman gains co-ownership of her husband's cattle, but her husband has rights to her property only during the period she is married to him.[2] Married women in Zaria and Nupe societies can also earn their own money separate from that of their husbands. From such private resources, Zaria women pay for their daughter's dowries and provide themselves with certain household essentials. It has been noted that a Nupe wife not only provides her family with certain food items from her private funds, but sometimes her earnings are substantial enough for her husband to be financially dependent on her.[3]

The precise nature of the relationship between a husband and a wife and its extension to the extended family has been of intense interest to

A happy couple smiles for the camera, Goree Island, Senegal, 1992. (Courtesy of A. Olusegun Fayemi)

researchers. The available data indicates the distinctive behaviors between married couples and the ways in which women affirm their own resolve and preference in the choice of marriage partners. The data also highlights how women balance their daily choices and responsibilities with that of the larger group, how they manage and control their homes, and the opportunities available to them in the acquisition and management of property. Against the above background, this chapter examines the role and influence that women have exercised—and continue to exercise—in African courtship and marriage arrangements. This chapter also examines how women have navigated their way in areas where they played either a minimal role or no role at all and had no influence. It also explores the effects of marriage on residential arrangements and the ones that modern market economies have had on contemporary marriage institutions and social relationships.

LOVE AND COURTSHIP

In general, discussions on African marriage systems often focus on structures, marriage payments, consequences, and changes in social organization. Attention given to the influences of kin in marriage, as well as rules governing prescribed and preferential marriages, have a limited number of researchers interested in such issues as individual choice of marriage partner, romantic love as consideration for marriage, consent, and interpersonal relationships between married couples. In particular, the idea of romantic love and courtship as factors in the choice of a marriage partner has not gained enough attention. The contention is that traditional marriage arrangements in Africa were a form of business transaction initiated and finalized by parents. Therefore, love was incompatible with or immaterial to marriage and therefore has no effect when we study African marriage institutions.

Alfred R. Radcliffe-Brown has argued that:

> The African does not think of marriage as a union based on romantic love although beauty as well as character and health are sought in the choice of a wife. The strong affection that normally exists after some years of successful marriage is the product of the marriage itself conceived as a process, resulting from living together and co-operating in many activities and particularly in the rearing of children. . . . Marriage is an alliance between two bodies of kin based on their common interest in the marriage itself and its continuance, and in the offspring of the union.[4]

A similar argument that has been made by some researchers is that although African societies exhibit plenty of lovemaking, there is seldom anything in their marriage institutions that correspond to what could be viewed as romantic love. Expressed differently, the argument is that the "primitive" African could not possibly possess the capacity to understand either sentimental love or its relationship with marriage.[5] Another argument that has been made regarding the absence of love in African marriages is that love in Africa is raw, motivated by animal instincts and animal passion. On the other hand, romantic sentiments and refined feelings are exhibited more frequently by people who are less primitive and more sophisticated.[6]

Although we cannot know exactly why Radcliffe-Brown and the others came to their conclusions on the absence of premarital love in African marriages, we can reasonably assume that the concept of homogenizing all African societies and the nature of their ethnographical questions may have accounted for their conclusions. In this case, questions specifically targeting ideas of courtship and love may not have been styled appropriately, or it is equally likely that people may have been unwilling to discuss freely such issues of a personal and intimate nature with strangers. In addition, the rejection of courtship and romantic love elements in African marriage appear to be rooted in a Eurocentric approach to issues of African sexuality and polygyny. This same approach helped codify what some have viewed as the lack of romantic love in African marriages.

The transfer of Western ideals of romantic love, which require couples to remain exclusive to each other, meant that polygyny, widespread in many

African societies, and romantic love are contradictory and hence cannot occur within the same system. On the one hand, African polygyny, it has been suggested, encourages sensuality among men; but on the other hand, it fosters immorality tempered with much jealousy and bickering among the women. Such conditions cannot engender companionship, love, honor, and conjugal fidelity that characterize marriage in Western societies.[7] The above views lay predominantly in the assumption that other than the Western ideal of monogamy and its romantic love exclusivity, any system of marriage must involve some sort of negative consequences for African women, regardless of whether they accept polygyny or not.[8] This view notwithstanding, some important studies have found evidence that romantic love is a near-universal cross-cultural phenomenon and therefore not exclusive to Western societies.[9]

The increased expression of romantic love as a condition in marriage arrangements in contemporary Africa does not mean that ideas of courtship and love have only recently emerged in African societies. A number of recent scholarships have acknowledged individual choice and love as important components in African marriage systems and its existence in precolonial African societies. In study after study, one finds that in spite of the general social conventions that have regulated African marriages, African cultural traditions have always been flexible enough to allow for the assertion of individual independence and choice.[10] One study among the Igbo of Nigeria confirms the existence of passionate love in that society since the precolonial days. The study asserts that both men and women were allowed the freedom to engage in courtship and sexual activities before marriage.[11] The main issue that has been raised is not whether love and sexual attraction has existed or exists now in African societies but rather how these elements are woven into the fabric of social life.[12] Here, we find that in precolonial African societies, ideas of love and courtship were often aesthetically expressed or performed, and we have to specifically target those forms before we can know the values, attitudes, expectations, and symbolism they reveal.

As is the case in Zulu society, a tradition of love songs performed by unmarried women existed and continues to exist today. The love songs were part of a highly institutionalized period of courtship with rules and regulations governed by women. When a girl reached a marriageable age, the *ukwemula* (puberty rite) initiation ceremony initiated her into womanhood. From hence, eligible young men in and outside of the community were free to court her. Throughout the period of courtship, a girl remained primarily under the influence and authority of other young unmarried women with minimal control or supervision from her parents. These women were responsible for sanctioning her choice of possible suitors and were the ones who approved when and where the couple met.[13] At marriage ceremonies and other social festivities, young people of different groups acquainted themselves with each other through song and dance. During informal singing and dancing at night, individuals were attracted to each other, and initial attachments were formed.[14]

From the initial meeting, the young girl's group of supervisors would arrange subsequent private meetings for the couple. When a girl finally made her decision, with the approval of her age group, to accept a particular suitor as a husband, she was responsible for initiating the formal process leading to marriage by officially "choosing" (*ukuqoma*) the young man. She accomplished this by raising a white flag in the courtyard of the young man's house, and then she would give him a gift of white beads (*ucu*) strung together. The young man demonstrated his willingness to marry the girl by holding the *umbongo* ceremony during which time he would officially express his gratitude to the girl for choosing him.[15] During the period of courtship, the lovers were required to remain separate from each other, and the longing experienced by the girl for her prospective husband found continued expression and release in the singing of love songs. This preliminary period was followed by a long period before the couple could be finally married, during which time the young man would pay the *lobolo* (dowry), usually in cattle, to the girl's father.

While pressure could be exerted in some cases for individuals to marry for particular reasons, it is evident that Zulu marriage custom had enough flexibility enabling young people to choose their marriage partners, with young women playing substantial roles in the achievement of the final marriage. In the same vein, it has been observed that with regard to courtship and marriage among the Mandari of southern Sudan, "the elaborate complex of custom, the express purpose of which is the bringing together of young people of the opposite sex, would have no function if marriages were arranged or enforced by the father."[16] Traditionally, among the Nandi of Kenya, it was the responsibility of the mothers of both the bride and groom to initiate the first steps that ultimately led to the contraction of a marriage, but both the bride and groom were given a fair chance to decide about the choice of their future spouses. The final marital arrangements would not be finalized without the girl consenting, and it was the duty of her kinswomen to find out if she was willing to marry the man her parents had selected for her.[17]

The Akan and the Krobo of southern Ghana have a similar courting system following their initiation ceremonies, with older women controlling the whole process. Prior to colonial rule in Ghana, the Akan celebrated the *Bragro* (menstrual celebration) ceremony to initiate a girl into womanhood. While this rite has practically disappeared among the Akan in recent years, it used to provide an opportunity for young men and women to court each other before they entered into marriage, be it arranged or not. Once a girl reached puberty, she was instructed in the art of womanhood and motherhood by an older woman in her family or in the community, and was secluded from the rest of the community until the day of her adornment at the *Bragro* ceremony. On this day, she was dressed in fine beads and cloth that only covered the lower part of her body. The upper part of her body, shining with shea butter, was left exposed to show the girl's physical beauty and her ability to bear and breastfeed her children.

This attraction was particularly for the benefit of young men of marriageable age, and families of eligible bachelors gathered around to watch. If a young man found attractive what he saw in the girl, he would instruct his relatives to initiate marriage arrangements while he used the period of negotiations to court the girl. The couples usually met late at night to share snacks prepared by either the girl or the boy, sing love songs, or play with their friends. According to Nzema (part of the Akan of southern Ghana) tradition, a man would sometimes polish a coconut for the woman he was courting—until they could see their images on the shell. Parents of young men could also initiate this process by encouraging their son to court the girl. Even though the *Bragro* ceremony was certainly not the only avenue of courtship and marriage for the Akan in the past (they also practiced child betrothal and arranged marriage without consent), it afforded young couples the opportunity to choose their future spouses and to experience intimacy and love before marriage. During the period of courtship, both the young woman and the man could assist their future in-laws with household chores and work on their farms to prove their value.

Like the Akan, the Krobo of the Ga-Adangbe group celebrated the *Dipo* (female initiation rite) to initiate girls who had reached puberty into womanhood. On this occasion, the initiates were paraded through the streets of the town with only their private areas covered with beads and cloth. Young men and families looking to marry any of the girls into their families could contact the family of the initiate to start the marriage process. While the parents and other family members handled the marriage arrangements, which could take several months or even years, the couples engaged in courtship. Among the Baule of the Ivory Coast, women were free to choose their own spouses. Marriage arrangements were not subjected to the manipulations of elders in each kinship group, even though elderly family members could influence choices by introducing young couples to certain social groups. In addition, they were called upon to sanction the choice of marriage partners, and were also involved in the prolonged and multiple phases of matrimony.[18] Nonetheless, they could not control, in any substantial way, the initial choice of a marriage partner by either the woman or the man nor could they force acceptance of a particular choice of spouse. Accordingly, the society had a built-in system that allowed premarital sexual relations to counter the manipulations of elders by preventing them from justifiably objecting to the contraction of the marriage should pregnancy result from the sexual contact.

Marriage arrangements undertaken by parents of both sides—in particular by the couples' mothers—could be broken without any consequence and at any time, if for any reason, the girl lost affection for the prospective husband, irrespective of the years of bride service that the groom may have rendered to the bride's family.[19] Therefore, regardless of the social, economic, or political considerations that may have been used to begin a marriage negotiation, initial love and courtship were key elements. It is not by any stretch of the imagination that one recognizes that marrying for love is not unfamiliar to Africans, and certainly not to the Baule. In many African societies, love and courtship occurred in a more subtle manner as demonstrated among the Mkako of Cameroon. In the past, Mkako women of Cameroon frequently employed delay tactics until they were convinced they loved the person selected for them by their fathers. These women would persuade their fathers to delay accepting the final bride-wealth payment, which would have finalized the marriage arrangement. The young women used the period to engage in a number of "mock or test marriages" in an effort to select someone they actually loved and wanted to marry.[20]

Thus, as indicated earlier on, even when arranged marriage exists in a society, it does not necessarily prevent courting and romantic love from occurring. A girl may be given in marriage at birth, but as exemplified among the Kissi of Guinea, once she grows up she is under no obligation to marry her future husband. A boy, on the other hand, must assume the role of a "fiancé" and court the girl his parents have chosen for him. He must express his love for her through gifts and other nice gestures, or he stands the risk of losing her. A young Kissi boy remonstrated that "girls don't realize how much fiancés have to suffer." She might say, "If you don't give me the headscarf I want for next feast-day, I know plenty of other boys who will be glad to give it to me."[21] Contesting assertions by A. Rançon of his conclusion that "the Coniagui never have love affairs, in the true sense of the term,"[22] Maupoil writes, "I have good reason to suppose that the love life of the Coniagui is rather a subtle affair. One has only to observe, in the bustle of the market or amid the silence of the bush, how a young man courts the girl of his choice, to become convinced that love and courtship"[23] exist as an element of marriage in this society.

Africa's rich oral traditions of love songs, poems, and courting rituals demonstrate that attraction and love form significant aspects of marriage in many African societies, although these expressions may sometimes be subtle. Nevertheless, we cannot ignore the fact that in some instances such emotions may not be a sufficient or necessary condition for marriage to occur. A study done among a sample of Luo women show that they had loved and courted one man but had accepted marriage from another. These instances resulted from the fact that sometimes the men they had loved were distant relatives, and they could not marry because of kinship ties. Other times, the woman's family had a strong feuding relationship with the man's family or his family was considered poor; or they had a reputation for witchcraft, infertility, or social problems.[24] A similar situation has been noted in a number of studies among the Igbo of Nigeria. In one study, what some elderly Igbo men revealed about their betrothals, their marriages, and about love, when relating personal stories and popular fables suggested a long tradition of romantic love. Both women and men endowed themselves in this romantic love irrespective of whether it resulted in marriage or not. Yet, the majority of the people involved in the study confessed that had they been allowed to "follow their heart," they would have married a different person other than their current spouse.[25]

WOMEN AND ARRANGED MARRIAGE

The exact point in time when the concept of selecting spouses became particularly individualistic and the privilege of romantic love became *the* major deciding factor in marriage in many African societies is hard to identify. Most likely, such transitions occurred first among the educated and elite populations in urban centers, rather than among populations in rural areas.[26] In spite of this increase in individual choice in recent years, many marriages are still arranged today. Even in instances where women and men meet on their own and develop affection for each other, their parents and some members of their kin still need to sanction their relationship before they can enter into marriage. Now, because of urbanization and social and economic mobility, arranged marriages are becoming as common as they were in the past. Individuals frequently contract someone, usually a friend, to seek a suitable partner for them or to inquire into a prospective partner's family character. For instance, the Luo in Kenya often rely on a family member or on a friend living in another community to find them a suitable partner. The key is to depend on someone who is capable of vouching for the character of the person and reputation of his or her family.[27]

In the past, negotiations for arranged marriages primarily occurred between two kin groups with varying degrees of consultation with the couples. As shown above, some societies entertained the concerns of the couples themselves, while others did not. The key consideration for most kin in arranged marriages was ensuring a successful and lasting union beneficial beyond the couples themselves and their children. To consolidate political power or establish peaceful relations with another group, precolonial African societies allowed a system where rulers and members of a ruling family received wives from subordinate chiefs and the general public. Such an arrangement was not exclusive to ruling families. Ordinary members of a society could enter their daughters into marriage, but such marriages were usually for social or economic benefits rather than for political purposes. The Ashanti, for example, allowed the use of women as pawns to secure loans. In the event that a borrower failed to repay a loan, the woman, used as collateral, became the wife of the lender.[28]

Some ethnohistorical studies on marriage in Africa suggest that among the Beti of Cameroon, the resultant effect of the increase in the ivory trade was a rise in polygynous marriages, as it became an opportunity to create and cement trading partnerships. This led to a situation where more and more marriages were arranged, with or without consent, than was usual in this society. However, once the Beti shifted their focus from trade in ivory to cocoa farming, polygyny and the increased incidences of arranged marriages declined.[29] As diverse and similar as African societies are, so are the reactions and attitudes of African women toward arranged marriages. While some women have readily agreed to enter into arranged marriages, others have used a variety of avenues to avoid them. The reasons that women have offered for accepting arranged marriages are numerous, but most of the common reasons included the following: arranged marriages prevented problems connected with spousal selection, parents and guardians who negotiated arranged marriages looked after the interest of the woman, some women entered as a result of family pressure or out of loyalty to family, and others accepted it out of the need to provide financial and social security to family members.

Different authorities have contested arranged marriages since the colonial period on the basis that such marriages disenfranchise women in their own private space. It goes without saying that marriage, since the precolonial era, has been also arranged for men who may or may not have liked the women they were to marry. Men have generally been portrayed as the supposed benefactors in arranged marriages. Thus, in recent years, women's organizations such as the Women and Law in Southern Africa Research Project are pressing for legislations that would require a woman's consent before any form of marriage could be instituted.[30] Yet, across Africa, the political wand cannot easily resolve problems associated with arranged marriages. As some researchers have suggested, "the situation is more complex and women's attitudes need explication."[31] Over the years, African women have used clever resistance strategies such as elopement, delay tactics, feigned sickness and laziness, adultery, and other marital violations to prevent themselves from being used as mere pawns in marital dealings. Kpelle women used their domestic role to informally maneuver marriage arrangements they wished to get out of, or they made things favorable to their needs. A woman could refuse to go to the farm or perform household chores such as cleaning, cooking, washing, and so on, until their marriage ended in a divorce or their complaints were resolved.[32] Sometimes these resistance strategies failed to achieve the desired result, in which case the consequences could be severe.

An illustration of the above is exemplified in the life stories of three Luo women. These women, after persistently refusing to accept their arranged marriages, were kidnapped by their prospective husbands and forced to have sex with them. Consequently, two of the women had to agree to the marriage, perhaps, out of the fear that no other man would want to marry them afterward or that their families might not take them back. The family of the third woman accepted her return, and most likely, without any compensation. The point here is that "the occurrence of premarital sex *per se* . . . [is not what bothered the women and their families], rather, it is the public character of the event, which might affect a woman's marital prospects."[33] Some African societies have developed strategies that minimize the stress that arranged marriages might cause women. For instance, a woman's first marriage may be arranged, but in case that marriage ended in divorce, she was allowed to choose her own husband should she decide to remarry. This practice was common among Swahili women and continues to be so even now.[34] The Rukuba in central Nigeria allowed women to take additional husbands after entering into an arranged marriage with their first husband and had the freedom to reside with whichever husband they preferred.[35]

In some societies, arranged marriages allowed women marrying into wealthy households to secure for themselves, their children, and other members of their family, financial resources and higher social status. Among the Zulu and the Swazi of southeastern Africa, although families of the bride and groom arranged marriages, the payment of *lobolo*[36] in cattle benefited women. This was because it provided a "direct economic asset and a means to generate kinship categories or units which were a basic source of security for women and their children."[37] The role that women played in marriage arrangements has a significant impact on the social structure in this society. Although Zulu women remained at the backgrounds of actual marriage negotiations conducted by men, they had various mechanisms to control kinship ties that marriage created in the larger social structure of the society. They used their feminine power to dissolve or emerge existing kinship units or created new units and decided the type of presents a groom's family could provide a bride's family. Women again controlled how the presents were to be distributed and what each interested party received.

In some cases in the past, as among the Asante of Ghana, women who accepted arranged marriage into the royal family could eventually become mothers of kings with substantial influence in the selection of successive kings. To some extent, this arrangement continues among the Asante. In precolonial Dahomey, women who entered the royal household as wives of the ruler did so through an arranged marriage or through slavery. Yet, opportunity existed in the political structure of the kingdom that allowed these women to "exercise power and authority, to make and influence policy, and to gain honor and wealth."[38] It has also been argued that even though each side of the family in an arranged marriage may indirectly gain economic or social benefit from it, the primary benefits usually went to the couples and their children. In recent years, men could take multiple wives to enhance their political and economic status; however, Kpelle women who were head wives could also initiate the acquisition of junior wives for companionship, to help with chores, and to help entrench their own status in the household. Head wives usually select junior wives for their husbands without much in the way of consent from them. Some women purposefully become wives in certain households just for the economic or political benefits such an arrangement affords them.[39] In a sense, there is a duality to arranged marriage, which in one instance restricts the needs and concerns of women, while in another, provides women with the opportunity to gain economic, social, and political stability for themselves and their kin.

MARRIAGE AND RESIDENTIAL ARRANGEMENT

In view of the fact that scholarships abound on family and women and marriage in Africa, it is surprising that we know and understand very little about the importance of residential arrangement for married women and its impact on their position and roles in extended family structures. The transition of a woman from her lineage to that of another has been marked by patterns of residential arrangement after marriage. While some societies practice matrilocal residence where married women remain at the compounds of their maternal families' side, in the majority of African societies, patrilocal residence was, and still is, the usual practice. In patrilocality, a woman resides with her husband's kin and usually remains with them even after her husband passes away. She may choose to marry another member of her late husband's descent group or just remain there with her children.[40]

Within the residential structure, particularly in patrilocality, women occupy various positions and play a myriad of roles based on hierarchy and a distinctive behavior pattern. For example, a woman marrying into a Yoruba family achieves a position of seniority in her husband's compound base on the order of her marriage in the event of her husband having multiple wives. If other women are already married into the household before her, not only is she junior to them but also to all children born in the household before her marriage. The Yoruba pay little attention to gender and place more emphasis on seniority. Hence, it is particularly important for a junior wife to show respect and reverence to senior wives in this hierarchical structure and to behave in accordance with her position in the household.[41] It follows from the above that senior wives have the benefit of light household chores and instruct junior wives, while junior wives, on the other hand, have the responsibility doing the dirtier and more difficult tasks in the household.

Similar hierarchical structures based on seniority can be found in other African societies, but those have characteristics distinct from that of the Yoruba. For instance, among the Luo society of Kenya, seniority establishes the position of wives in the husband's compound as well as the order in which sons marry, but unlike the Yoruba form, it does not determine the behavioral pattern of members of the household.[42] Behavior has more of a ritual and spiritual significance than of a physical one. The influence of one wife over the other is also determined by seniority, but it extends only to farming activities. Senior wives have the responsibility of initiating stages in the farm cycle, with junior wives following in reference to their positions. Senior wives also have the sole right to start a new homestead when the husband decides to establish a new residence. Besides these reservations for senior wives, each wife controls her own activities.[43] In precolonial times, some senior wives may have received their husbands' authority and support to form joint farming units with junior wives to which she had control. Additional power may have been granted a senior wife that allowed her to act as a liaison between her husband and the other co-wives, resolving conflicts and reporting on their daily needs. Such instances are becoming rare in recent times since few women today are willing to allow their husbands to control them, let alone another woman.

Mariages are global, with an African married to an American. (Courtesy of Toyin Falola)

In other societies, such as among the Nguni, wives who, in the past, lived in a patrilocal extended family structure were ranked and had specific roles according to principles distinctive to this group. Among the Pondo (members of the Nguni group), a wife's status in her husband's household was based on the length of her marriage and the presence of her mother-in-law, rather than on the position of other wives in the household. A young bride in the initial years of her marriage was subjected to strict regulations, but as time passed, many of the restrictions and regulations became less strict.[44] At first, she had no hut of her own, no field, cooked in her mother-in-law's hut, and worked in her field; and her mother-in-law could allocate to her any task she desired. It was customary for the new bride to be responsible for the heaviest duties in the compound. In addition, she was not allowed to go out to social gatherings and was required to observe a strict formal behavior toward her husband's relatives. As her marriage progressed, she was allowed a hut of her own, and her mother-in-law granted her permission to attend social functions.[45] Each new wife that married into the household went through the same process.

A similar structure existed for the Kgatla, also of the Nguni cultural group. Here, a new wife was not subjected to the same restrictions as in the case of the Pondo, but she also went through a period of practical servitude in the household of her husband's parents.[46] Nevertheless, a new wife was allowed, in the early stages of her marriage, her own hut separated from that of her in-laws where she exercised absolute authority. She had a recognized place in her husband's family councils and was especially influential in marriage arrangements of her children.[47] The Kgatla marriage institution allowed a husband and a wife an opportunity to enjoy an outward display of affection and a degree of daily intimacy in the public sphere. They could sit together when entertaining visitors, eat together, and enjoy each other's company during social gatherings. This level of public displays of affection between a husband and a wife appeared to be less among the Pondo probably because wives were restricted from going into public places to socialize without the consent of their mother-in-laws, who normally would not grant such permissions.

The Pondo example is indicative of the influence and implications mother-in-laws had on the status and roles wives exercised in their husbands' household in patrilocal settings. In a similar example, although more contemporary, a Luo woman starts her married life under the supervision of her mother-in-law. She has no farm of her own and works on the farm of her mother-in-law. As new wives marry into the household, they take over working for the mother-in-law, and she is given her own field and gains a degree of autonomy from her mother-in-law. The song sung by the bridegroom's mother during the ceremony when a wife takes residence in her husband compound also signifies the role of wives and the expectations of mother-in-laws among the Dogon of Mali: "I shall no longer go to fetch wood and to fetch water and I shall no longer pound the grain."[48]

In Dogon Society, the moment a new wife arrives in her husband's home, she is almost immediately regarded as a stranger and barely tolerated. In particular, her mother-in-law may wish to seek retribution for herself for the treatment she once had to endure when she married. A mother-in-law's sphere of influence may also involve arranging the marriage of her sons. This practice was very common among the Coniagui of Guinea in the past where it was a mother's duty to choose a fiancée for her son when he was still an infant. In recent years, the occurrence of mothers choosing wives for their sons has declined; nonetheless, it remains the traditional form of initiating marriage in this society. The importance of the mother's role is underscored by the fact that if a girl wants to marry, she must obtain not only her father's consent but also that of her mother and her mother's family.[49]

Western influences and contemporary situations in many African societies are weakening the power mother-in-laws exercise over other women in residential arrangements based on patrilocality. Luo wives, in recent years, no longer work for their mother-in-laws for extended periods as they used to do, and this is especially so if the couples reside in a different locality because of job requirements. This notwithstanding, it has been pointed out that mother-in-laws in Luo society continue to exert considerable influence in such areas as child care. In instances where a husband lives and works outside of the town his wife resides in, it is his mother who stands in for him in decision making when a child is ill. In fact, a Luo wife "may need her mother-in-law's . . . permission to obtain medical care for her children or herself," and she would be criticized severely if she failed to acquire the consent of her mother-in-law.[50]

Patrilocality is often common in polygynous societies. Most African women raised in such societies do not consider it as an indignity to be one of several wives, yet many women accept the fact that polygyny provides ample opportunity for indignation and jealousy between wives. Rivalries and competition among co-wives may be expressed in firm insistence on equal sharing of a husband's lands and other resources as well as his affection and favor, in spitefulness towards co-wives' children, in the harsh treatment of a new wife by an older wife, and in suspicion and accusations of witchcraft.[51] In some cases, co-wives go out of their way to exceed the execution of their domestic duties just to displace or discredit one another. Suspicion of a husband's partiality toward a particular wife may aggravate rivalry between co-wives, and with contemporary economic and educational expenses in many African countries, the situation is made worse if a husband does not have sufficient economic resources to cover the expenditure of his household alone.

Jealousies and rivalries between co-wives should not, however, be construed as an index of all polygynous households; for as it will be demonstrated, in some instances, women married to one man and living together coexist peacefully and sometimes even collaborated for their own economic prosperity. Kpelle head wives were receptive of polygyny and often initiated the acquisition of junior wives for their husbands since it afforded them the chance of controlling the labor of such wives. A number of senior wives in Nandi society in an interview with Regina S. Oboler told her, "They urged their husbands to take second wives, helped to find appropriate candidates, and were members of the marriage negotiation parties."[52] This attitude by the Nandi women is perhaps influenced by the reduction of their own household duties and companionship that additional wives brought them. In the precolonial period, wealthy Igbo women, bearing the title *Ekwe*, practiced *igba ohu*. *Igba ohu* was a system of woman-to-woman marriage, which allowed the *Ekwes* to take other women as their wives. The system was intended to allow a potential *Ekwe* woman to take on several women as "wives" into her household whom she not only claimed their services to increase her wealth but also gave birth to children in her name. The influence of colonial rule changed the Igbo woman-to-woman marriage practice and in its place, a new system emerged in which wealthy women provided the bride-wealth for their husbands to marry additional wives whose services they likewise had control over.[53]

In the Sherbro society of Sierra Leone, polygyny allowed senior wives engaged in trading activities to gain more wealth by setting up economic ventures for the junior wives, which they ultimately controlled. Some Sherbro women in polygynous marriages resided neither with their husbands nor with their other co-wives. This arrangement allowed them a greater degree of cooperation. A wife living in a fishing village, for example, could supply her co-wife in a marketing town with dried fish to sell. The wife in the marketing town reciprocated by supplying the co-wife in the fishing town with items such as rice, sugar, and salt to sell in the fishing town.[54] In other arrangements, a senior wife owning her own ovens for smoking fish in a fishing community might not resent her husband for marrying additional wives since such junior wives could help her business with their labor. While such arrangements favored senior wives, which therefore, encouraged them to urge their husbands to marry more women, it increased the incidence of junior wives leaving their marriages to seek other households where they would not be under another woman.

Among the Ewes of southern Ghana, co-wives residing in a patrilocal household generally rotated cooking for their husband. This arrangement granted other wives the opportunity to use their off-days to engage in trading activities. As indicated earlier on, even though patrilocality is widespread in Africa, it is not the only form of residential arrangement for married couples. Different societies have different forms of residence that suits their needs and customs. For example, the Akan of Ghana do not traditionally practice matrilocality, where women will have to remain with their maternal kin after marriage. However, Akan women in polygynous marriages have developed a preference for remaining with their maternal family after marriage. To avoid the prevalence of co-wives disputes, jealousies, and other domestic squabbles, many Akan women as well as men favor residing on their own or with their own kin. Co-wives living under this residential understanding prepare their husbands' meals in their own homes and deliver it to his residence. Husbands, in turn, rotate visiting and sleeping patterns among the wives.[55] A woman maintaining her residence with her matrilineal kin gains the advantage of getting additional help from her younger sisters and nieces in caring for her children. Yao women of Malawi also remain in their matrilineal homes after marriage. The organization of the Yao society is based on mothers and their children, and husbands are the ones who marry into the households of their wives.[56]

Residential arrangements play a significant role in the position and roles African women enjoy in their various extended family structures. While some societies practice matrilocality, it is not as widespread in Africa as compared with patrilocality. A combination of the two structures may even exist within the same society, or an aspect of either or both may exist. In instances where polygyny necessitates patrilocality, some women coexist cordially and sometimes cooperate for their economic and social well-being, but this picture is not universal in all patrilocal households. Co-wives residing together sometimes engage in vicious competitions, quarrels, jealousies, and other activities to offset each other's position in the household. In addition, while all the various in-laws may influence new wives in various ways, a mother-in-law, in particular, influences the life of a new wife in a more substantial way.

WOMEN AND MARRIAGE IN MATRILINEAL AND PATRILINEAL SYSTEMS

In many African societies, matrilineal and patrilineal systems establish the line of descent and inheritance. These social delineations also hold an important key to the role women play in African marriages. Both systems offer different avenues for a man to become the lawful husband of a woman and her children, and hence, entitle himself to their services. The various avenues all entail some form of payment by the man or his family to the parents or the family of the woman. Previous scholarships on African marriages focused on the "strangeness" of this payment requirement, and many theorized that it was equivalent to the sale of a woman. It is only with recent scholarships that the record is being set straight by the reexamination of imperial narratives and its tools of analysis. These new scholarships now provide us with a better understanding of the importance and the symbolism of marriage payments and the position and roles of women in matrilineal and patrilineal systems. Some researchers have pointed out that the transfer of goods or money "form a pledge of the maintenance of the marriage, since they must be returned if [the marriage] is dissolved . . . the payment does not make the wife her husband's property, or place her in the relationship of a slave to him."[57]

Indeed, the requirement to pay a bride price is more adequately understood as recognition of the wife's value both to her husband and to her own relatives, and to indicate the importance of the marriage contract to all the parties involved.[58] Within certain matrilineal societies, such as among the peoples of northeastern Zimbabwe (Rhodesia) and Malawi (Nyasaland), a husband is obligated to work permanently at the village of his wife's father both before and after his marriage, regardless of how much he paid to his wife's family. In matrilineal societies, people trace their ties of kinship through women, and lineages deem their descent as having emanated from a common ancestress. Children born into matrilineal societies belong to the mother's family, whereas in patrilineal societies, the reverse is typically the norm. Accordingly, marriage does not involve any act that would possibly transfer children from their mother's kinship to that of their father. Therefore, the responsibility of raising children and caring for the well-being of sisters usually lies with brothers and maternal uncles and not with husbands.

Men in matrilineal families arbitrate and protect their sisters in conflicts and act as intermediaries and guarantors in marriage arrangements. Among the Bemba, who are matrilineal and practice matrilocality, a woman's brothers and uncles are more accountable than a father for coming up with reparations if a child commits an offense and is unable to pay the remunerations demanded by him- or herself. Some old Bemba informants described the care and support of children by fathers as "charity" but as "duty" on the part of uncles.[59] Among the Cewa of Malawi, if a man wants to discipline his children, he needs the consent of his wife's brother. Failure to obtain this consent might cause his wife's relatives to demand compensation from him—particularly if the punishment is severe.[60]

The constant presence and influence of brothers and uncles in matrilineal marriages also signify that wives have more bargaining power and solidarity to navigate and negotiate issues with their husbands than perhaps is the case in patrilineal marriages. In most people's mind, the general conception about the position of a wife turns out to be that of submissiveness to her husband. However, in reality, the "real master" of the household is the one who has the stronger personality or who knows how to take advantage of his/her own strength and that of the larger kin group.[61] Thus, a husband who cannot adequately provide for his family and has to depend on the labor of his wife for the family's subsistence living may appear in public as the head, but his position is relatively fragile compared to that of his wife at home. For her domestic duties to her husband and his family, a Nyamwezi wife generally has the upper hand in her husband's household. Inside the house, she acts supremely and is acutely aware of her superiority; she asserts her independence and takes initiatives. In addition, not only does she know how to stand up for her rights, but also she is unafraid to do so.[62]

In the event that a husband makes the regrettable mistake of beating his wife, she could return to her own kin, and he would be reduced to begging her, visiting her, and heaping gifts on her before she may be persuaded to return to his home. The same strategy can be said of women married in patrilineal societies. The Nkundo of central Africa, for instance, acknowledge a husband's right to discipline his wife by beating her, but he must opt for this kind of punishment as the last alternative, and even with that, he cannot beat her excessively.[63] A wife who is beaten excessively by her husband can complain to her relatives who might take her side. This may lead to dispute between the two kin groups. The Dzing, the Kongo, and the Yombe use a different approach in which they may urge, or even pressure, a wife to return to her husband after incidences of beating in order to avoid reimbursing the husband his marriage payment. On the other hand, since the children of a Yombe woman belongs to her family, her family head could encourage her to leave her husband if she remains childless and is subject to his constant beating.

The roles women play when they marry into patrilineal societies are no different than those played by married women in matrilineal societies; however, in matrilineal societies, women have access to their own families' solidarity and the degree of control their husbands wield over them is probably what differentiates the two groups of women. Although debatable, the mold of inheritance in matrilineal societies offers women the chance of commanding positions of authority, and in such cases, women "ignore their consorts in the ordering of their social and political life."[64] Elderly women, in particular, enjoy high social statuses and are generally the first to be consulted in issues regarding marriage and divorce. In patrilineal groups such as the Nkundo and the Ngoni, a wife has the responsibility of undertaking all domestic duties, including cooking, cleaning, gardening, and caring for the children while her husband provides shelter, clothing, and clearing the field during the farming season. Until recently, husbands were responsible for making all household utensils except cooking pots, which were made by women. Now almost all household utensils are readily purchased from the market. With the Nkundo, women had the sole responsibility of planting and harvesting crops, fetching firewood, cooking meals, making mats and pots, and taking care of all other essential household chores.[65]

A woman dances during a wedding celebration in Dakar, Senegal, 1992. (Courtesy of A. Olusegun Fayemi)

WOMEN AND SOCIAL AND ECONOMIC TRANSFORMATIONS IN MARRIAGE

Included in the several attributions of Western influences on African cultures are the changing marriage outlooks and definitions as well as the roles women play in it. There is now a constant combination of traditional African values and standards with those of foreign origins. Western cultural ideals have had massive effects on African marriage institutions, but the degree of their influence differs from region to region and from one group to another. Although arguable, the complexities in attitudes and practices that constitute African marriage institution no longer endure in its totality in many African societies. Some practices and values are still held high and considered essential, even though contemporary conditions and consequences make them less effective to practice. Others have become redundant and have therefore been abandoned. Christianity and, to some extent, Islam have also succeeded in condemning and eroding African religious beliefs and other practices associated with marriage. The institutions of polygyny, initiation rites, marriage payments, and arranged marriages have been at the center of Christian religious and political attacks.

Yet, the effects of modern economic conditions have been more invasive to African marriage structures than anything political authorities and religious groups could have done to disrupt it. The resultant effect of these economic conditions in African is that it breaks up the organization of families; and as a result, family members can no longer depend solely on each other for social and economic support. This is especially so when relatives travel individually seeking economic opportunities to satisfy their daily needs. Not only do these changes have the consequence of restructuring household organization, but it is also changing the economic securities and social ties associated with marriage throughout Africa. The increased social mobility in search of economic security is applicable to both women and men, but it also implies that married couples are now more than ever removed from the control and scrutiny of their elderly family members. Couples' behaviors and their treatment of each other, which in the past, parents and other family members had the responsibility of ensuring it was in some form of equilibrium, is now left to the couples' own devices.

The new economic conditions have also indirectly caused marriage payments, particularly in some parts of eastern Africa, to increase dramatically, causing the reduced desire of men to marry multiple women. The governments of Kenya, Uganda, and Tanzania have put into place measures to limit marriage payments, but such measures are not always effective without constant enforcement. Nevertheless, the increase in the amount demanded for marriage payments are, in themselves, serving as disincentives for many men to marry. A Kenyan official circular explains the above issue well:

> Young men often cannot afford to pay the big dowry demanded and as a result young women form unions without the consent of either of their families or with a modified consent, which, in the absence of the usual customary ties, may result in the complete break-up of the family at a later date.[66]

Perhaps, it is as a result of such occurrences that some researchers are quick in generalizing about the fact that African parents "sell" their daughters into marriages, regardless of whether a society requires a marriage payment as part of its marriage procedures or not.

The recent economic conditions are, however, not without benefits, particularly for the roles and positions of African women in their various marital homes. Harsh economic conditions in many countries as well as the increased unemployment rates for men have necessitated that women, who previously were restricted to domestic duties, take up supplemental activities to help in the survival of their households. Indeed, some women have become the sole breadwinners of their families. For example, in the past,

Nupe women who engaged in trading activities were confined to certain locations near their homestead. Now, not only are such trading activities conducted in far-off places, but these women may be gone for weeks, months, or even years from their husbands and homes. More than ever before, an ever-increasing number of Nupe women, including those with infant children and very young themselves, independently travel around the country to carry out their trading activities with no social restrictions.[67] There are instances in northern Nigeria where middle-class Hausa wives, in spite of being required to live in seclusion (*purdah*) have found inventive ways to supplement their families' income and to gain some form of autonomy from their husbands. They accomplish these by trading among themselves and by engaging in sewing, embroidery, hairdressing, etc., to generate income.[68]

More than ever before, women are increasingly interested in engaging in economic activities either because their families' survival obliges such actions or because they have personal desires to gain economic independence. Contrary to popular views that African women are pawns of men and societal regulations, they are social actors who seek power and opportunities by any means available. Therefore, women may occasionally bond together as in the case of co-wives doing cooperative ventures or market women forming trade unions. We must point out, however, that women do not necessarily have a natural inclination to connect among themselves unless the relationship benefits them. Caroline H. Bledsoe points out that "the model woman of my argument . . . is not the affectionate daughter, hardworking wife, or loving mother . . . but the cold, calculating female who uses all available resources to control the world around her."[69] It is therefore a reasonable deduction from the above that whenever possible, women use each other and the institution of marriage for their own personal advancement. The probability of this deduction may be confined, depending on region and society, but given the general social and cultural structures that regulate women's lives in the institution of marriage in Africa, women are likely to operate independently or collaboratively when such actions result in benefits. For example, some women may divorce their husbands on the grounds that acquiring additional wives increase the social and economic hardships on them, or equally, they may instigate their husbands to take on additional women for the advantages co-wives bring with them. In contemporary situations, women are adopting different strategies to become "equal" partners in marriage, or more frequently, they are choosing to become independent single-parent family heads. The increased number of women who are combining careers and the traditional requirements of a wife are beginning to serve as a reference guide for other women, and it would come as no surprise that such women would eventually initiate revolutionary ideas and practices regarding the roles and positions of women in the institution of marriage in Africa.

NOTES

1. Arthur Philips (ed.), *Survey of African Marriage and Family Life* (New York: Oxford University Press, 1953).

2. Marguerite Dupire, "The Position of Women in a Pastorial Society," in Denise Paulme (ed.), *Women of Tropical Africa* (Berkeley: University of California Press, 1971), 47–83.

3. Siegfried Frederick Nadel, *A Black Byzantium: The Kingdom of Nupe in Nigeria* (London: Oxford University Press, 1942), 252–254.

4. Alfred R. Radcliffe-Brown and Daryll Forde, *African Systems of Kinship and Marriage* (New York: Oxford University Press, 1950), 46.

5. Edward Evans-Pritchard, *The Position of Women in Primitive Societies and Other Essays in Social Anthropology* (London: Faber and Faber, 1965), 37–58.

6. Cécile McHardy, "Love in Africa," *Présence Africaine*, Vol. 68 (1968): 52–60.

7. Harold J. Simons, *African Women: their Legal Status in South Africa* (London: C. Hurst, 1968), 81.

8. Since Simon's work, researchers such as Paulme (1963), Bohannan (1964), and Mair (1969) have challenged Western-oriented views on African polygyny.

9. William Jankowiak and Edward Fischer, "A Cross-Cultural Perspective on Romantic Love," *Ethnology*, Vol. 31 (1992): 149–155.

10. Lucy Mair, "Freedom of Consent in African Marriage," *The Anti-Slavery Reporter and Aborigines' Friend*, Vol. 11 (1958): 63–65.

11. Victor C. Uchendu, "Concubinage among the Ngwa Igbo of Southern Nigeria," *Africa*, Vol. 35 (1965): 187–197.

12. Emmanuel N. Obiechina, *An African Popular Literature: A Study of Onitsha Market Pamphlets* (Cambridge: Cambridge University Press, 1973), 34.

13. Rosemary M. F. Joseph, *Bulletin of the School of Oriental and African Studies, University of London,* Vol. 50 (1987): 90–119.

14. Ibid.

15. Joseph indicates that her research shows it was the girl who hoisted the flag, but Kohler (1933) stated that it was the young man who hoisted the flag while Msimang (1975) argued that the hoisting of the flag could be done by either the young man or the young woman.

16. Jean Buxton, "The Significance of Bride-wealth and the Levirate among the Nilotic and Nilo-Hamitic Tribes of the Southern Sudan," in Isaac Schapera (ed.), *Studies in Kinship and Marriage.* Dedicated to Brenda Z. Seligman on her 80th Birthday (London: Royal Anthropological Institute of Great Britain and Ireland, 1963), 67.

17. Regina Smith Oboler, *Women, Power, and Economic Change: The Nandi of Kenya* (Stanford, CA: Stanford University Press, 1985), 99.

18. Mona Etienne, "Contradictions, Constraints, and Choice: Widow Remarriage among the Baule of Ivory Coast," in Betty Potash (ed.), *Widows in African Societies* (Stanford, CA: Stanford University Press, 1986), 241–283.

19. Ibid.

20. Elizabeth Copet-Rougier, "Etude de la Transformation du Marriage chez les Mkako du Cameroun," in David Parkin and David Nyamwaya (eds.), *Transformations of African Marriage* (Manchester, UK: Manchester University Press, 1987), 75–93.

21. Denise Paulme, *Women of Tropical Africa* (Berkeley: University of California Press, 1971), 9.

22. Dr. A Rançon, *Dans la Haute-Gambie, Voyage d'exploration Scientifique 1891–1892*, Annales de l'Institut Colonial de Marseille, *Soc. D'Editions Scientifiques*, Vol. 1 (1894): 592, cited in Denise Paulme, *Women of Tropical Africa*, 25.

23. Unpublished accounts by Maupoli, cited in Paulme, *Women of Tropical Africa*.

24. Betty Potash, "Women in the Changing African Family," in Margaret Jean Hay and Sharon Stichter (eds.), *African Women South of the Sahara* (New York: Longman Publishing, 1995), 85.

25. Daniel Jordan Smith, "Romance, Parenthood, and Gender in a Modern African Society," *Ethnology*, Vol. 40 (2001): 129–151.

26. Peter Marris, *Family and Social Change in an African City* (Evanston, IL: 1962); Kenneth Little and Anne Price, "Some Trends in Modern Marriage among West Africans," in Colin M. Turnbull (ed.), *Africa and Change* (New York: Knopf, 1973), 185–207.

27. Potash, 82.

28. Dorothy D. Vellenga, "Who is a Wife? Legal Expressions of Heterosexual Conflict in Ghana," in Christine Oppong (ed.), *Female and Male in West Africa* (London: George Allen and Unwin, 1983), 144–152.

29. Jane Guyer, "Beti Widow Inheritance and Marriage Law: A Social History," in Potash (ed.), *Widows in African Societies* (Stanford, CA: Stanford University Press, 1986), 193–220.

30. Alice Armstrong, *Women and Rape in Zimbabwe* (Roma, Lesotho: Institute of Southern African Studies, National University of Lesotho, 1990).

31. Potash, 83.

32. Caroline H. Bledsoe, *Women and Marriage in Kpelle Society* (Stanford, CA: Stanford University Press, 1980), 112–113.

33. Potash, 83.

34. Pamela Landberg, "Widows and Divorced Women in Swahili Society," in Potash (ed.), *Widows in African Society* (Stanford, CA: Stanford University Press, 1986), 107–131.

35. Jean-Claude Muller, "Where to Live? Widows' Choices among the Rukuba," in Potash (ed.), *Widows in African Society* (Stanford, CA: Stanford University Press, 1986), 175–193.

36. Marriage payments among the Nguni are expressed by the term *lobolo*. The payment is usually in cattle but sometimes in money. This is done before the marriage can be finalized. See Clement Martyn Doke and Benedict Wallet Vilakazi, *Zulu-English Dictionary* (Witwatersrand, South Africa: Witwatersrand University Press, 1948).

37. Harriet Ngubane, "The Consequences for Women of Marriage Payments in a Society with Patrilineal Descent," in David Parkin and David Nyamwaya (eds.), *Transformation of African Marriage* (Manchester, UK: Manchester University Press, 1987), 173–181.

38. Edna G. Bay, "Servitude and Worldly Succession in the Palace of Dahomey," in Claire C. Robertson and Martin A. Klein (eds.), *Women and Slavery in Africa* (Madison, WI: Heinemann, 1997), 341–342.

39. Bledsoe, 85.

40. Jeremy S. Eades, *The Yoruba Today* (Cambridge: Cambridge University Press, 1980), 52–53.

41. Ibid.

42. Potash, 74.

43. Ibid.

44. Monica Hunter, "Effects of Contact with Europeans on the Status of Pondo Women," *Africa*, Vol. 6 (1933): 259–276.

45. Ibid.

46. Isaac Shapera, *Handbook of Tswana Law and Custom* (London: Oxford University Press, 1938), 103.

47. Schapera, 107.

48. Denise Paulme (ed.), *Women of Tropical Africa* (Berkeley: University of California Press, 1971), 11.

49. Monique Gessain, "Coniagui Women," in Paulme, *Women of Tropical Africa*, 17–44.

50. Potash, "Female Farmers, Mother-in-law and Extension Agents: Development Planning and a Rural Luo Community," *Working Papers on Women in International Development*, Vol. 90 (1985).

51. Schapera, 202–203.

52. Oboler, 125–126.

53. Ifi Amadiume, *Male Daughters, Female Husbands: Gender and Sex in an African Society* (Atlantic Highlands, NJ: Zed Books 1987), 42.

54. Carol P. MacCormack, "Control of Land, Labor, and Capital in Rural Southern Sierra Leone," in Edna G. Bay (ed.), *Women and Work in Africa* (Boulder, CO: Westview Press, 1982), 37–38.

55. Katherine Abu, "The Separateness of Spouses: Conjugal Resources in Ashanti Town," in Christine Oppong (ed.), *Female and Male in West Africa* (London: George Allen & Unwin, 1983), 156–169.

56. Margaret Jean Hay and Sharon Stichter (eds.), *African Women South of the Sahara* (New York: Longman Scientific and Technical, 1995), 77.

57. Lucy Mair, *African Marriage and Social Change* (London: Frank Cass & Co., 1969), 5.

58. Ibid.

59. Audrey I. Richards, "Bemba Marriage and Present Economic Conditions," *Rhodes-Livingstone Paper*, No. 4 (1940): 35.

60. W. Rangeley, "Notes on Cewa Tribal Law," *Nyasaland Journal*, Vol. 1 (1948): 47.

61. Günter Wagner, *The Bantu of North Kavirondo* (London: Oxford University Press, 1949), 44.

62. P. Bösch, *Les Banyamwazi: Peuple de l'Afrique Orientale* (Munster: Anthropos Bilbiothek, 1930), 341–342. Cited in Mair, *African Marriage and Social Change*, 74–114.

63. Richards, 85–87.

64. Ibid.

65. Mair, 92–95.

66. Kenya Administrative Circular (1948), unpublished. Cited in Mair, *African Marriage and Social Change*, 68.

67. Nadel, 334.

68. Catherine Coquery-Vidrovitch, *African Women: A Modern History* (Boulder, CO: Westview Press, 1997), 106–108.

69. Bledsoe, 180–181.

SUGGESTED READING

Bledsoe, Caroline. *Women and Marriage in Kpelle Society*. Stanford, CA: Stanford University Press, 1980.

Coquery-Vidrovitch, Catherine. *African Women: A Modern History*. Boulder, CO: Westview Press, 1997.

Hay, Jean Margaret and Sharon Stichter (eds.). *African Women South of the Sahara*. New York: Longman Scientific and Technical, 1995.

Mair, Lucy. *African Marriage and Social Change*. London: Frank Cass & Co., 1969.

Oppong, Christine (ed.). *Female and Male in West Africa*. London: George Allen & Unwin, 1983.

2

—∞∞∞—

Women and Family

For many historians, an important aspect of understanding society has been through the area of the "ordinary," such as in family systems, changes in family structures, and in the patterns of daily living. The changes in the structures of family and its material manifestations, in particular, have been important in understanding historical developments in the institution of marriage in any society. As noted by some scholars, historical research on family has shown the significance of such issues as fertility, age at marriage, and household size in preindustrial societies. These issues have been influential in the ways in which societies have tamed, utilized, and distributed resources. Yet, unlike in Europe and America where the history of the family has received detailed attention from researchers since the 1960s, historians have virtually neglected the African family—let alone the roles of women in it.[1] One explanation for this state of affairs is perhaps the large number of anthropological studies on African kinship systems, which has captured our interest for decades on the static categorization of kinship instead of the material manifestation of kinship structures, the changes it has undergone over the years, and how those outward manifestations and changes help in the understanding of the social, economic, and political organizations of societies.

The existing literature on family suggests that on the one hand, researchers who support Africa's struggles to reaffirm and preserve its identity in the face of Western economic and cultural onslaughts have fallen to the lure of romanticizing the African past manifested in the way they discuss Africa's social institutions. On the other hand, those with nostalgic feelings for the so-called authentic African family have been caught up in an immovable state, which prevents these scholars from coming to terms with the extent of the changes that have taken place in the African family. It has been argued that the ironic reality is that "nostalgia is precisely a reaction to change."[2] Indeed, talking about or remembering with nostalgic feelings may historically stand for neither an idea of pan-African cultures, nor something that is natural to humans, but something that seems "almost as 'natural' to us as motor reflexes."[3] From here, we can somehow understand nostalgic feelings, which may frame a researcher's perspective as a natural way of dealing with change, particularly if adjustment to that change is not smooth or pleasant. In other instances, the often-mentioned male perspective bias in African history hides the female factor in discussions on domestic units and the family although as many would agree, reproductive and much of productive labor has been, and continues to be, predominantly the responsibility of women in the African family.

The African continent has an uncountable number of cultures and covers a wide range of different types of familial societies. There is hardly a

A grandma celebrates with her grand and greatgrand children—family continuity is very important. (Courtesy of Toyin Falola)

single model that can best describe an African family or the roles women play within it. However, there are some main similarities and generalities that provide some degree of understanding of the structures and functions of the African family and the roles women play in it. In this chapter, we will analyze the complex roles women play in African family and kinship systems. We will provide details about the various family and kinship structures, such as matrilineal, patrilineal, and bilateral systems and women's experiences within these structures. Since the era of hunter/gatherer societies in Africa, the family has been at the center of production, reproduction, and domestic life. Family systems may have started with just a few individuals—husband, wife, children, and probably grandparents and a few cousins—but as time went on and the demand for cooperation increased, the family grew to include a larger circle of individuals. A lineage was thus born consisting of individuals who recognized themselves as kin based on descent from a known common ancestor.

We can make a reasonable assumption based on anthropological and other research findings on African social life that in African precolonial societies, family and kinship were the units that socialized the individual and provided people with a sense of belonging. The family is, indeed, a universal social condition found in almost every society around the world and the most efficient means of checking and balancing the human need for food, shelter, security, companionship, and for the expression and regulation of sexual reproduction and socialization. The African family may contain several generations of people and utilize the sanction of kinship obligations to reward members and to bind them to an acceptable mode of behavior and action. The key importance of kinship in precolonial societies, and even today, was expanding and augmenting the social, cultural, economic, and political positioning and survival of the group. Igor Kopytoff puts it this way:

> Traditionally, African kin groups had an almost insatiable demand for people and jealously guarded those they already had. Socially, this meant the existence of corporate groups of kinsmen, collectively holding resources, carefully enforcing their rights in membership . . . every newborn was legally spoken for and eagerly appropriated at birth by one or another autonomous kin group . . . similarly, the reproductive capacity of every woman was a resource to be appropriated at birth.[4]

Family and kinship systems, therefore, became vital to every group— triggered by such forces as economic issues, political tensions, migrations, and the need for social order. Indeed, structures within family and kinship systems direct rights and responsibilities of individuals and define the limits within which members must confine their behaviors and activities. To understand women's roles and the situations that required their duties, let us turn to a brief overview of conceptual issues in African family and kinship systems.

FAMILY AND KINSHIP STRUCTURES

The African family institution, as with other familial institutions around the world, provided people in the past, and continues in contemporary times, to provide people who share kinship ties with sociocultural, economic, and political subsistence through a shared need and cooperation. The general definition affixed to family has been expressed in terms of relationships that result from marriage. Many researchers have rejected this approach of looking at the family. In particular, feminist writers have called for an all-embracing definition that disassociates the family from marriage. To them, the family should be conceived of in terms that accommodate diverse groupings of permanent or semipermanent families.[5] Two major types of family systems have been identified in African societies: one based on sexual relations and the other on descent. There are *conjugal* families in which marriage serves as the key element that ties the unit together, and there are *consanguineal* families, where the groups' relationship is based on their descent from a common ancestor.[6] A descent group emerges when membership in a family extends into generations—generally around three of them. While the particular descent adopted by a group differs from society to society, the major ones identified include patrilineal descent, matrilineal descent, and bilateral descent.

In the above descent systems, the most reckoned one in many African societies is the patrilineal, where descent is through the male line. In this descent system, children are members of their father's family, and it is there that they exercise their primary rights and responsibilities. In matrilineal systems, sometimes referred to as uterine systems, descent is recognized through the female line. As with patrilineal descent, children belong to their maternal family and enjoy their rights and responsibilities there. Matrilineal descent occurs in societies such as the Akan, Bemba, Tonga, and Tuareg. In a few societies, stress is placed on neither patrilineal nor matrilineal: both are given equal recognition. This descent arrangement is commonly referred to as bilateral, practiced in societies such as among the Afikpo of eastern Nigeria and the Birifor of the Ghana-Ivory Coast border.[7] Recent studies suggest that contemporary social and economic changes and Western influences in Africa have given force to a shift in a bilateral direction. In particular, the pursuit of economic goals that have become accessible to people are eroding the importance that people used to attached to patrilineal or matrilineal ties. Essentially, people could form interpersonal relationships that had no precedence to descent ties in pursuit of their economic objectives. It has also been indicated that the practice of conjugal family principles appear to be minimal on the African continent dating back to the precolonial period. In conjugal families, because marriage holds the family together, any breakage in the conjugal relationship turns to break up the family structure. Even when the marriage remains intact, the family may still disintegrate when older children leave to establish their own families and households without strings of generational ties with one another.

In contrast, consanguineal families endure across generations because of individuals marrying in and their children maintain collective kin ties regardless of the existence of marriage. Before the interference of European colonization, many African societies appeared to have favored consanguineal family systems. Although recent social and economic conditions have made the conjugal family structure a more desirable alternative, consanguineal family continues to endure in many African societies. In the past, consanguineal family also allowed a cyclical replacement of labor as children took over from their parents when they got older or died. Older children, upon marriage, usually left their parents' household to form their own in nearby locations although they continued to connect and cooperate with one another for sociocultural, economic, religious, and political reasons.[8] It is important to note here that in both conjugal and consanguineal family structures, polygyny may be practiced, which gives rise to a polygynous family structure. Polygyny has been practiced in various societies in Africa since the precolonial era and continues to exist in many places today. The polygynous family allows a man to marry multiple wives and to have legitimate claims to their productive and reproductive labor. Other structures such as patrilocality and matrilocality, discussed in the previous chapter, may exist in the above family systems. The various variations use by different groups make it difficult to establish distinct spheres or boundaries that define the African family, household, or residential arrangements from one another, since a group may practice one form—or a combination of two—or just some aspects of the structures.

The diversity of arrangements in African family systems means that women's rights and responsibilities in their descent groups are equally as varied. However, as with other African histories, we know more about men's roles and positions in lineage groupings than we do of that of women. Nonetheless, many studies have suggested that African women since precolonial periods have actively participated in their kin group activities and taken on essential roles. In many cases in precolonial Africa, women have held important political and religious offices and have taken on more responsibilities in recent years with women's education and empowerment agendas to better the general social and economic status of them. Indeed, contemporary economic conditions have allowed more women to assume increased responsibilities in subsistence farming and trading as well as in other economic ventures to help maintain their immediate and extended families.

WOMEN'S ROLES IN THE HOUSEHOLD

Until recently, the majority of Africans who lived in rural areas were generally only concerned with the basic necessity of caring for themselves and their families. Their activities included farming; cattle herding; trading; and in a few instances, hunting and gathering as in the cases of the Mbuti Pygmies of the Ituri Forest and the San people of the Kalahari Desert. In these activities, a distinct but fluid division of labor existed between men and women. In general, men took on the responsibility of clearing the land for farming, long-distance trading, hunting, and public affairs. Women were almost exclusively responsible for reproductive activities. They were expected to be fertile and to bear enough children for their husbands. Indeed, the value and status a woman acquired in a society may very well be dependent on her fertility. In addition, women were responsible for household or domestic duties such as fetching water and firewood, cooking, cleaning, gardening, subsistence farming, and small-scale trading. Nonetheless, the distinguishing line between the activities reserved for each sex was sometimes blurry, allowing both men and women to engage in the duties of their other. For example, among the Fon of Benin, although it was considered inappropriate for women to be working the land, they sometimes did so beyond their own domestic duty of gardening, dying indigo, and transporting goods for trading.[9]

Women's management of the household did not necessarily equate control of the decision-making process regarding the affairs of the family. However, in the polygynous joint family where co-wives lived by themselves, the household usually consisted of a woman and her children. In such instances, each wife enjoyed some level of autonomy, which allowed her to have control of over her food stores, manage her fields, and take charge of her daily choices. Three different stages have been identified between women in a household system where women lived with the families of their husbands. There was the young bride expected to prove her value to her husband's kin by being shy, respectful, and hard working; the mature wife who competed with others for resources and tried to safeguard her children's interests; and the mother of adult sons who wielded considerable influence and power in the household.[10] Once women became mothers of adult children, they not only exercised their power over their daughter-in-laws, but in many cases, they controlled the affairs of their sons. They directed how their sons spent their resources and on whom they spent it.

In matrilineal societies, in particular, the roles of the older women were especially emphasized and tended to create a hierarchy among the group of women in the household. When older women reached menopause, they gained particular authority and influence, which sometimes allowed them to take on ritual and political roles generally restricted to men. While such women may have exerted this power over both men and women, they usually exerted more over women within their households. They structured and supervised the activities of their daughter-in-laws and that of their younger co-wives for their husbands. In reaction to how women exercised such powers within the household, some researchers have argued that postmenopausal women were responsible for reproducing, within the community of women, the hierarchical relations that governed the relationships between elders and their dependents. In all the various levels of social organization, this reproduction of social hierarchy occurred from the basic household unit to the level of state.[11]

Widowhood also affected women's responsibilities within the household. In matrilocalities, changes in household responsibilities that occur as a result of a deceased husband may be very subtle. This is because only the personal duties that a woman rendered to her husband ceased. She continued with her domestic responsibilities toward her children and the other members of her maternal kin who may be living in the household. Among the Akan, for example, a woman, in the past and also today, could remarry a couple of times, but she usually resided with her maternal kin for the entire period of her marriages. In systems where widows were allowed to remarry, they could leave their late husband's household if they chose to do so, or they could just return to their own kin and take up residence there.

However, if remarriage was forbidden, a relative of the late husband could take on the widow as one of his wives, if he already had some, or he could also become just the sexual partner of the widow. In such cases, a number of things, including the woman's age, the number of co-wives of the new partner, the number of children the widow already had, her prior relationship with her husband's relatives, and the value of property of the late husband determined the widow's status and responsibility in the household. If neither of the above scenarios was possible, the widow could just be absorbed into the family as one of the women of the household. In systems that allowed remarriage, widows could choose to continue residing in the late husband's compound if they did not remarry. In these instances, such widows became the heads of their households and could be responsible for managing their husband's property—generally with the approval of her husband's family and usually for her children until they reached maturity. Her status as an independent woman made it possible for her to engage in private economic ventures. She could use her resources to seek counsel from outside both her maternal family and her husband's family, and she could reallocate her resources according to her wishes.

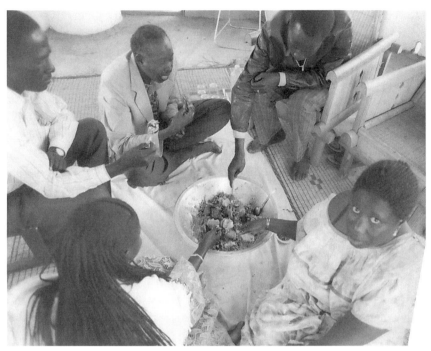

A family sits down to a meal in Niaga, Senegal, 1992. (Courtesy of A. Olusegun Fayemi)

Studies also show that in contemporary times, women in Burundi society sometimes collaborate with their husbands in business ventures: in which case a husband must consult his wife in every business decision, and her decisions must be respected. Outside of their economic partnerships with their husbands, some women also manage to establish themselves well within their husband's household, which allow them to serve as the link between their husbands and those who seek the goodwill of their husband. A wife's position as an intermediary enables her to receive gifts, especially pots of beer, from persons who wish to influence her to intercede on their behalf with her husband. Some women in this position have shown themselves to be very crafty by selling the excess gifts that she will need for her husband's persuasion and for the household and keeping the proceeds from the sale for herself.

Interestingly, some Burundi husbands appear to take immense satisfaction in a wife who uses her wits to become wealthy: for a wife's wealth not only indicates her ingenuity and creativity, but also the husband does not have to worry about laying down any income or bearing any financial burden. More importantly, a man gains reverence from his peers as a result of the hospitality his wife provides to his visitors, and a wife shows her satisfaction with her husband by seeing to it that visitors to their home are welcomed with opened arms and leave with a good impression of the man. She equally seeks out the enemies of her husband and devises ways to defeat them. A high social status of a husband and a wife means that visitors who pay them homage equally have high social status and are likely to be wealthy. Women of such households profit from the stream of visitors she entertains by asking them for gifts and favors for her children.[12] In the past, some of these women managed to attain high political offices as judges and councillors at the court of a ruler through the means by which they managed their household affairs and becoming rich in the process. Through their offices, these women may receive additional gifts in the form of cows, clothing, and jewelry, and may occasionally accrue more wealth than their husbands.

Men in Burundi society are noted for their frequent long absences, which gives women the opportunities to take control of their husbands' property and to show themselves as capable women. Women of wealthy and powerful family backgrounds could also help their husbands' social and political positions by assisting them in forming beneficial alliances with her family and with other wealthy families. While women of the lower caste in Burundian society may not enjoy the same privileges and opportunities to amass wealth as those of the upper castes, there are many opportunities and a variety of optional roles through which they can earn money for themselves and their families. Many of the lower caste women earn income through basket weavings, working as a midwife or as an assistant to a physician or a pharmacist, and working as a governess for upper class families who can afford their services.[13] Essentially, as the Burundi and the other examples illustrate, women play important social, economic, and political roles within the confines of their households, which eventually reflects in both subtle and flamboyant ways in the public arena.

WOMEN'S ROLES IN KINSHIP GROUPS

As members of diverse kinship groups, African women maintain some rights and responsibilities, but their particular roles and positions depend on the pattern of system practiced by their group. Such roles and positions may be expressed in a symbolic manner, especially in rituals regarding funerals. For example, among the Luo society in Kenya, the category of womanhood has for generations been identified with wifehood to such an extent that upon the death of a married woman, her body was not returned to her natal family but buried in her husband's compound. Even in the event that a woman died in her maternal home, whether visiting or separated, she was still not buried within the compound of her natal family but outside of it.[14] This tradition still exists today although due to Christian influences, some women are buried at the church cemetery. The reverse is true of Igbo society in Nigeria, where a woman's descent group always retains the right to her body for burial.[15] The same is the case among the Akan of Ghana, where a woman maintains her membership in her natal family from birth until death, and her natal family has the responsibility of interring her remains upon her death. The above symbolic positioning not only informs us of how women may envision themselves within their descent or kinship groups, it may also indicate the factors that dictate or facilitate women's responsibilities. For instance, in circumstances where women, regardless of what marriage structure they have married into, feel part of their natal lineage, they may be more obliged to render their services readily to members of their kin. In matrilineal systems, in particular, where women have the support of their own kin they maintain a greater influence in their husband's family.

The role of queen mothers among the Asante in Ghana reflects, to some degree, the political roles women play in their descent groups. Asante queen mothers are not only pivotal in the selection of chiefs, but they also ensure that the group's interest is protected at all times against the male leadership. They do this by attending political meetings of the group and voicing their concerns.[16] Almost every Akan lineage has an *obaa payin* (elderly woman) who may not necessarily be a queen mother; her position allows her to serve not only as the "mother" of the entire lineage, but she also helps in selecting the male leaders of the lineage and ensure that women within the group conform to certain behaviors. Women also bear financial responsibility in their descent groups. In the past, many women accepted or were forced into marriages so that their group would gain financially or maintain certain status. For example, in the 19th century in Ganda society in central Africa, any lineage hopeful of gaining political office had to "sacrifice" some of its females by way of giving to the king several of its daughters.

While such practices have not completely died out in many African societies, women in recent years have garnered for themselves economic statuses that allow them to contribute financially to funeral rites, housing projects, and other activities of their group. More importantly, women's improved financial positioning has made it possible for some of them to gain political offices. In precolonial Igbo society, women were organized into two groups entrusted with the responsibility of protecting women's interests, sanctioning their behaviors, and for maintain their general affairs. The two groups consisted of daughters of the lineage while the other was made up of women who married into the lineage. Although the daughters exercised a greater degree of influence as compared to that of the wives, both groups worked together to guarantee the success of their work.[17]

In matrilineal societies where inheritance passes from a father to his sister's children, rather than from a father to his children, women enjoy a unique position power brought on by their children's inheritance. However, it has been suggested that instead of women in these societies exercising the power themselves, they transfer that power to the men in their families, which may sometimes earn them titles such as "mother of the chief," or "mother of the family."[18] Sometimes social stratification of kinship groups affected the roles that women played in their kinship group. For instance, in Rwanda and Burundi in central Africa—where society has been hierarchically structured—the upper class of herding Tutsi rule over a lower class of Hutu farmers. As a result of this structure, Tutsi noblewomen could supervise work done by both Hutu men and women.[19]

Women's rights to property in descent groups also affect their productive and reproductive roles and the level of their participation in the affairs of the group. In instances where women have rights to property in their own natal family or to acquire their own property, they enjoy a greater of level of independence in their conjugal relationships. They do not have to depend entirely on their husband's family in caring for their children, and they may actually be the source of their husband's wealth. In West Africa, women involved in trading activities have the capacity to accumulate wealth on their own. In such cases, not only do their own kin consult them regarding their property, but their husbands have to tread carefully with them in order to maintain their financial resources in his family. This has been illustrated among the Nupe people of northern Nigeria. In Nupe society before colonial rule, female trading—especially itinerant, long-distance trading—was ideally limited to women with no children. However, under British colonial rule, economic activity grew, causing mothers to become traveling traders.

Many Nupe mothers contributed a greater share of the family income than their husbands, who were often poor farmers. Husbands were often heavily in debt to their wives because the latter assumed many of the financial responsibilities in the household. Indeed, this reversal of roles traditionally reserved for men caused many husbands to be resentful, yet they remained helpless and unable to remedy the situation.[20] On the other hand, in descent groups where women did not have the right to own or acquire property, and their access to housing and land was only by way of marriage, they competed with other wives in polygynous families and/or kowtow to the wishes of the husband's mother in order to gain land and property. This may also have been their only source of economic support for themselves and their children; and therefore, they may have been forced to remain in the relationship regardless of any marital difficulties and the amount of domestic responsibilities they had to take on.

A grandmother surrounded by her grandchildren in Addis Ababa, Ethopia, 1997. (Courtesy of A. Olusegun Fayemi)

As in the past, kinship ties in recent years have allowed women to access the help of their natal kin or from that of the husband's family. In fact, women have long relied on their family members to be able to carry out their domestic and reproductive roles. Sisters may help each other; co-wives may form cooperatives in their farming and trading activities; daughter-in-laws help mother-in-laws; and mothers depend on their children for support. In particular, the help that mothers get from their children allow those engaged in trading activities to do so over distances and to spread their activities to many places. Older children may take the responsibility of looking after younger siblings or elderly relatives while their mothers are away on trading activities.[21] An illustration of this cooperation and dependence has been found among some Muslim communities in northern Nigeria where as a result of the practice of *purdah* (seclusion and veiling of women), women rely on their children for their trading activities.[22]

In recent years, with the introduction of the Western system of education, many children have been enrolled in school and are unable or have limited amount of time to assist their mothers in their trading activities. Moreover, due to the nature of current market economies, relatives may live too far away from one another to be able to offer any substantial assistance. The result is that not only are women left alone to accomplish their domestic responsibilities, but they must also perform their productive activities with no or a limited amount of help.[23] Yet, such changes have not left women without alternatives. Many women now enlist poor relatives whose parents could not afford the cost of education to assist them as domestic help. In return, such relatives may be allowed to learn a trade skill in areas as hairdressing, dressmaking, culinary, carpentry, masonry, and vehicles mechanics—in the case of boys—or they may be given a monthly stipend, which they can save and use to start a petty trading venture after they leave. In other instances, women who do not have junior relatives to rely on may employ on nonrelatives for the same purpose.

WOMEN'S ROLES IN THE CHANGING AFRICAN FAMILY

Unquestionably, change is perhaps the most characteristic feature in the history of modern Africa. The most obvious change the continent has experienced, and one that has affected almost every aspect of the social, cultural, economic, religious, and political life of Africans, was one brought on by European colonization and imperialism. In many instances, change meant abrupt and painful alterations in the ways of life. In other cases, change was more gradual, allowing social and cultural systems and institutions, in particular, to remain unaltered while people adapted to the effects of new elements without drastic departures from their way of life.[24] Still, in some instances, change has been a welcome relief for some sectors of society. As with all of these sectors, colonial rule transformed family systems and relationships as well as women's roles in these institutions. While some researchers have argued that the change from subsistence farming to cash-crop economy, urbanization, labor migration, and new legal codes of marriage have placed women in a disadvantageous position, African women have also benefited from the new opportunities available as a result of the social and economic changes.

One of the fundamental changes in the African family today is labor migration. Employment opportunities, overexploitation of resources, lack of employment, and work requirements have led to men, more so than women, leaving their families for other places and often for long periods of time. This has given women a newfound independence as the effective heads of their families in place of their husbands and other men of the family. In the past, married women could step in for their husbands or for the male leaders of their group. However, in recent years, women have tended to take complete control of managing every aspect of the family's daily activities and property in the absences of their male counterparts. More importantly, a woman's responsibility in making the daily decisions and managing the family's affairs not only binds herself and her children, but also her husband, as well, on his return. In the extended patrilocal family, such a woman is less likely to submit to the wishes and the authority of its male head than she would in her husband's presence because of the fact that the network of command has become reordered.[25]

In the same vein, bitterness between co-wives may reduce, and they may cooperate more on family matters for the simple reason that the object of their jealousies and competition is not around.[26] Admittedly, while labor migration potentially increases the level of the workload and stress that women face in managing their families almost single-handedly, the significant aspect of this change is that women's roles in the family have become even more vital to the very survival of the institution of family in African societies. As indicated above, the downside to the male migration has been the forced responsibility placed on many African women to accomplish alone various tasks that required the assistance of a husband or other male family members. Some women have responded by migrating themselves into towns and urban centers to seek avenues of economic and social success. However, not all have found city life rosy and greener at the feet. Many have had to succumb to force labor, underpaid employment, prostitution, and homelessness while others have had to take on male lovers for their financial support and their very survival.

Married women are expected to dress with grace and elegance. (Courtesy of Toyin Falola)

Because most African societal regulations and customs provide no sanction for a lover's responsibility toward a woman and her children, women in such relationships can hardly seek both legal and traditional compensation from the family of the man. The decision to move to an urban center could potentially end a woman's marriage and jeopardize the position of her children in the family. In addition, such women are almost completely isolated from the support they would otherwise have enjoyed from their family and other kin members, and they have to rely on their own oars for survival. The sharing of childcare and other domestic duties with, for instance, co-wives and other siblings is generally not available to urban women. Single women who have children but are not financially sound may find it difficult to bring younger siblings from the country to help them, and they may not be able to hire a stranger for childcare and other domestic support. Such women must find effective ways to combine managing her domestic responsibilities with working outside the home. Research reports on Kenya suggest that in precolonial Kenyan societies, a wife was likely to get help from a junior co-wife, a slave girl, or older female children for childcare and domestic duties. Today, changes in family arrangements resulting from geographical and economic factors have closed women's access to each other's unpaid labor. Now the relationship is primarily a wage one.[27]

For some African women, the reverse of the above is true in the sense that they relish the independence and the flexibility that contemporary changes have engendered in the African family structure. A study among women factory workers in Jinja, Uganda, in the 1950s found that some women left their villages for the independence that urban life offered as well as to avoid entering into arranged marriages. The anonymity of urban life also afforded the women an avenue to evade traditional opposition to a wife working in the public space to earn money: a notion that was quite common in the rural areas. According to the study, many men held strong reservations against this new crop of women factory workers for the fear that they might reject their traditional roles of child bearing and child rearing, their roles in looking after the needs of their husbands, and taking care of the household responsibilities.

In particular, they strongly objected to women—regardless of whether it was their wives or not—working under the supervision of another man they were not married to, and extended the opposition to the employers of these women.[28] Another reason for the men's objection to allow their wives to earn an income working was that a wife's financial stability might eventually result in her leaving her husband, especially if the husband was not financially sound. Such women could also be a potential threat to their husbands' authority in the household reduce their capacity to control the family affairs.[29] Other researchers have found similar conventional views about women's mobility and employment and the relationship between these factors and their family life in places like South Africa, Ghana, and Nigeria. One study among Ghanaian women found that the employment of women in factories was mainly restricted to younger women, because a large percentage of the general population, perhaps including a portion of women themselves, considered factory work and family life—child bearing in particular—as incompatible. In spite of these constraints, independent women are now a feature in the African urban scenery.

In the towns and urban centers and away from the scrutiny and meddling of family members, women can conveniently enter into flexible heterosexual bonds and enjoy the advantages that loosened kinship ties bring to individuals. In spite of the added financial burden and domestic responsibilities that they have to sometimes carry out single-handedly, many women enjoy the opportunity to make decisions about their lives and the welfare of their children without fear or favor. It has been suggested that heterosexual bonds in Africa have historically had a long and central economic element for both couples and, in the African context, their extended family members. However, "what is new is not that heterosexual bonds are a source of resources and opportunities, but rather the bonds between kin groups that marriage represented have disappeared."[30] This development has allowed both women and men to enjoy more freedom and flexibility in their choice of partners and to divorce their spouses or leave incompatible relationships—a fact found in almost every African society and which has been noted by a number of researchers in their respective studies.

In Abidjan, Côte d'Ivoire, it has been found that changes in how people perceive heterosexual bonds is not limited to any particular group or class of people; rather such changes can be found among the various social classes.[31] In other words, not only are upper class/elite women redefining conjugal relationships to suit their needs and lifestyles, but women of lower social statuses and positions are picking and choosing what type of family relationship would be best for them. Professional women, in particular, are more likely to choose a single, independent lifestyle over the option of saddling themselves with the inconveniences of marital life. Many professional women now choose to enter into heterosexual relationships that they considered realistic rather than ideal.[32] In the same way, many professional women now object to entering into polygynous marriages for a number of reasons.

First, they may be contributing equally to the family's resources and do not wish for their husbands to share these resources with his other wife/wives; and second, they may just be appalled at the idea of sharing a husband. Third, the idea of being a co-wife may socially stigmatize them because of their high educational attainment. And fourth, the presence of co-wives may threaten their future security and the security of their children in the marriage. For many of these women, if marriage becomes an

Grandmother and daughter, a bonding that is promoted as part of African culture. (Courtesy of Toyin Falola)

option for them, their ideal marriage would be a monogamous relationship in which they share responsibilities equally with their husbands. However, as it has been suggested, "more often than not, the reality does not meet the ideal."[33] While many men in theory may sign up for a monogamous relationship with a woman, in practice, they are likely to oppose the sexual and financial exclusivity monogamy imposes on them and enter into extramarital relationships.

The odds are usually against women whose husbands engage in extramarital affairs, for in many African societies, social/customary regulations have little or no censorship against men engaging in such activities; and many of these women generally get nothing in return. Some studies suggest that elite women are more likely to keep quiet over their husband's extramarital relationships for fear of losing their social status in the event of a divorce or for the fear of being labeled as a "neglectful" wife. In recent years, although many African women have experienced significant changes in their social statuses, reinforced by improvements in women's legal rights, very few women have been able to take advantage of these changes because of the lack of knowledge about their legal rights. More and more, divorce is becoming accessible to many women in many African countries, yet in some selected few, a wife seeking divorce because of an adulterous husband or a wife getting her matrimonial rights implemented through the courts usually entails a lengthy and costly processes. Adultery is especially slippery grounds for women in the court system, for while it is generally accepted as grounds for both wife and husband to seek divorce, the courts are more sympathetic toward an adulterous husband than they are toward an adulterous wife.

Courts' gender biases that favor men over women prevents or puts stumbling blocks in women's willingness to seek help through the courts, and women who do not want to endure the processes and the ridicule and derision of the public may hesitate or avoid the courts altogether. Some women, however, avoid getting divorced for social reasons. As will be discussed later on, the social title that marriage endears on women causes some to want to hold onto the marriage even when the marriage is both physically and psychologically unbearable. For such women, seeking divorce would cause them to not only lose their status as married women, but they will, as a rule, forfeit their title as "Mrs. X, the wife of so and so—an important consideration in the emerging class system."[34] One of the consequences of the African embrace of the Western-style marriage model is that men whose wives seek divorce through the courts may request for the payment of alimony and other maintenance support. Although there is no guarantee that when the courts grant such requests, the men will feel obligated to comply with the ruling or that law enforcement agencies would be willing to enforce the ruling.

The conflict between men's lack of commitment to sexual exclusivity and women's insistence on having single partners comes from the fact that African social structures provide no such models to follow. Those striving for such exclusiveness are unwilling or unprepared for the fact that monogamy entails more than just the reduction of the number of women a man may wish to marry.[35] As a number of researchers point out, any blind adoption of foreign marriage systems is bound to cause troubles for couples for they entail values and principles that people are inherently not accustomed to, are unwilling to get accustomed to, or unable to get accustomed to because of existing sociocultural precedents already established in that society. Laura Longmore expressed this well when she wrote:

> The chief difficulty encountered by urban African is that they are striving after a culture of which they seldom have inside knowledge, practical experience, or guidance. No doubt, the emerging middle class strives consciously for the values of the white group, but it is no easy task under existing conditions. It would seem that in adopting western marriage the African has taken over some of the external trappings without the inner significance; the values and ideals of western monogamy are lacking in their Bantu form, and the

new and modified forms are not holding their own under urban conditions. They are inadequate and point to a disequilibrium in urban African domestic institutions. Western monogamy, without its accompanying values and ideas, is meaningless and ineffective.[36]

Many scholars have come to similar conclusions. That is, when some African men meet their potential spouses, most would readily accept the new domestic roles of a husband that comes with Western-style marriages without any real commitment to carrying them out once they get married. They live their lives in the same ways as most African cultures ascribe to a man—taking no part in household chores, caring for children, spending their free time away from the household,[37] or just relaxing while watching their wives juggle a million household tasks with little or no help. Like women, men equally want the contemporary social prestige attached to monogamous marriages but find it, inconvenient to put any real efforts into making it work for both themselves and their spouses, which often leads to conflicts revolving around unfulfilled spousal expectations.

A study among teachers in Kinshasa reveals that discrepancy exists between the general qualities men ascribe to the modern woman and what they personally hope to find in their wives—a situation that can lead to expectation conflicts in the conjugal family relationship. In principle, the majority of the young teachers agreed that there must be equality between women and men and that women must also have equal social and political responsibilities. To them, the ideal modern woman should adopt Western-style dressing; must be able to speak French; and must be a professional women working in media, teaching, and in other socially acceptable fields. Ironically, the men envisioned different qualities in their future wives and in situations where the supposed wife already has a profession or is behaving in the ways of modernity, the men would require that such values be set aside. Therefore, a woman who has been trained as a teacher, for the sake of wifehood and motherhood, involuntarily becomes a housewife restricted to the affairs of domesticity. Clearly, the men envisioned their wives to be, above everything else: housekeepers, obedient and respectful companions, mothers, and sexual partners. This is in addition to the view that even when women are educated, their education would be more useful in the domestic space than in the public space. In effect, educated women would be better housekeepers and mothers than uneducated women would, even though it is not hard to tell that the men's position comes from their fear that an educated wife would be more willing to question a husband's authority.[38]

The changes that have occurred in African family structures have also played out in the level of domestic responsibility that used to exist between a wife and a husband. An illustration of the changes in family responsibilities between women and men has been documented among the Igbo of

Afikpo in eastern Nigeria. In precolonial Igbo society, women were responsible for pot-making and small-scale trading while men engaged in yam farming and slave trading. The European colonial rule brought with it new sets of crops onto the African scene. Of the new crops introduced, cassava became vital to the family in rural Afikpo. This was because Afikpo men who traditionally farmed yams, considered a prestigious activity, refused to farm cassava allowing women instead to grow it. Cassava eventually became a staple crop and gained market value.

From the proceeds women made from selling cassava, they were able to provide for themselves and their children with little or no help from their husbands. In recent years, Afikpo husbands have almost lost the authority to restrict the activities of their wives to the domestic sphere and to subjugate them.[39] The changing family arrangements between husbands and wives have not been restricted to rural Africa. In many urban centers in Africa, social, economic, educational, and cultural changes initiated by the European contact, and reinforced by the recent Western cultural influences in African societies, have affected women's roles within the urban family both positively and negatively, which we turn our attention to next.

WOMEN'S ROLES IN THE URBAN FAMILY

The most distinguishing features in women's roles in the urban African family have been the increased responsibilities women have taken on and the growing number of women in single-headed households. Contemporary educational and employment opportunities, added to women's empowerment agendas, have resulted in the fact that African women are no longer the face of a stereotypical "housewife" who is only good for domestic duties and uncontrolled reproduction. As indicated above, many African women have entered into professional careers and are employed as teachers, nurses, doctors, technicians, lawyers, politicians, and in almost every sector of public life. This means that not only are many women capable of single-handedly supporting themselves and their children, but also, they are finding marriage as perhaps, an impediment to a peaceful existence, rather than as a necessary lifestyle.

Financial security has allowed women to buy their own homes, live an independent family life, and to have children outside of marriage without so much of a social stigma—at least not one that money cannot cover. This is because most of the time family members, and to some extent, the larger community are more amiable to turning a blind eye to a person's behavior and activities if that person is financially stable and can help others. A study done in 1947 showed that in Langa, South Africa, some of the most highly educated women who held various positions in the public sector never married or got divorced almost immediately after marriage. Most of these women had children whom they financially supported alone. Notwithstanding the fact that the majority of these women came from patriarchal societies, which traditionally have tough social regulations on women, they managed to gain financial autonomy, and this security allowed them to establish and become the effective heads of their domestic units.[40]

Recently, there have been an increased number of studies done on the subject of female-headed households, and the majority has found similar situations across different regions of the continent. For instance, female-headed households are now a permanent feature of many urban centers in West Africa, particularly in Nigeria, Ghana, and the Ivory Coast. To avoid social stigmatization and to legitimize their social status, some women in Nigeria enter temporarily into marriages to earn the right of being referred to as "Mrs.," a title they never give up even after divorce. And it is very common to find women adding this marital title to their academic titles, for example, as in "Dr. (Mrs.) Z." Depending on their secured social status, financial resources, and their own kin, such women provide for their children's needs, and they may cut ties with the husband's family completely. Indeed, the ability of a woman to maintain her own household without the support of a male partner and without the strings of marital commitment could potentially liberate her from the controls of traditional family responsibilities and obligations that would have been expected of her in marriage.

As in many societies around the world, the majority of the time women choose to enter or remain in marital relationships than outside of it. However, the conjugal family household in the urban center, in particular, has experienced some profound changes. Women can now meet their partner's financial contributions for the upkeep of the family on an equal footing, if not more. Arguably, some men find significant drawbacks in the agency that women have found in their family lifestyle. Contemporary working conditions in many sectors of public employment have required that women give up some of their domestic responsibilities traditionally reserved for women, and husbands are picking up those responsibilities. An increasing number of husbands now have to babysit, cook, clean, and wash while their wives are at work. This situation has not only resulted in some men being resentful of women's newfound positions, but they have also developed an incensed fear of losing control over their families. Men have found various ways of maintaining their hold over women. As with the Jinja example cited above, Luo men in Nairobi who, because of the fear they have of women's independence, have resorted to controlling their wives' income by requiring that they deposit their income into a joint bank account in which only they have access.[41]

In another example, Zambian and Nairobi husbands achieve control over their wives' finances by giving them money for household expenses or an allowance in what is referred commonly to as "chop money" in Ghana. In Kenya, the majority of men conceal from their spouses their actual incomes; nonetheless, these same men are eager to know how much their wives are earning, and they may demand that their wives' salary or wages be deposited into their own accounts. Some men even take the added step of buying the household needs with their wives' money regardless of whether the women like this arrangement or not. A husband may take part of his wife's income to support his own kin while at the same time preventing his wife from financially supporting her extended family members. In the view of these men, once they marry a woman, they, in effect, have complete control over her, including the products of her labor.[42] The reaction by Kenyan and Zambian men to women's financial independence in the family is, however, not a reflection of what is happening in other African societies. In many places, husbands are supportive of their wives working outside the domestic sphere and of their financial independence. For example, in Ghana nowadays, men specifically target working women as potential partners for the added income they would bring to the household. Many Ghanaian couples have separate accounts, control their incomes privately, and very often spouses do not know the exact earnings of their partner.[43]

Another aspect of the urban family dynamics is the relationship between spousal financial contribution and power sharing in the household. This is based on the fact that wage income is the main economic resource of most urban families, and it affects how couples disburse it or use it as an advantage within the household. In other words, economic resource contribution influences the power relationship in a conjugal family. For example, when couples make equal financial contributions in purchasing their house as well as in bearing the financial burden of the family's upkeep equally, they also share the domestic responsibilities equally. The husband takes the responsibility of the family car, the family garden, and any general repairs or decorations the house might need. The wife takes the responsibility of cooking the family meals, cleaning, and washing, which she accomplishes with the assistance of a domestic servant. The couples do together the task of bathing the children and assisting them with their schoolwork. Essentially, the distribution of work and power in such a household is mediated by the fact that the women is a trained professional and is earning income to support the family.

From the above example, it is clear that women who bear equal or larger shares of financial responsibility of the family tend to share both the daily domestic responsibilities with their husbands as well as share the decision-making processes of the family. In addition, in conjugal family relationships in urban areas, the level of a woman's education, her occupation, and income in comparison to that of her husband drives the power relationship in the family.[44] In a study among Nairobi's middle-class families, it

Prominent women in a socialization process at a community celebration. (Courtesy of Toyin Falola)

was found that wives were more likely to put a greater proportion of the resources they earn, either through wage employment or self-employment, into a household pool than did their husbands. Concerning what couples allocated their resources to, it was found that in the majority of the cases, husbands were more inclined to spend their incomes on the more expensive expenditures of the household including such things as paying the rent or mortgage and paying school fees and hospital bills. Women, on the other hand, tended to spend their incomes on paying the wages of the household help, groceries, and other smaller items for household use. However, unlike in the previous case scenario where women achieve some level of financial autonomy and power equity in their families because of their income contributions, Kenyan women's contributions did not earn them equal power sharing with their husbands.[45] That is, the Nairobi study found no significant frequency that these women in middle-class families exercised any financial autonomy by the simple reason that they were also earning money for the support of the family as their husbands. Nor did it find any notable matrimonial parity in power sharing, in financial contributions, and in how a wife and a husband cooperated with one another in the family.

There is no denying that contemporary changes in the African family structure have come to stay. The family system that has emerged has both positive and negative implications for women's roles in the urban family. In some places, women who have embraced urban life and the Western way of life have left behind some of the constraints of traditional marital requirements prevalent in the rural areas, or at least, the effects have minimal impact in their lives. In some other places, regardless of entering into a monogamous marriage and living in the city away from the influences of kin, nothing really has changed much for women—they live in their marital homes as though servants for their husbands and their husbands' kin. Yet still, in some places continuity of traditional marital values and contemporary changes have been merged together in the dynamics of the urban family. Nevertheless, as with all the hurdles they have had to overcome, African women have, for the most part, embraced the Western concept of family and are willing to go the extra mile to overcome the challenges this family model presents. They are establishing themselves in the new social order speared on by urbanization, technological improvements, and the economic and political opportunities that are increasingly becoming available to women.

As a unit of production and reproduction and a site of socialization, the African family is as vast as women's roles in it. From the precolonial, through colonial, to the postcolonial era, women's roles have been key in both conjugal and consanguineal family systems and in structures such as matrilineal and patrilineal. Through these systems, women have been in constant contact with various kin and non-kin members, whose positions in the household significantly affect what roles women play in the family. In many precolonial African societies, with the exception of a few powerful women who had political responsibilities, women were responsible almost exclusively for domestic and reproductive duties in the family and were shielded from the public space. The era of colonial rule, with its resultant economic, social, cultural, political, and ideological notions, set the African family on the course of change with important implications for women's roles and positions in the family.

Undoubtedly, colonial interference devastated many aspects of African social institutions. Nonetheless, the Western educational and economic ideologies the colonizers brought with them found ground and reinforcement in postcolonial Africa, allowing many women to achieve Western education and to find employment in the public sector. Urbanization has also encouraged women to form nontraditional social alignments and relationships and to define what they perceive to be the family of their choice. In general, many African women have taken advantage of the new opportunities to improve their statuses and to become financially independent in their families. Today, many African women share equal, if not more, financial responsibilities in their families, and sometimes they are the family's sole provider. Many women have taken the additional step of avoiding conjugal marital ties altogether in order to be free of patrilineal obligations that marriage sometimes imposes on them and to be able to head their own households.

NOTES

1. Shula Marks and Richard Rathbone, "The History of the Family in Africa: Introduction," *The Journal of African History,* Vol. 24 (1983): 145–161.

2. Sharon B. Stichter, "The Middle-Class Family in Kenya: Changes in Gender Relations," in Sharon B. Stichter and Jane L. Parpart (eds.), *Patriarchy and Class: African Women in the Home and the Workforce* (Boulder, CO: Westview Press, 1988), 177–178.

3. Renato Rosaldo, "Imperialist Nostalgia," *Representations,* Special Issue: Memory and Counter-Memory (1989): 107–122.

4. Igor Kopytoff (ed.), *The African Frontier: the Reproduction of Traditional African Societies* (Bloomington: Indiana University Press, 1989), 43.

5. T. R. Nhlapo, "The African Family and Women's Right: Friends or Foes?" *Acta Juridica,* Vol. 135 (1991): 135–146.

6. Ralph Linton, *The Study of Man: An Introduction* (New York: Prentice Hall, 1936).

7. For more on the classification of bilateral descent societies in Africa, south of the Sahara, see Jack Goody, "The Classification of Double Descent Systems," *Current Anthropology,* Vol. 2 (1961): 3–25.

8. Betty Potash, "Women in the Changing African Family," in Margaret Jean Hay and Sharon Stichter (eds.), *African Women South of the Sahara* (New York: Longman Group Ltd., 1995), 69–91.

9. Catherine Coquery-Vidrovitch, *African Women: A Modern History* (Boulder, CO: Westview Press, 1997), 11.

10. Potash, 78.

11. Coquery-Vidrovitch, 16.

12. Albert Ethhel, "Women of Burundi: A Study of Social Values," in Denise Paulme (ed.), in *Women of Tropical Africa* (Berkeley and Los Angeles: University of California Press, 1963), 212–214.

13. Ibid.

14. Potash, 79.

15. Ibid. Also see Ifi Amadiume, *Male Daughters, Female Husbands: Gender and Sex in an African Society* (Atlantic Highlands, NJ: Zed Books, 1987).

16. Agnes Akosua Aidoo, "The Asante Queen Mother in Government and Politics in the Nineteenth Century," in Filomina Chioma Steady (ed.), *The Black Women Cross-Culturally* (Rochester, VT: Schenkman Books, 1985), 65–78.

17. Amadiume, 31, 180.

18. Elizabeth Colson, "Family Change in Contemporary Africa," in John Middleton (ed.), *Black Africa: Its Peoples and their Cultures Today* (London: The Macmillan Company, 1970), 152–158.

19. Ibid.

20. S. F. Nadel, "Witchcraft in Four African Societies: A Comparison," *American Anthropologist,* Vol. 54 (1952): 18–29.

21. Potash, 69–91.

22. Ibid. Also see Enid Schildkrout, "Age and Gender in Hausa Societies: Socioeconomic Roles of Children in Urban Kano," in Jean Sybil La Fontaine (ed.), *Sex and Age as Principles of Social Organization* (New York: Academic Press, 1978), 109–137.

23. Potash, 85–88.

24. Colson, 152–158.

25. Ibid., 155.

26. Ibid.

27. Stichter, *Patriarchy and Class*, 199–200.

28. Walter Elkan, *An African Labor Force: Two Case Studies in East African Factory Employment* (East African Institute of Social Research, 1956), 41–46.

29. Colson, "Family Change in Contemporary Africa," *Annals of New York Academy of Sciences*, Vol. 96 (1962): 641–647.

30. E. Frances White, "Women in West and West-Central Africa," in Iris Berger and E. Francis White (eds.), *Women in Sub-Saharan Africa: Restoring Women to History* (Bloomington: Indiana University Press, 1999), 122.

31. Claudine Vidal, "Guerre des sexes à Abijan: Masculin, Feminin, CFA," *Cahiers d'Etudes Africaines*, Vol. 8 (1977): 121–153.

32. Claudia Dinan, "Pragmatists or Feminists? The Professional Single Woman in Accra, Ghana," *Cahiers d'Etudes Africaines*, Vol. 65 (1977): 155–176.

33. White, 123.

34. Kenneth L. Little, *African Women in Town: An Aspect of Africa's Social Revolution* (Cambridge: Cambridge University Press, 1973), 153–154.

35. Ibid.

36. Laura Longmore, *The Dispossessed: A Study of the Sex-Life of Bantu Women in Urban Areas in and around Johannesburg* (London: Cape, 1959), 15–16.

37. Barbara Harrell-Bond, *Study of Marriage among the Professional Groups in Sierra Leone* (Unpublished Report to the Department of Social Anthropology, Edinburgh University, 1971).

38. Guy Bernard, *Ville Africaine: Famille Urbaine: Les Enseignants de Kinshasa* (Paris: Mouton, 1968), 126. Cited in Little, 168.

39. Phoebe V. Ottenberg, "The Changing Economic Position of Women among the Afikpo Ibo," in William Russell Bascom and Melville Jean Herskovits (eds.), *Continuity and Change in African Cultures* (Chicago, IL: University of Chicago Press, 1959), 205–223.

40. Ruth Levin, *Marriage in Langa Location* (Cape Town, South Africa: Cape Town University, 1947), 31–39, 95.

41. Potash, *Widows in African Societies: Choices and Constraints* (Stanford, CA: Stanford University Press, 1989), 44–62.

42. Diane Kayongo-Male and Philista Onyango, *The Sociology of the African Family* (New York: Longman Group Ltd., 1984), 68.

43. Christine Oppong, *Marriage among a Matrilineal Elite: A Study of Ghanaian Civil Servants* (Cambridge: Cambridge University Press, 1973).

44. Ibid.

45. Stichter, 177–200.

SUGGESTED READING

Gonzalez, Ana Marta, Florence Oloo, and Laure DeRose (eds.). *Frontiers of Globalization: Kinship and Family Structures in Africa.* Trenton, NJ: Africa World Press, 2010.

Hafkin, Nancy and Edna Bay (eds.). *Women in Africa: Studies in Social and Economic Change.* Stanford, CA: Stanford University Press, 1976.

Oheneba-Sakyi, Yaw and Baffour K. Takyi (eds.). *African families at the turn of the 21st Century.* Westport, CT: Greenwood Press, 2006.

Oppong, Christian (ed.). *Male and Female in West Africa*. Boston, MA: Allen and Unwin, 1983.

Paulme, Denise (ed.). *Women of Tropical Africa*, trans. H. M. Wright. Berkeley: University of California Press, 1971.

Potash, Betty. "Women in the Changing African Family." In Hay, Jean Margaret and Sharon Stichter (eds.), *African Women South of the Sahara*. New York: Longman Publishers, 1995.

3

---∞∞∞---

Women and Religion

The religiousness of the African life is well known. The limits and inter-connections fostered between spirits and humans, men and women, adults and children, and between communities are of the highest religious impor-tance in the life of Africans.[1] However, this religiousness has generally been communicated not just in terms of the ways in which men protect their social, religious, economic, and political dominance, but it has also been compared and unduly valued between men and women. The valuation has largely been presented on a scale of nurture/nature, active/passive, reason-able/unreasonable, and organize/disorganize, with women filling the latter category. Indeed, in African religious scholarship, when women are pres-ent, what we know of their participation and roles in the many religions on the continent is sketchy and, at best, paradoxical. On the one hand, re-ligion has been a source of reverence and equality for women, but on the other hand, it has been a source of subordination and oppression. Some re-ligious belief systems classify the female sex as sacred and a vital life force, while others only serve to keep women subordinate to men—particularly in instances where women's biological functions such as menstruation and childbirth are seen as sources of religious sacrilege and contamination.

This chapter crosses between the physical and the metaphysical and con-nects ambiguity to certainty to provide an insightful description of women's roles in Africa's three main religious bodies—African Traditional religions, Christianity, and Islam. Particular attention is focused on the ways in which religious beliefs and ideologies and social constructions have affected wom-en's religious roles in relation to the social, cultural, economic, and political institutions in Africa, south of the Sahara. Indeed, the need to be conscious of the influence of religion in the lives of African women is not just to satisfy the fundamental interest scholars have in religion but also to understand the capacity of religion to construct meaning, shape community, and influence behavior and self-esteem of people.[2]

Thus, this chapter begins with the idea that religious beliefs and values open a window of understanding into a society's gender constructions and outlook toward women. Regardless of the religiousness of women, their participation and activities in religion are influenced by such constructions and ideologies. The performance of African women's religious roles may sometimes be sexually restrictive, but it may also be comparable or complementary to men's religious roles. To make sense of the distinctiveness of women's roles, the connections between women's and men's roles and how both sexes cross boundaries and reverse roles require a comprehensive look at women and religion both in the past and in the present. In both historical and contemporary context, we will look at the complexities, ambiguities, and various aspects of women's religious interactions not only with men but also with the wider society, as well as the ways in which women's religious development have been both enhanced and hampered by gender constructions. We acknowledge women's strengths and weaknesses in indigenous African religions, Christianity, and Islam stretching from precolonial to postcolonial Africa. We focus especially on the effects of Islam and Christianity: with their own editions of the appropriate place for men and women, initiated religious divisions in many African societies. This chapter observes that the widespread involvement of women in African religions as ritual specialists, cult leaders, priestesses, healers, diviners, and spirit mediums have a connection to how women have negotiated, and continue to negotiate, their role in the social, cultural, economic, and political realms in African societies.

WOMEN'S ROLES IN AFRICAN
TRADITIONAL RELIGIONS

The major focus in African traditional religions is protecting the welfare of society by fostering a harmonious relation between the physical and the spiritual worlds. Religion is such a crucial force in African societies that it has been suggested to be the reason that in many African languages there is no word for religion.[3] In other words, religion is synonymous with daily living and as such, no special word is required for its description. In addition, African traditional religion concerns itself with the "transcendental significance of everyday life."[4] It routinely deals with issues concerning food production, festivals, chieftaincy, diseases, invasions, and life transitions and rites of passage such as birth, puberty, marriage, and death. In many African societies, although men dominate the performance of such religious activities, wide varieties of religious roles are open to women based on the belief that they possess certain creational and supernatural powers. While women have found their own inventive ways to exercise these powers, how society views the nature and sexuality of "femaleness" has influenced women's spiritual positions as ancestors, deities, or witches and has directed the roles they have been ascribed including guardians of shrines, "wives/husbands" of deities, ritual specialists, and healers.

The Metaphorical World

In many African myths of origin, humans at the beginning of time co-existed with gods; however, the two became separated in a series of events resulting from the insensitivities of humans. In these myths, the metaphysical status of women was cast either in a positive or negative light, but some scholars have argued that the majority of them place the blame on women for the physical divide that exists between heaven and earth. According to an Akan myth of origin, a woman constantly knocked the pestle she used to pound her *fufu* (pounded yam or cassava and plantain) against *Oyankopong* (the Akan Supreme Being), causing him to retreat deeper into the sky and eventually separating himself from the earth.[5] There is also a Yoruba creation myth in which the withdrawal of God higher into the sky was the result of a woman using the sky to clean her dirty hands. The Dogon of the central plateau region of Mali believe death came into the world when a woman discovered the fibers of cloth that originally clothed the earth.[6] The above notwithstanding, not all of African creation myths portray women in a negative way. For instance, the Akan, in spite of their creation myth that blames women for the separation between heaven and earth, believe that a mother-goddess gave birth to the universe. Their earth goddess, known as Asaase Yaa, is highly revered and considered a provider, protector, owner, and mother of her people. She not only controls land, productivity, and fertility but is also responsible for public morality. Anyone caught defiling the land in such cases as incest, adultery, or having sexual relations in the bush is severely punished by her. Other groups of people such as the Zulu, the Fang, and the San peoples of the Kalahari Desert all celebrate their separation from the gods for the division of the two spheres removed from their midst the constant threat of "divinity's unrestrained proximity."[7]

Ideas about women as divine or as deities can be found in a variety of instances in African traditional religions. For example, the supreme deity known as Mawu-Lisa of the Ewe people of the Republic of Benin is personified as both female and male. Mawu, generally believed to be a creator god, a mother, gentle, and forgiving, and the eldest of the two personifications is female and identified with the moon. Lisa, the male part and identified with the sun, is believed to possess all the opposite qualities of Mawu.[8] In Togo and central Benin, Nana Buku is also portrayed as a female god responsible for creation. The Uzo people of Nigeria view their supreme deity in female terms. The four main ways the Uzo view their deity include Temearu (a female creator god/molder of all), Ayeba (the foundress of the universe), Woyingi or Oyin (our mother), and Oginarau (she who dwells in the heavens).[9] Among the Akan, the queen mother's position in state affairs and her ritual roles reflect her divine identity.[10] Whether venerated as the source of creation or as the source of social disorder, the above ideas about women's religious roles and position originates from ideas about the complex nature of women.

The Physical World

Outside of the metaphysical world, yet functioning with it, African women play significant roles as healers, spirit mediums, cult leaders/participants, priestesses, diviners, and ritual specialists, among other roles. Examples from East African societies demonstrate both the essence of cults in women's religious experiences and the avenues through which female mediums and diviners exert their control and influence in society. In places such as Uganda, Burundi, Rwanda, and northeastern Tanzania, spirit cults were very common in the past where women served as mediums and diviners. These spirit cults continue to exist to some extent in contemporary times. In many of the cults, female mediums dealt with problems regarding childbirth, agriculture, sterility, and marriage. In their role as mediums, these women achieved flexible physical mobility unavailable to other women and provided the opportunity to gain some degree of wealth through the fees they collected. A classic example was the female medium of Ndahura spirit among the Kitara in Uganda, who not only had territorial control of her lands and wealth but played an essential role in the installment of a new *mukama* (king). It has been observed that even though very few female mediums attained such a level of influence, the prestigious position of the few brought "ordinary" women an alleviated status and an increased respect within their localities and even outside of it.[11]

The call to mediumship had multiple implications for African women's religious experiences. A woman's refusal to accept such a call often resulted in unexplained illnesses, social isolation, witchcraft accusations, and death. At the same time, women who accepted calls to mediumship had to sometimes give up on their personal needs and preferences in order to be in the service of a deity. In societies where mediumship, was indicated in marital terms, that is, the woman becomes a "wife/husband" of a deity—as was the case in the main deities of Bunyoro and Buganda kingdoms in East Africa where women were dedicated as wives—these women had to remain unmarried. Nonetheless, mediumship brought enormous power and influence to women. Among the Ga people of Ghana, cults of deities and divinities were in the hands of priests and mediums. This practice continues to this day. Since the olden days, priesthood has been the preserve of particular predetermined kinship males who, in the spirit world, represent humans. Ga females have had to achieve mediumship in order to serve as the channel through which humans communicate their needs and messages to the gods. It has been argued that it is only during spirit possessions that Ga female mediums exercise social and political authority and influence, and outside of such possessions, these women have no influence.[12]

The majority of the Ga female mediums have no formal education and often have no children. But spirit possessions afford them insights in dealing successfully with many of the social and economic problems of the people. Through their achievements, they are able to address indirectly some of the social inequities and injustices they normally would have experienced as illiterate and childless women in Ga society.[13] In the past, and also now, female mediums across Africa achieved higher social status by appropriating traditionally ascribed male roles to gain authority over others. An example is that of a female medium named Kunzaruwa, who under the influence of Nehanda Mhondoro spirit, gave strategic advice to the guerilla warriors during the Zimbabwean war of independence (1971–1973) to help them win. She imposed ritual prohibitions on the fighters (both men and women) regarding food choices, sexual relations, and paths to utilize in the war.[14] In contemporary Senufo society of Côte d'Ivoire, female diviners, also called *Sandobele,* intercede on behalf of clients who have accidentally committed offenses against particular spirits. These women are highly respected for their capacity to heal people from illnesses and troubles that result from punishments melted to them by the spirits.[15] Among the Temne of Sierra Leone, although divination is predominantly a male role, certain women have managed to gain acceptance as respectable female diviners in charge of mainly the private and individual domains.[16] Women diviners in Azande society achieve social authority to intercede on behalf of humans in the spirit world when they claim to have experienced a symbolic death and resurrection.[17]

In their roles as ritual specialists, African women, since precolonial times, have dominated the rituals of status transformation and life cycles rituals such as marriage, puberty, death, birth, fertility, kingship, and the rest.[18] They have also used their ritual positions to appropriate for themselves higher social positions and political status. Among the Qua people of southeastern Nigeria, the responsibility of crowning a new ruler falls on the queen mother who acts as the representative of the people.[19] The

Lovedu, for example, had a rain queen mother who was believed to combine her divinity with her knowledge of medicine and charms to control rain and guarantee a consistent cyclical occurrence of the seasons. Oral traditions suggest that not only did she use her ritual powers to sustain her people, but her very position as ruler elevated and maintained the status of women in a highly patriarchal society.[20] African women also play significant social and religious roles that affect their private lives as well as the life of their communities. Ideas about the women's *Poro* (women's secret society) in Senufo society indicate that these women provide public displays during funerals and initiation rituals for audiences.[21]

Like the *Poro,* the *Bondo* and *Sande* are women's initiation societies found among some groups in Liberia and Sierra Leone. These females-only initiation societies are influential associations with social, cultural, political, and religious goals.[22] Sande tradition indicates that the female figure signifies the foundation of fertility, prosperity, and productivity. To some extent, not only do women in Sande exert strong spiritual influence over people in the community, but they also have a monopoly over certain sacred knowledge crucial to the development, happiness, and success of individuals and the well-being and prosperity of the community.[23] The Sande is one of the few female-exclusive societies that uses masked female ancestral figures during their ceremonies, and it is through these figures that they demonstrate their power in the community.[24] The Sande also display two different sets of decorated figures. One set denotes health, righteousness, and womanhood while the second set guards against evil doers of both sexes and of all ages. The purpose of this set of figures is intended to reinforce to the general public the Sande's power to reprimand evil doers. Besides their importance in the social and cultural structures of the community, Sande provides social solidarity, community, and respect for women. And both men and women generally respect Sande's laws, which are legitimized by religious sanctions.[25]

WOMEN'S RELIGIOUS ROLES
IN CHRISTIANITY

An integral part to the expansion of colonial rule in Africa was the introduction and spread of Christianity. As early as the 16th century, Portuguese priests began missionary work at the various Portuguese ports. Missionary activities grew in the 19th century with the formal establishment of colonial rule. Africans converted to Christianity for various reasons including the failure of traditional spirits to protect them from the foreign invasions, mission education, Western culture, and the like. As with other aspects of colonialism, Christianity brought its own gender notions with the separation of roles and spaces between women and men. Nineteenth-century

Western ideals and Christian views conceived of the role of women as mothers and wives—roles that were considered as vital in maintaining the home as a sanctuary from the complexities and hassles of the public life in which men functioned. Essentially, any activity in the public sphere, including running the church, belonged to men and women and were limited to the periphery of church activities. The missionary churches, after establishing themselves in African societies, excluded women from mainstream authority such as priesthood and other leadership positions and restricted them to roles that revolved around women's issues such as women's organizations, singing groups, and cleaning and arranging of church facilities, fundraising, catechizing to children, and cooking for church functions.

Many researchers have noted that nowhere are the roles of women and men more defined and rigidly set than in Christianity—even more so than in secular activities. For while some contemporary changes have forced societal perception toward women to change to a certain degree and opened up previously men's-only roles for women's participation, many Christian congregations continue to prevent women from attaining certain positions and performing certain religious roles. It appears that the recent calls for social, economic, religious and political equality for women have bypassed the leadership of some churches. Interestingly, in most Christian churches in Africa, women are in the numerical majority. They are probably the very force that sustains many of these congregations.[26] Nonetheless, the large numbers of women have not served in any significant direct leadership positions or authoritative roles, and they continue to serve at the periphery of church activities. In fact, it has been women, more so then men, who have always availed themselves for church activities and have taken responsibilities for the success of the various social organizations in the church. It is quite common to find that men, who are usually in the minority, are frequently selected as leaders and representatives of these social organizations in spite of their minimal participation. Based on its interpretations of the Bible on who a woman is and what her capabilities entail, the church has positioned women in a childlike state and effectively rendered them as needing care; attention; and most importantly, directions in order to function properly in society and to live a righteous life.

In fact, this conception functions not only on the assumption that Christian women are not interested in aspiring to higher positions in the church, but also it challenges them to accept their lot and to obey church doctrines as "good" and "faithful" Christian women. Furthermore, for much of its history in Africa, the Bible's authority regarding the roles of the sexes has not been questioned much within missionary churches. Any attempt aimed at questioning biblical understanding and interpretations most certainly would result in either a schism or the accusation of heresy and lack of faith. As a result, women themselves are generally careful not to question the

Bible or challenge church traditions for the fear of being labeled unbelievers, accused of heresy, or being expelled from the church. Christianity established itself in Africa, and elsewhere, on the premise of bringing salvation to the multitude of people living in "darkness" under "false" religions. While Christian churches have made major strides in establishing themselves in African societies, they did not or could not completely annihilate indigenous African religions and belief systems.

To maintain their distinctiveness and authenticity, churches in Africa have ensured that contrary biblical interpretations and understanding are not tolerated, and they fight against any sign of syncretism on the part of its members. To avoid jeopardizing their own faith, the majority of Christian women in missionary churches accept their exclusion from ordained ministry and other leadership roles. Some scholars have pointed out that throughout the history of the Christian church, it has in a systematic way, excluded its women members from ordained ministry, and in doing so, has prevented them from participating in significant roles that only ordained ministers could perform. Furthermore, the limitation on women's

A Gambian woman, Fatou Njie, in an Islamic attire for her wedding ceremony. (Courtesy of Toyin Falola)

roles in the church is not because of their lack of ability to function at the top; rather they are limited because of gender ideologies. For such a position, some scholars hold the church responsible for inflicting injustice on women.[27] This is not to say that all Christian churches prevent women from entering into ordained ministry. In a more recent development, some missionary churches have allowed women to be ordained as priests, and many more women are serving in other leadership capacities. Nonetheless, even in denominations that ordain women, they are still excluded from acquiring certain higher positions[28]—particularly if such positions grant them authority of men—and are generally stationed in small congregations and in places with less significance for the church.

One area that African women in Christianity, in particular those in the Catholic faith, found some level of opportunity to gain some recognition and respect among their fellow Africans, if not among the top leadership of the church, was through the life of contemplation in a nunnery. The idea of a life of contemplation for women in the Catholic faith was late in coming to many African countries, even in places where the church had been established for many years. As compared with the French colonies, the English colonies had very few monasteries founded. Even in places like Malawi, where the English had political control, the French were the ones who established a monastic life for women. One reason that has been given for this development was that a life of contemplation had been a vital and a well-developed aspect of French Catholicism.

The Dominican sisters were probably among the first group of nuns to establish themselves on the continent. They were first invited to southern Rhodesia (Zimbabwe) in 1877, but it was not until the 1920s that they finally accepted the first five African women to become part of their group. Race relations in Rhodesia at the time caused this move by the Dominican sisters to draw the dissatisfaction of the Catholic bishop at Salisbury where the sisters were located. Shortly after the acceptance of the African women, the bishop ordered the sisters to start a separate congregation for African women in the diocese. It has been reported that the Dominican sisters were displeased with the decision, but they agreed that the prevailing attitude of European in southern Rhodesia, who hated any close association between members of the African race, made establishing a different place for the African sisters seemed to be the right choice.

Therefore, in 1932, the Dominican sisters established a novitiate at Makumbi mission in the Chinamora district, which was close to Salisbury for the African women. At this new location, the five young women who had first joined the Dominican sisters became the pioneer members, although reportedly, a number of them left and got married,[29] probably because of the way the Catholic Church treated them. As time passed, the Dominican sisters began to free themselves from racial prejudices toward Africans,

and sometimes they were even prepared to defy the Rhodesian government, if not their own leadership, on its regulations on racial separation
and educational opportunities. For example, to counter the commonly held
opinion of the European community that Africans should perform only unskilled labor, the Dominican sisters insisted that the African women they
accepted into their congregation were trained academically so they could
work in the teaching and nursing fields. In such positions, they would be,
in every respect, the equals of their fellow European sisters. Therefore, all
African women who applied to the convent were first sent to secondary
schools and teacher training and nurse training colleges before being accepted into the sisters' religious training program.[30]

In West Africa, the best-documented contemplative convent that accepted African women was the convent of the Poor Clares established by
Sæur Marie de Jésus in 1958 in Cameroon. In 1967, Marie de Jésus com-
mented: "I believe that Africans are by nature ideally suited for the contemplative life. They stand in a constant dialogue with the invisible and are
deeply sensitive, like a harp, to the touch of the supernatural."[31] Like the
Poor Clares, the Carmelite monastery of Zaza, which was established in
Rwanda in 1952, is also well documented.[32] In both the Poor Clares and the
Carmelite, the European women who founded these convents denounced
their own European cultural backgrounds in order to allow the African
women who had accepted their faith to find their own religious expression.
Therefore, African customs such as dancing were introduced into liturgical celebrations. To ensure that they were fully incorporated into the social
setup of their African neighbors, the Carmelite sisters in 1967 abandoned
their monastery. They left it to the poor and built themselves huts in the
same style as those used in the area.

Accordingly, the rejection of the European way of life as well as the
adoption of African architecture brought the sisters close to the people,
causing a great number of African women to be attracted to them. It has
been noted that so many African women applied to both of the above monasteries that they were forced to open daughter foundations to accommodate their new members.[33] By the mid-1970s, a number of other monastic
orders, including the Benedictine nuns, had also established themselves on
the continent. At present, almost every African country where the Catholic
Church has been established has a monastic order established for Catholic
women. Many researchers have expressed their opinions on investigated
the benefits of a life of contemplation for African women, especially when
such an action is placed within the context of the value African societies
put on women to have children in order to help perpetuate the family line.
On the one hand, some have argued that African women who enter these
organizations enjoy a high prestige among their people because of the fact
that they end up becoming teachers and nurses and Africans, in general,

greatly admire the teaching and nursing professions.[34] On the other hand, it has been suggested that monastic life provides these African women an avenue to serve God and to participate in the activities of the church without worrying about the power struggles and the lack of opportunities other women often encounter in the church. In addition, women who otherwise would have been social outcasts because of a physical or emotional disability have found a place where they could become successful in their careers and respected in society.

WOMEN'S RELIGIOUS ROLES IN AFRICAN INDEPENDENT CHURCHES

From the late 1950s, dissatisfaction with European control of church governance, exclusion of women from ordained ministry and other leadership roles, and the need to incorporate certain aspects of African religious practices and belief systems into Christianity resulted in the emergence of new religious movements in many regions in Africa, particularly in areas south of the Sahara. Established primarily by Africans and for Africans, these movements or churches ranged from neotraditional religions, prayer-healing movements, spiritual/independent churches, separatist churches, Christian revivalist movements, Zionist movements, prophetic/syncretistic movements, nativity churches, and messianic movements. Collectively, these churches are often referred to as African Independent Churches/African Instituted Churches/African Indigenous Churches/African Initiatives in Christianity, but the more common name used is African Initiated Churches. The two main categories that researchers have identified are the spiritual/prophetic type and the nonprophetic type. The emergence of African Independent churches not only initiated a challenge to the Eurocentric interpretation and understanding of biblical text, but they also set themselves up as a true reflection of how Africans perceived Christianity and an objection to the very presence of European rule on African soil.

Many researchers have attributed the surge and persistence of these new religious movements to their social and cultural innovations and transformations as well as their ability to unify the sacred with the secular and the old with the new. For African women, the need to leave missionary churches to join an African Independent church or to establish one originated from the church's unaccommodating outlook toward women, although in some cases, external factors contributed. African women have always wanted to retain their membership in the mainstream churches; however, the patriarchal tendencies in the church prevented them from attaining their spiritual fulfillment. Thus, they either had to leave to express their spirituality elsewhere in a new church or join one that accepted women in leadership roles.

Other reasons that have accounted for the emergence of African Independent churches included the translation of the Bible into local languages, which allowed Africans to make sense for themselves of their importance in biblical text and the significance of their indigenous institutions, which Europeans wanted to discredit in order to replace them with their own. The following factors, among others, have been cited as instrumental in the establishment of African Independent churches. First, European missionaries did not meet African Christians on brotherly terms and failed to understand the complex nature of African social and cultural values and belief systems to be able to differentiate between the good and the bad. Second, because the missionaries attacked social institutions such as marriage and family structures, women were the most affected in terms of their security and status at home. But when they could not find status positions in the church, they became the most disenchanted with Western Christian values.[35] In addition, it is apparent that just as the failure of African traditional healing mechanisms to provide cures for the inflictions of people led to the acceptance of Christianity, the inability of Western medicine to provide cures for the diseases of Africans led them to leave missionary churches to seek and to establish their own healing and spiritual churches.

Providing faith-induced healing and spiritual answers to the many social, economic, and political hardships that people face is perhaps the most distinguishing feature of African Independent churches, and the healing is the leading reason people join these religious movements. In this regard, many of these movements have established healing centers and prayer camps where people who may not necessarily be members of the church go to receive healing. People sometimes wait for extended periods (even years) until they receive their healing or are provided with the answers they are seeking. Typically, in African Independent churches, two factors are essential for healing to take place. First, the patient must believe in the spiritual causes of diseases and other hardships, and they must have faith that they will be healed. The second factor is that the prophet or prophetess provides healing through intense prayer regiment, fasting, ritual bathing, laying of hands on patients, oil anointment, ritual bathing, and the drinking of holy water. Many of these movements place emphasis on the Holy Spirit and engage in exorcising patients of evil spirits and deliverance from other malicious forces. Their prayer sections have been noted as occasions for forcing witches to confess.

Other features of African Independent churches include the incorporation of African music and indigenous musical instruments such as drums into their services accompanied by dancing, singing, and clapping. Most of these churches do not forbid polygyny, and polygynous families may serve in important leadership positions. Their sermons integrate biblical text with African social and cultural values and belief systems such as beliefs in dreams, evil forces, and nature. African Independent churches are also distinctive for the prominent roles and positions women hold in these movements. Indeed, women have demonstrated their role in religion by rejecting both the patriarchal and leadership traditions as well as the gendered tendencies of the missionary churches by founding or co-founding their own African Independent churches.[36] Examples of some of these movements include the Lumpa Church founded in 1954 in Zambia by Alice Mulenga Lenshina. Lenshina started the Lumpa Church after the Presbyterian Church threw her out for her beliefs and utterances. It quickly became one of the most flourishing churches in Northern Rhodesia until the new Zambian government in 1964 undermined its dominance. The first recorded religious movement in Africa was founded by a woman called Dona Béatrice (Kimpa Vita) in the late 17th century in the former kingdom of Congo (now Democratic Republic of Congo).

Dona was widely known for her healing powers but became even more famous for her challenge of the Portuguese Roman Catholic Church and its doctrinal and liturgical hegemony, causing her to be burnt at the stake in 1706. As with Dona, Lenshina was especially revered for her healing capabilities. She was an example of a woman focused on reinterpreting both indigenous and external traditions and establishing a new community that provided a sense of security mainly for women in a period of social and political upheavals. In Zimbabwe, the story of the prophetess Mai Chaza, who founded the Church of Mai Chaza, bears resemblance to the above account, but more importantly, Chaza's story emphasizes the gendered aspect of healing and women's spirituality. Unlike their male counterparts, most women involved in spiritual and healing activities have to take extraordinary measures to substantiate their right to lead and to heal. After proclaiming that God had chosen her as a new Moses, Mai Chaza became a ritual leader focusing on healing; however, in order to authenticate her special spiritual powers and her healing abilities, she had to separate herself from "customary accepted conceptions of women" and renounced all sexual relations and marriage.[37]

There are other less-known women who have also established their own movements in various regions in Africa. Examples of some of these women include Gaudencia Aoko who, with the help of Simon Ondeto, founded the *Legio Maria* (Legion of Mary) among the Luo of Kenya. This movement focuses on healing by faith and liberation of women and their children from the constant threat of death and sickness.[38] Besides the fact that the founder was a woman, women, in general, play important leadership roles and positions in the church. These roles include holding important church offices, earning the status as mothers in God, prophetesses, pastors, healers, and ordained ministers. The significance of women's roles is linked to the role of the Virgin Mary in the history of Christianity. There was also Mother Christianah Mokotulima, an Ndebele woman from South Africa who founded the St. John's Apostolic Faith Mission of South Africa; and in Kenya, Senaida Mary Akatsa, a Luhyia woman who conducted faith-healing sessions in the Muslim village of Kawangware. In June 1988, Akatsa attracted massive media attention with her claim that Jesus himself had attended one of her healing sessions and thus sanctioned her as a "true representative of the 'most high.'"[39]

In West Africa, the Harrist movement was started by William Wade Harris from Liberia who preached against faith in African traditional religious gods and certain practices against women. As the movement expanded, many women began to form their own versions and to exercise leadership roles. In Ghana, Harris "Grace" Tani and Kwesi "John" Nankabah formed a branch of the Harrist movement, popularly called "Nankabah" or the Twelve Apostles church. While both Tani and Nankabah share leadership roles, it was Tani who exercised the power of healing. The Harrist movement, like others of its kind that have spread throughout West Africa, focuses on providing both spiritual and physical healing, particularly conditions that affect women the most: infertility, poverty, and lack of social and economic support. In Nigeria, the women of the Ladies Christian Improvement Society lead the United Native African cathedral church

Women meet in a private home in Soweto, South Africa, for a weekly prayer service, 1996. (Courtesy of A. Olusegun Fayemi)

located in Lagos. There are numerous examples of women establishing African Independent churches in the Ivory Coast, Zimbabwe, South Africa, Uganda, and Kenya.

These churches offer women a greater degree of spiritual freedom, prestige, power, and religious participation than they possibly could have accessed in missionary Christianity. For the most part, gender balance is maintained in the leadership as well as in the various roles of African Independent churches, which gives women a sense of belonging and accomplishment. Sometimes, even when men are the founders, women can be found playing dominant roles out of the public view. An example is the case of the Divine Healer's Church in Ghana whose founder, Brother Lawson, is the public face of the church; however, many have noted that his wife, Sister Lawson, is the one who actually controls the affairs of the church. In a social environment that marries African beliefs in the unique spirituality of women with the spirituality offered through Christianity, the importance of women to these churches cannot be emphasized enough. It is no wonder that two thirds of all members in African Independent churches are women, which makes them a vital force to be reckoned with in these movements.

WOMEN'S RELIGIOUS ROLES IN ISLAM

The spread of Islam to Africa occurred as early as the 12th century, spreading along the east coast of Africa to North Africa and then to the rest of Africa, south of the Sahara. Because of the lack of leadership control issues in the Islamic religion and the successful onslaught of colonialism, many Africans converted to Islam during the colonial period. However, like Christianity, Islam holds certain ideological beliefs on gender roles and on the position of women in society. Within Islamic religious practices, women have been excluded from holding authoritative leadership positions that directed the affairs of both women and men, as well as being denied participation in certain religious roles within Muslim communities because of the practice of *purdah* and the belief that men have the responsibility to supervise the affairs of women. The prevention of women from attaining certain leadership positions and playing specific religious roles pushed women into actively participating in unorthodox spirit cults. Among the well-known spirit cults in Muslim communities included the *zar* cult among the Sudanese, the *bori* cult among the Hausa, and the *pepo* among the Swahili. There are other examples in Qadiriyya communities in Bagamoyo and Tabora in Tanganyika (Tanzania) where women have been, and continue to be, involved in cults and brotherhoods. Women have been noted to play significant roles within some *tariqas* (brotherhoods). These are groups generally organized around charismatic leaders and unlike in orthodox Islam where minimal emphasis is placed on mystics and emotional elements of religion, *tariqas* focus on them.[40] Essentially, Muslim women have had to resort to unconventional avenues in order to access important positions and roles, a factor that has been echoed in different ways by many researchers.

In the last few decades, although academic interest in women's studies has increased, it appears that the position and role of women in Islam is still uncertain, as many researchers have taken for granted that Islam is a male religion.[41] Hence, the impact of religious roles does not penetrate into the private world of women. The role women play in Islam reflects a greater association with Africa's indigenous past than with Islam itself. That is, Muslim women are, indeed, largely restricted to the domestic space, responsible for all the tasks normally associated with such a role in traditional Africa, including childbearing, adult care, cooking, and cleaning.[42] In other cases, women in Islam are responsible for preserving the culture that existed before the introduction of Islamic religion, which gives them some degree of independence and authority in their relationship with men.[43] These two suggestions indicate that not only does the religious world of African women lie in pre-Islamic Africa, but also the introduction and development of Islam in African societies appear to have created a world in which men have absolute authority. Women's spaces of control are, therefore, limited to a cultural community that exists on the outskirt of mainstream Islamic practices.

Within this cultural community, Muslim women's only opportunity for autonomy is to depend on pre-Islamic African notions, which they use to undermine, in covert ways, Islamic rules that have excluded them from leadership roles and kept them in subordinate positions. Furthermore, it has been argued that the introduction of Islam into African societies weakened women's ritual importance and roles. For example, when the Pokomo, (Wantu wa Dzuu) who inhabit the area along the Tana River in the Tana River District of northern Kenya, adopted the Islamic religion, conflict broke out involving Muslim leaders and women who have traditionally been in charge of burying infants who died at birth. In accordance with Muslim practices and customs, the Muslim leaders, who are males of course, demanded that a male Muslim official, selected purposefully for this ritual, must wash and bury these babies. The two sides reached a compromise whereby the women took the initial responsibility of the deceased infant and later sent it to the official for the performance of the Muslim rituals. By stepping in to control a local custom, which gave the responsibility to women to bury infants who died within 30 days of birth, the Muslim leadership within the Pokomo community was not only interfering in women's rights and responsibilities, but they inadvertently allowed Islam to erode the position and status of women in the traditional system.[44]

Yet, in the fight over religious control between women and men, women have not necessarily been submissive to the tactics employed by men.

As with the example with the *zar, bori,* and *pepo* spirit cults, women, in a variety of instances, have resorted to pre-Islamic indigenous African rituals to reassert and maintain their independence. In other words, while the official structures and religious authorities may seek to control and contain women's roles in religious practices, women have a variety of arsenals they use to circumvent, either openly or covertly, the agendas of men. Sometimes they involve themselves in the less-orthodox aspect of religious practice, or they may depend on indigenous religious traditions to reaffirm their rights.[45] An illustration of this happened in the 1960s among the Dioula in Bobo-Dioulasso, located in the southwestern part of Burkina Faso. In describing the challenges women encounter in their attempt to achieve formal status in religious groups and their actual capacity to attain positions of spiritual power and influence, Lucy Quimby points out the conflicting effects that new religious norms in African religious practices have on both sexes. According to her, Dioula women wanted to continue a traditional Dioula warrior dance, which men had given up as a result of becoming Muslims. A conflict arose when the male Muslim leadership in the community publicly announced that the dance was contradictory to Islamic practices. Dioula women countered the men's objection and effectively justified their position with the argument that before the introduction of Islam, the Dioula traditional religion sanctioned the dance.[46]

Some scholars are of the view that contrary to the general assumption that women occupy inferior positions in Islam and that Islam, perhaps, has little or no room for women, Islam is flexible and fluid enough to respond to local changes and conditions.[47] Their argument is that despite women's perceived inferior position in Islam, they are not completely barred from playing significant roles in the religion. The involvement of women in Islam is not restricted to the domestic realm, and their primary religious beliefs are not based exclusively on indigenous African traditions. Indeed, in their own ways, Muslim women not only participate, but they also accommodate and sometimes manipulate certain Islamic practices to suit their own needs.

Few studies that focus on female religious expression indicate that Muslim women play crucial roles in the Islamic religion both as *marabouts* (Muslim religious scholar/teacher) and as patrons of *marabouts* and shrines. Muslim women also form the greater portion of participants during the annual pilgrimage of the Senegalese Mourides at the Magal in Touba. For the women who participate in these pilgrimages, the occasion is a perfect time to visit their *marabouts,* organize religious chants, or just wander about in the holy city wearing their special *boubous* (a flowing garment worn by both women and men).[48] A significant number of women have been identified as having worked as important *shaikhs* (Islamic scholar). For instance, in northern Senegal, several women worked as shaikhs and were famous for their scholarship and Baraka (blessing).[49] Khadija of Ahl-al-Aqil was one such woman who was believed to have been the teacher of Abd al-Qadir of Futa-Toro who was the leader of the Torodo Revolution that occurred in the late 18th century in the middle valley of the Senegal River.[50] In recent years in northern Nigeria, literate Muslim women play important roles in ensuring that the cults of the shaikhs grow through the utilization of educational tools. Notions of gender in Islam have also directed what roles women play. Gender constructions in Islam govern issues regarding women's rights in marriage, divorce, and property and their observation of *purdah* (women's seclusion and veiling) as well as women's exclusion from formal governance in Muslim communities. In spite of women's exclusion from formal offices in Islam, they have found ways to exercise leadership positions in Muslim societies. Examples of women who have excelled as Islamic scholars and leaders included two Hausa women of Kano society in Nigerian: Hajiya Maria Mai Tafsiri, master of "Qur'anic exegesis"; and Hajiya Laraba Karaba, leader in the Qadiriyya Muslim brotherhood.[51]

The work of these female religious elites neither constitute nor support the marginalization theory about Muslim women, and as argued by some scholars, Islam has undergone, to some degree, religious reform, which has promoted the education of women and made them moral guardians of the religious movements. Similar examples can be drawn from other Muslim societies across Africa. For example, in Senegal, some Muslim brotherhoods encourage the employment of women in Islamic education.[52] Women also use their financial resources to sponsor brotherhoods, *marabouts*, and *shaikhs*, and as such they exercise considerable influence in the religious circles of these groups. As with any religious body, distinct spheres of influence may exist for both men and women, yet, flexibility often exists to allow both sexes to cross their gender-specified boundary. Women's religious activities in Islam cannot be absolutely relegated to the domestic sphere, for as we have seen, Muslim women have embarked, and they continue to do so today, on pilgrimages to holy sites and have provided Islamic education to others, which can be considered as public expression of women's religious roles. Although opportunities for religious expression in the public sphere may be subtle, they do exist, and they allow women to engage not only in important religious roles but also to circumvent the prescribed peripheral spaces into which Islam sometimes confines them.

THE PARADOXES OF WOMEN'S ROLES IN THE RELIGIONS OF AFRICA

As seen in the above discussions, many African societies have specific roles for both women and men. The delineation of these roles is often fluid and differs according to social, cultural, economic, political, environmental, and historical factors.[53] Throughout the continent, women regularly collaborate within their own spheres through associations and institutions that parallel those of men, yet, in instances where women and men group or act together, perceived, or apparent male domination and power inequity exist. Some scholars attribute these imbalances to biases towards male superiority, which have been emphasized particularly by Christian and Islamic theologies, women's lack of access to resources, and social and cultural notions that keep women in subordinate positions. Some scholars maintain that the distinction between women and men is often emphasized through religious ideologies and related ritual practices detailed from the male perspective.[54] Not only does this view portray men as central to religious activities and to society itself, but it "others" women by placing them on the outside of society.[55]

Regardless of these social differences, other scholars have argued that men and women complement each other's activities more than it has been portrayed in literature. Interrelations, rather than social equality, characterized many religious activities allowing both men and women to rise above everyday hierarchical social relationships. Some researchers have insisted that ideas of women's subordination, particularly in African traditional religious systems, are the result of Western imposed values and its objectified interpretations. Although religion may serve to legitimatize or privilege male dominance, it equally provides avenues for women to communicate their interests, challenge male authority, and express their identities.[56] When we focus on women's religious roles as subordinate to that of men by the mere fact of women's sexuality and biological functions, we oversimplify the many roles women have played and continue to play in religion.[57] The perceived marginalized world of women may be deceptive and misleading to both inside and outside observers, for although African women may not always be at the center stage, their exclusion in some aspects of religious practices should not necessarily be characterized as powerlessness. In many instances, African women may display tolerance of, or even pretense of male power, while enjoying their own form of autonomy. Abundant complexities and ambiguities exist in symbols, rituals, and sexual representations marked by fluidity as men could be "wives" of deities in the same way as women could be "husbands" of gods.

It is this very ambiguity and fluidity that stimulates academic discussion over whether religion gives women greater or special powers or works to estrange them, or whether female ritual authority questions or challenges male authority. Indeed, uncertainty seems to characterize any attempt at providing insights to these questions. As seen above, African women's mystical roles equip them to serve in various religions as diviners, mediums, ritual specialists, and as healers and may generate power and respect for them. Yet, at the same time, such roles may lead women to be considered as sources of evil and misfortune, often under the pretense of witchcraft, and as agitators of social and political unrest. In instances where a strong female deity exists, it does not necessarily assure female ritual authority. An example is the case of the cult of Ala, a female earth goddess in Igbo society whose followers are almost exclusively males.[58] Some researchers have analyzed the paradoxes surrounding women and religious power, and they have highlighted how eastern and southern African women compete for and achieve higher statuses and power in African traditional religions.

To these researchers, divination, healing, ritual specialization and initiation, and spirit mediumship offered mystical women, in the past, not only the greatest possibilities for active religious participation but also the means of exerting authority over other women and men in community affairs.[59] As indicative of Kunzaruwa's story, female mediums relying on the tradition of Nehanda-Charwe spirit assisted in the Zimbabwean political struggles dating back to the 1890s when the Shona began resisting colonial oppression. Important scholarships in Shona literature have discussed this woman's spiritual agency and its significance in understanding gender perceptions. For example, Ruramisai Charumbira has contested David N. Beach's assertion that during the 1896–1897 central Shona uprising in Zimbabwe against colonial rule, Nehanda-Charwe, acting in the capacity of a spiritual leader, was unfairly accused and prosecuted because of gender bias. Beach notes that male spiritual leaders such as Kaguvi-Gumboreshumba had more to do with the rebellion than Nehanda-Charwe since available sources on the event mentions him more than her.[60]

In her reexamination of the same sources, Charumbira indicates that Beach's characterization of Nehanda-Charwe as a victim of gender partiality emanates from the fact that he failed to consider the broader spectrum of women and gender history before and during the uprisings, which would have allowed him to understand and articulate Nehanda-Charwe's actions better.[61] Considering the events of the 1896–1897 uprisings from a gendered perspective in terms of the dynamics of power between the colonizers and the colonized and between women and men, Charumbira concludes that Nehanda-Charwe was anything but a victim. In fact, she used her position and influence to rally rebels and to urge people to take part in the rebellions.[62] In many African societies, women's power of intercession was so powerful that it often changed the course of events—sometimes determining whether there would be peace or war. This crucial, yet "dangerous," power was so feared by men that they invented appropriate rituals and practices to benefit themselves of such powers, while making sure they were protected against it.[63] There is a belief among the Mbuti Pygmies that women once controlled their *Molimo* (an important festival), but men stole it from women and have since then prohibited them from participating in it or even watching it.

A similar story is found among the Ibibio of southeastern Nigeria, where women initially started the Ekpo Society, which is now an exclusive male organization. According to the accounts, men persuaded the women who started the society to admit them, but once the men were initiated, they passed a law permitting only men to participate and to witness the rites.[64] In some instances, including the afterlife, beliefs and practices have been instituted in African traditional religions to define and articulate women's morality and power. Among the Swazi of southern Africa, a woman may have a moral character in life, but in death, she automatically becomes a source of natural evil and is therefore denied the privilege of being recognized as a full ancestor. A wife, in death, joins her husband's ancestors; nonetheless, her position as an ancestor is uncertain. Her burial place, just outside of the entrance to the cattle kraal, reflects her dissociation from her own natal ancestors while not fully being recognize as an ancestor in her husband's line of ancestors.[65] From society to society, the perception of women's power may vary, but it is clear that there is usually a degree of ambiguity and fear attached to their power. The Bambara of Mali compare women to "darkness" or "night" by the fact that she is difficult to understand and mysterious by nature.[66]

Indeed, if the fear that men have for women's spiritual powers caused them to institute restrictive religious ideologies on women, they may have failed to escape it entirely. There are many instances where men have often worshipped, depended on, and even followed female figures. Men may have retained the routine management of religion; but they have depended on women's spiritual ability to give life, provide good harvest for the society through fertility rituals, and their ability to heal. Tswana women of South Africa have used witchcraft, oracles, and spirit possession to predict rain, drought, famine, or war in their communities.[67] In the lake regions of East Africa, in places such as Uganda, Burundi, Rwanda, and northern Tanzania, female mediums are known to wield uncommon influence in issues relating to childbirth, agriculture, and healing, etc. For these women, their ritual roles afford them greater physical mobility to places normally restricted to women. For instance, in the southern region of precolonial Kitara society (Uganda), a priestess known as Muhumusa, personifying Nyabingi, a female deity of the area, led men in an anti-European attack in 1911.[68]

In spite of the above, it is difficult to conclude precisely whether women's spiritual roles are just a veneer they put up to escape male dominance or whether they are a genuine source of power for women. It has been suggested that spirit possession and its related symptoms are traceable to the innate power struggles between women and men in which men generally monopolize the many social, cultural, and political structures in African societies. This monopoly creates subjugation and dispossession prompting women to create or flock to spirit possession cults, which have been

labeled as "peripheral" or "tangential" because their only purpose is to provide therapeutic backing to "powerless" women or to compensate for their
otherwise low status.[69] For example, Muslim women in many East African
societies—particularly women in Somalia—participate in zar cults where
women's ailments are interpreted by other women as zar spirit possession
requiring husbands of the afflicted women to provide luxurious items and
expensive healing rituals and dances in order for their wives to recover.

Ironically, the spirit possessions usually occur during periods of neglect
and abuse in conjugal relationships; forcing men to comply with the demands of the women of zar cults. Furthermore, it is suggested that deprav-
ity and marginality generate hostility between men and women, which
women express in spirit possession, as there is no formal avenue for them
to air their grievances and gain a measure of control. Consequently, spirit
possession forms part of an ongoing "war between the sexes."[70] A different interpretation of these cults and why women utilize them is that contrary to the sex war argument, spirit possession and other similar forms
are closely allied with social structures that frequently give rise to conflicts,

A woman kisses a cleric's cross on the streets of
Lalibela, Ethopia, 1997. (Courtesy of A. Olusegun
Fayemi)

competition, tension, rivalry, or jealousy between members of the same sex, rather than between members of the opposite sex.[71]

In other words, since spirit possession occurs mainly among women, and in particular, among married women, it is the structural context of married life and its specified "performative" roles required of wives, which potentially cause women to engage in such activities. Women's individual performances in social arrangements may be publicly questioned; therefore, seizure by spirits and the resulting rituals performed publicly provide an arena for women to compete with one another either to remove the ambiguity of their statuses or to change them. In other words, spirit possession is a form of "rite of passage" through which social identity and statuses may be challenged, changed, defined, or redefined.[72] Yet still, there are other perspectives that criticize the above positions. That is, the social/functional perspectives employed in these arguments depict women negatively as "pawns" or "agents of conflict." On the contrary, in societies such as among the Luvale of Zambia, spirit possession is a way women treat their physiological displacement and bind themselves together into a wider symbolic community.[73]

The predicament many African women found themselves in during the period of apartheid in South Africa illustrates the above argument. In apartheid South Africa, social, economic, and political situations forced many women to live separately from their families. Women were in constant fear that family members could be arrested and detained for political activity or for minor violations of apartheid laws. To give themselves some form of psychological relief from the pressures of daily living and to collectively deal with problems associated with gender roles allocated to them, many women turned to spirit cults to create a community of "sister sufferers."[74] Besides strong feelings of communication, equality, euphoria, and empathy, women who led such cults gained a measure of control while offering a place of retreat and safety to others.[75] Whether the above is the case or not, what is obvious is that ideas about women, gender, and power in African religions poses ambivalent, and often contradictory, meanings—especially when linked with recent deluge of new Christian-related religious movements and contemporary social, economic, and political conditions.

In other cases, the special healing powers some women possess are generally viewed with uncertainty until such women find ways to validate themselves and their powers.[76] In other words, for women to become sacred professionals, they must somehow masculinize their powers and adopt more nonstandardized feminine roles. The reverse of this argument can also be true. Women healers who manage to masculinize their ritual powers and "liberate" themselves from their domestic obligations may still take advantage of the inscribed gender roles by inculcating powerful female symbolism such as maternal nurturing and fertility into their healing practices, thereby increasing their own ritual powers. In spite of contention that women healers, whether in traditional African religions, Islam, or in the newer independent churches, have to validate their powers, and that their healing activities exploit conditions of massive poverty and acute political oppression, these women have created the environment where healing can be given and received uninhibitedly.[77]

This chapter, while surveying the various discussions on women's roles in the religions of Africa, also provides insights into the interplay of women, power, gender, and healing. Understandably, such a synthesis can raise more questions than provide answers, given the different social, cultural, economic, environmental, historical, and political contexts in Africa. Yet, in viewing religion as a major avenue of cultural ingenuity, expression, interpretation, and transformation, it is possible to see how social groups negotiate or enforce their identities and mission through the medium of religion. Colonial rulers used Christianity to entice and establish their leadership over Africans; in the same way, Africans used African traditional religions to resist colonial rule. Since the colonial period, African women have relied on the rubrics of religious notions and beliefs to analyze society, expand women's views, challenge gender roles that restrict women to certain religious activities, and establish their own agency by establishing a myriad number of new religious movements.

Certainly, religion may serve to determine gender-related behavior, but it may also enable people to act independently of the stereotypes that define their gender. Women, in particular, have utilized Africa's new religious movements to shape the perception of themselves; their relations, not just with men, but also with the larger society; their ability to act and garner power; and provide strategies for surviving social, economic, and political hardships. Even so, we cannot lose sight of the complexity of the whole issue—not just the diverse roles and positions of women and men in Africa's religions, but also the configuration of forces that have shaped those diverse roles and positions in any given time. As demonstrated in resistance and liberation wars as well as with social, economic, and political inequities between those with power and those without it, different configurations of forces can have serious implications for how we view and understand people's participation in religion. In the same vein, while theological notions regarding women, power, gender, and healing and many other religious symbols and practices in African traditional religions, Christianity, and Islam may be seen as ambivalent, the new Pentecostal, evangelical, and revivalist movements may equally perpetuate many of the ambiguities and paradoxes prevalent in the "old" orders.

In spite of the attempt made in this study to provide a broad synthesis of women's religious roles in the three major religions of Africa and the various dimensions of gender and power in religious discourses, it has not been possible to cover every perspective. For instance, within mainstream churches and Islam, women do not often exercise power as priests and pastors or as Imams but as leaders in the various women's organizations and prayer groups. An examination of how these semiautonomous groups constitute a powerful voice within the respective churches and the Muslim community is of essence in understanding religious developments and transformations in Africa. Another area of near-neglect has been the ways in which religion was often the language through which gender and race were articulated in the colonial context, especially in the relationships between colonizing and colonized women.

This is vital because not only was the interaction of race and religion one of the chief means by which two groups of women encountered each other, but it prevented any meaningful exchange between them, especially when we factor in social classifications. More insight is also necessary for understanding the role that environment plays in religious practices as it relates to sacred sites, prayer grounds, and the like. The Lele of Zambia, for example, regard the forest as an exclusive male sphere; women are forbidden from entering it on religious occasions. Although Lele women have control over grasslands and that their ritual exclusion from the forest revolves around religious conceptions of women's fertility powers as both vulnerable and polluting,[78] it is unclear as to whether the spatial separation based on gender roles restricts men from entering the grasslands as it restricts women from entering the forest.

In particular, we must hear from women themselves as they configure and reconfigure their own power or rights to power, their religious experiences, and the effects of women challenging religion-induced sex-role expectations. This is important because women's ability to liberate themselves from sex-role expectations may not necessarily be equivalent with religious autonomy and self-determination. Studies in religions of Africa as it relates to women and gender issues, and those beyond it, must therefore seek all the nuanced perspectives and multiplicity of voices in order to evaluate more clearly, or even reconstruct, women's religious lives not just in contradiction to but also in interaction with men's religious lives.

NOTES

1. Evan Zuesse, *Ritual Cosmos: The Ritual Sanctification of Life in African Religions* (Athens: Ohio University Press, 1979), 11.

2. Rosalind I. J. Hackett, "Women in African Religions," in Arvind Sharma (ed.), *Religion and Women* (New York: State University of New York Press, 1994), 61.

3. Hackett, 64.

4. Zuesse, 3–7.

5. John S. Mbiti, "Flowers in the Garden: the Role of Women in African Religion," in Jacob K. Olupona (ed.), *African Traditional Religions in Contemporary Society* (New York: Paragon House, 1991), 57–72.

6. Hackett, 63–64.

7. Zuesse, 55.

8. A number of researchers have provided various accounts of Mawu-Lisa as a supreme god among the Ewe and the Fon. See Edwin William Smith (ed.), *African Ideas of God: A Symposium* (London: Edinburgh House Press, 1950), 226–227; Edward Geoffrey Parrinder, *West African Religion* (London: Epworth Press, 1961), 16–18.

9. Hacket, 67.

10. Eva L. Meyerowitz, *The Akan of Ghana* (London: Faber and Faber, 1958).

11. Margaret Strobel, "Women in Religious and Secular Ideology," in Margaret Jean Hay and Sharon Stichter (eds.), *African Women South of the Sahara* (New York: Longman Publishing, 1995), 102–103.

12. Margaret J. Field, *Search of Security: An Ethno-psychiatric Study of Rural Ghana* (Evanston, IL: Northwestern University Press, 1962).

13. Marion Kilson, "Ambivalence and Power: Mediums in Ga Traditional Religion," *Journal of Religion in Africa*, Vol. 4 (1972), 171–177.

14. David Lan, *Guns and Rain: Guerillas and Spirit Mediums in Zimbabwe* (London: James Currey, 1985), 3–7.

15. Anita Glaze, "Dialectics of Gender: Senufo Masquerades," *African Arts*, Vol. 19 (1986): 37.

16. Rosalind Shaw, "Gender and the Structuring of Reality in Temne Divination: An Interactive Study," *Africa*, Vol. 55 (1985): 289.

17. Dominique Zahan, *The Religion, Spirituality, and Thought of Traditional Africa* (Chicago, IL: University of Chicago Press, 1979), 83.

18. Kilson, "Women in African Traditional Religion," *Journal of Religion in Africa*, Vol. 8 (1976): 138–39.

19. Rosalind I. J. Hackett, *Religion in Calabar: The Religious Life and History of a Nigerian Town* (Berlin: Mouton de Gruyter, 1989), 35.

20. Eileen Jensen Krige and Jacob Daniel Krige, *The Realm of a Rain Queen: A Study of the Pattern of Lovedu Society* (London: Oxford University Press, 1943).

21. Anita Glaze, "Woman Power and Art in a Senufo Village," *African Arts*, Vol. 8 (1975): 65.

22. Sylvia A. Boone, *Radiance from the Waters: Ideals of Feminine Beauty in Mende Art* (New Haven, CT: Yale University Press, 1986), 13.

23. Ibid., 16.

24. Carol P. MacCormack, "Sande: The Public Face of a Secret Society," in Bennetta Jules-Rosette (ed.), *The New Religions of Africa: Priest and Priestess in Contemporary Cults and Churches* (Norwood, NJ: Ablex, 1978), 35.

25. Ibid., 34.

26. David Crabtree, "Women Liberation and The Church," in Sarah Betley Doely (ed.), *Women Liberation and The Church. The New Demand for Freedom in the Life of Christian Church* (New York: Association Press, 1970).

27. P. N. Wachege, *African Women's Liberation: A Man's Perspective* (Kenya: Kiambu, 1992), 93.

28. Daniel Kasomo, "The Role of Women in the Church in Africa," *International Journal of Sociology and Anthropology*, Vol. 2 (2010): 126–139.

29. Terence O. Ranger and John Weller (eds.), *Themes in Christian History in Central Africa* (Berkeley: University of California Press, 1975), 223.

30. Ibid.

31. Jean de Menasche, "Contemplative Life and Missions' Supplement to Doctrine and Life," *International Review of Mission*, Vol. 56 (1967): 3330–3337.

32. Werner Zerfluh, "Rundhutte fur Gott," *Bethlehem-Kalender*, (1971): 38–43.

33. Ibid.

34. Ibid.

35. Kasomo, 126–139.

36. Jules-Rosette, "Privilege Without Power: Women in African Cults and Churches," in Rosalyn Terborg-Penn, Sharon Harley, and Andrea Benton Rushing, *Women in Africa and the African Diaspora* (Washington, DC: Haword University Press, 1987), 99–116; Jean Comaroff and John L. Comaroff, *On Revelation and Revolution: Christianity, Colonialism and Consciousness in South Africa*, Vol. 1 (Chicago, IL: University of Chicago Press, 1991).

37. Jules-Rosette (ed.), *The New Religions of Africa* (Norwood, NJ: Ablex, 1979), 75.

38. Nancy L. Schwartz, "World Without End: the Meanings and Movements in the History Narratives and 'Tongue-Speech' of Legio of African Church Mission among the Luo of Kenya," (PhD Dissertations, Princeton University, 1989).

39. Ursula King, *Religion and Gender* (Cambridge, MA: Blackwell, 1995), 277–281.

40. Strobel, *Muslim Women in Mombasa, 1890–1975* (New Haven, CT: Yale University Press, 1979), 77–78.

41. Christian Coulon, "Women, Islam and Baraka," in Donal B. Cruise O'Brien and Christian Coulon (eds.), *Charisma and Brotherhood in African Islam* (Oxford, UK: Clarendon, 1988), 113.

42. Mark R. J. Faulkner, *Overtly Muslim, Covertly Boni: Competing Calls of Religious Allegiance on the Kenyan Coast* (Boston, MA: Brill, 2006).

43. See M. Bovin, "Muslim Women in the Periphery: the West African Sahel," in Bo Utas (ed.), *Women in Islamic Societies* (London: Scandinavian Institute of Asian Studies, 1983), 66–103.

44. Robert L. Bunger, *Islamization among the Upper Pokomo* (Syracuse, NY: Program of Eastern African Studies, Syracuse University, 1973), 96.

45. Strobel, "Women in Religious and Secular Ideology," 112–114.

46. Lucy Quimby, "Islam, Sex Roles, and Modernization in Bobo-Dioulasso," in Bennetta Jules-Rosette (ed.), *The New Religions of Africa: Priests and Priestesses in Contemporary Cults and Churches* (Norwood, NJ: Ablex, 1979), 203–218.

47. Jennifer Kopf, "Repression of Muslim Women's Movements in Colonial East Africa," in Karen M. Morin and Jeanne Kay Guelke (eds.), *Women, Religion, and Space* (New York: Syracuse University Press, 2007), 11.

48. Coulon, 116–132.

49. Charles C. Stewart and Elizabeth K. Stewart, *Islam and Social Order in Mauritania: A Case Study from the Nineteenth Century* (Oxford: Clarendon Press, 1973), 22–24.

50. John Ralph Willis (ed.), *Studies in West African Islamic History: The Cultivators of Islam* (London: Frank Cass, 1979), 12.

51. Strobel, "Women in Religion and Secular Ideology," 110–111.

52. Jean Boyd and Murray Last, "The Role of Women as Agents Religieux in Sokoto," *Canadian Journal of African Studies*, Vol. 19 (1985): 283–300.

53. Nancy J. Hafkin and Edna G. Bay (eds.), *Women in Africa: Studies in Social and Economic Change* (Stanford, CA: Stanford University Press, 1976), 7.

54. Shaw, 286–303.

55. Susan Reynolds Whyte, "Men, Women and Misfortune in Bunyole," in Pat Holden (ed.), *Women's Religious Experience* (London: Croom Helm, 1983), 180–181.

56. Holden (ed.), *Women's Religious Experience* (London: Croom Helm, 1983), 3–4.

57. Judith Hoch-Smith and Anita Spring (eds.), *Women in Ritual and Symbolic Roles* (New York: Plenum Press, 1978), 2–4.

58. Hackett, 76.

59. Iris Berger and Francis White, *Women in Sub-Saharan Africa: Restoring Women to History* (Bloomington: Indiana University Press, 1999).

60. David N. Beach, "An Innocent Woman, Unjustly Accused? Charwe, Medium of the Nehanda Mhondoro Spirit, and the 1896–97 Central Shona Rising in Zimbabwe," *History in Africa*, Vol. 25 (1998): 27–54.

61. Ruramisai Charumbira, "Nehanda and Gender Victimhood in the Central Mashonaland 1896–97 Rebellions: Revisiting the Evidence," *History in Africa*, Vol. 35 (2008): 103–131.

62. Ibid.

63. Catherine Coquery-Vidrovitch, *African Women*, trans. Beth Gillian Raps (Boulder, CO: Westview Press, 1997), 49.

64. Hackett, 74.

65. Jim P. Kiernan, "The 'Problem of Evil' in the Context of Ancestral Intervention in the Affairs of the Living," *Man, New Series*, Vol. 17 (1982): 194–195.

66. Dominique Zahan, *The Religion, Spirituality, and Thought of Traditional Africa* (Chicago, IL: University of Chicago Press, 1979), 93–94.

67. Coquery-Vidrovitch, 47.

68. Berger, 35–40.

69. Ian M. Lewis, "Spirit Possession and Deprivation Cults," *Man, New Series*, Vol. 1 (1966): 307–329.

70. Ibid.

71. Peter J. Wilson, "Status Ambiguity and Spirit Possession," *Man, New Series*, Vol. 2 (1967): 67–78.

72. Ibid.

73. Spring, "Epidemiology of Spirit Possession among the Luvale of Zambia," in Hoch-Smith and Spring (eds.), *Women in Ritual and Symbolic Roles* (New York: Plenum Press, 1978), 4–15.

74. Mukonyora has suggested that the issue of women binding together as a result of socioeconomic and political dispossession was not restricted to apartheid South Africa, but widespread throughout the whole region of southern Africa. See Isabel Mukonyora, *Wandering a Gendered Wilderness: Suffering & Healing in an African Initiated Church* (New York: Peter Lang, 2007), 57–66.

75. Susan Middleton-Keirn, "Convivial Sisterhood: Spirit Medium-ship and Client-Core Network among Black South African Women," in Hoch Smith and Spring (eds.), *Women in Ritual and Symbolic Roles* (New York: Plenum Press, 1978), 191–201.

76. Walker, 87–97.

77. Mukonyora, 106–121.

78. Mary Douglas, "The Lele of the Kasai," in Cyril Daryll Forde (ed.), *African Worlds: Studies in the Cosmological Ideas and Social Values of African Peoples* (Piscataway, NJ: Transaction Publishers, 1999), 7.

SUGGESTED READING

Blakely, Thomas D., Walter E. A. van Beek, and Dennis L Thomson, et al. *Religion in Africa: Experience and Expression.* Portsmouth, NH: Heinemann, 1994.

Callaway, Barbara. *The Heritage of Islam: Women, Religion, and Politics in West Africa.* Boulder, CO: Lynne Rienner, 1993.

Frahm-Arp, Maria. *Professional Women in South African Pentecostal Charismatic Churches.* Boston, MA: Brill, 2010.

Hinfelaar, Hugo F. *Bemba-Speaking Women of Zambia in a Century of Religious Change (1892–1992).* New York: Brill, 1994.

Hoehler-Fatton, Cynthia. *Women of Fire and Spirit: History, Faith, and Gender in Roho Religion in Western Kenya.* New York: Oxford University Press, 1996.

Morin, Karen M. and Jeanne Kay Guelke (eds.). *Women, Religion, and Space: Global Perspectives on Gender and Faith.* Syracuse, NY: Syracuse University Press, 2007.

Pohl, Florian. *Modern Muslim Societies.* Tarrytown, NY: Marshall Cavendish, 2010.

Sackey, Brigid M. *New Directions in Gender and Religion: The Changing Status of Women in African Independent Churches.* Lanham, MD: Lexington Books, 2006.

Saidi, Christine. *Women's Authority and Society in Early East-Central Africa.* Rochester, NY: University of Rochester Press, 2010.

Soothill, Jane E. *Gender, Social Change, and Spiritual Power: Charismatic Christianity in Ghana.* Boston, MA: Brill, 2007.

4

—✴—

Women and Work

Throughout the course of Africa's history, women have been at the helm of domestic and agricultural production and distribution. African families have depended on, and continue to depend on, the work of women for their very survival. In precolonial African societies, in particular, many women worked from dawn to dusk. They invested an extensive number of hours in subsistence farming activities and in domestic duties. With the exception of a few powerful women who had political and ritual responsibilities in their societies and thus worked in the public sphere, women's domestic responsibilities restricted them to the homestead and effectively stripped them of any active public roles. This, however, does not cancel out the fact that for the most part, African women have found their domestic and family responsibilities rewarding. With the onset of the European colonial invasion and its resultant socioeconomic changes, African women had to confront simultaneously the difficult task of balancing the conflicting pressures to fulfill their domestic roles and the need to embrace the public-oriented colonial market economy.

For many women, the colonial disruption of the balance in the economic systems of African societies made it increasingly necessary for them to work outside the home in order to help provide food and shelter for their families and education for themselves and their children. Yet, both African and colonial objections to women working outside the domestic sphere provided a powerful stamping block to the efforts of many women. Not only were women associated with domesticity and required to maintain the family, but also their very status was defined

by it. Indeed, gendered delineation of work has been part of African social and economic structure with different degrees of fluidity and flexibility. Colonial rule, however, reemphasized gendered work, making it
even more difficult for women to transcend from their domestic roles to
public roles.

As many researchers have attested to, the discrepancies in the type of
work available to women and men during the colonial period continued
through to the postcolonial periods. The inequity in work availability and
access restrictions hampered women's ability to get high-paying jobs, low-
ering their economic progress and contributions toward economic developments in their societies. The above notwithstanding, changes in the last
few decades in many African societies have brought some significant improvement in women's access to work in the public sector and their control
over economic resources. In this chapter, we will look at African women's
work through history in both the domestic and public arenas, focusing on
their roles in agricultural production and distribution and their access to
and control of economic resources.

Although we cannot do diligence to the subject of women and work
without highlighting the predominant control men have over economic

Ibadan marketplace. (Courtesy of Toyin Falola)

resources in many African societies, our emphasis is placed on the numerous avenues of enterprise, agency, and autonomy women appropriate for themselves: sometime tacitly, other times overtly to challenge and subvert patriarchal authority. This chapter also examines women's involvement in the African market economy from precolonial to contemporary times, analyzing the various avenues through which women have generated income and continue to generate income. Our emphasis not only focuses on women's participation in trading activities but also their roles as trained professionals and as producers of goods and services. In view of the fact that the majority of African women predominantly work in the domestic sphere and in agricultural production and distribution, and the importance of these sectors to African families and to national economies, we stress women's roles in these sectors.

WOMEN'S ROLE IN DOMESTIC AND AGRICULTURAL PRODUCTION AND DISTRIBUTION

Africa's precolonial societies were mostly based on subsistence agriculture and/or livestock rearing in pastoral societies. Every household grew all or most of its consumable food items and hand made almost every necessary tool and utensil needed for daily living. In most instances, gender ideologies and the nature of work determined the organization and allotment of productive tasks between men and women. In farming societies, food cultivation depended on hoe culture, which was labor intensive for both men and women. The hoe was the basic tool for cultivating the land. As a result, small tracts of land were cultivated at a time, requiring the clearing of a new area of about one to two acres every so often. A form of shifting cultivation developed where a farmed land was left for long periods to fallow before being used again. The major role men played in this type of agricultural setting was the heavy work of clearing the land for cultivation. In addition, men were usually responsible for making cloths from the bark of trees, hunting, fishing, and defending the group. Women's work entailed both domestic and agricultural responsibilities. Farming tasks such as planting, weeding, harvesting, and storing foodstuff all fell under the responsibility of women. Furthermore, women were in charge of processing food items for immediate and prolonged use, as well as cooking; washing; cleaning; making pottery, baskets, and mats; and raising and caring for children and the elderly.[1] In some societies, women were able to engage in agricultural activities that supported subsistence living as well as generate wealth depending on the flexibility of gender norms in that society. For instance, women in Amhara society (Ethiopia) were able to procure their own land and by so doing control the agricultural production process.

These women took charge of preparing the land for planting, harvesting, and controlling the proceeds the land generated.[2] Like women in Amhara society, Tswana and Xhosa women had control over their agricultural production and the wealth it generated. They, however, had to contend with gender norms that restricted them to the domestic sphere. These women were prohibited from engaging in the affairs of the public and in legal issues, and in the case of Xhosa women, they remained legally subjected to the whims and caprice of the men in their society.[3] Yet the above instance is not reflective of women's positions in every African society. Varying degrees of flexibility and fluidity existed in many societies to allow both sexes to engage in socioeconomic and political activities of the other. The Lovedu had a political and social system that allowed both women and men to engage in public life and to have control over their own property. Women could act as district heads and as healers and could own livestock.[4]

It has been argued that in pastoral economies, such as among the Bororo, it was unlikely for a woman to gain the title of *jom-na'i* or "master of the herd." This arrangement, however, had nothing to do with gender ideologies and everything to do with practicality. Women naturally do not have the physical strength required in looking after the semidomesticated humped cattle of the Bororo. This duty was physically demanding, requiring long-distance treks to find and fetch water and grazing lands for the animals during the dry season, protecting the herd against wild animals and thieves, castrating bulls, and training the oxen. In addition, motherhood requirements made it near impossible for women to leave the camp for extended periods. Bororo women, therefore, took responsibility for duties that allowed them to stay at home. They milked and made butter and took care of minor ailments of the animals left behind by the men. Bororo men lacked any knowledge of butter making or milking, but if need be, they would have learned to perform "this feminine role."[5]

The pattern of livelihood among the Bororo, therefore, determined its gendered delineation of labor. The same was true of the seminomad Fulani of Niger where men had the knowledge and responsibility of milking while the women took care of making butter. Fulani men performing this presumed "feminine role" resulted from the fact that they spent extensive amount of time away from their settlements looking after their herd and thus needed to know how to milk for consumption. In the village, older men took charge of milking the cows left behind. It has been argued, "Much of these habits, which sometimes persist long after there has been a change in the mode of life, are functional in origin, and not based on any magico-philosophical concepts of irreducible differences between the sexes."[6] The division of labor based on sex did not carry any inferiority clause for women in this pastoral society as normally found in agricultural-based societies. Nonetheless, men's control of the herd—the lifeline of pastoral societies—allowed them greater socioeconomic benefits as compared to those achieved by women.

Bororo women may have had responsibilities that required the exertion of less physical strength, yet their domestic duties bordered on monotony and required the investment of extensive hours to complete. Food preparation alone required that they get up at dawn, and whenever they needed to sell their milk and butter, they often had to walk about 20 to 30 kilometers to the nearest village to do so. Bororo women were also in charge of building the groups' temporary dwellings, decorating calabashes, making mats and fans, and plaiting the light ropes used in making the fire for the dwelling.[7]

It has also been found that among the Hausa Muslims of Kano, Nigeria, the practice of *purdah* restricted women's work to the domestic space; yet, in recent years, Hausa Muslim women have found ingenious ways of navigation around this restriction to earn income outside the home to support themselves and their families. The women's control of domestic labor has allowed them to establish and participate in a complex system of economic exchange. In a typical Hausa Muslim household, women and children are

Street trading is common in all of Africa, and child labor is regarded as part of socialization to strong work ethics. (Courtesy of Toyin Falola)

consumers, not producers. Women's domestic roles revolve around reproductive responsibilities, cooking and cleaning, and taking care of the
household. Because the practice of *purdah* requires that women do not
work—at least not outside the home—Hausa men have the duty of providing all the food items for eating, and in most cases, they do so by giving
their wives cash allowances. Married Hausa women undermine the *purdah*
rule by diverting cash intended for domestic consumption and investing it
in income-generating activities.[8]

For instance, instead of cooking three meals a day for their families,
women usually cook once a day and purchase the rest of their daily meals
from their neighbors, or they would cook once a day for the families and
cook the rest of the day for sale. Besides selling cooked food, these women
also engage in petty trading of raw food and other small items. They may
also participate in embroidery making and sewing, plaiting hair, and in ro-
tating credit societies. These economic practices by women in *purdah* are
important in many ways. That is, in diverting their domestic allowances
into a paid production, these women are in effect making income for their
domestic labor, in addition to the fact that they are freeing their time to
engage in income-generating activities. The women have complete control over the incomes they generate, which allow them to establish support
groups with other women through the exchange of gifts. The income also
gives these women a certain level of social mobility and freedom, making
it possible for them to supplement their husbands' incomes; negotiate in
their daughters' marriages; and more importantly, being able to manage on
their own after divorce or widowhood.[9]

The above studies suggest that the gender division of labor, which determines women's domestic and subsistence agricultural responsibilities, may
equally provide a space for women to gain or lose control over their labor.
In recent years, researchers have deepened our understanding of the nuanced dimensions of a gender-based division of labor and the fact that African women have not necessarily accepted claims on their labor, particularly
as it pertains to exertions and demands imposed by colonial rulers. The
colonial restructuring of African economies have researchers in hot debate
over whether it affected women's socioeconomic activities positively or
negatively.[10] On the one hand, some argue that the effects of colonial capitalist exploitation and their ideologies about proper gender roles eroded
African women's socioeconomic independence.[11] On the other hand, others have suggested that colonial rule rather freed African women from the
stringent patriarchal grip men had over women, allowing women access to
divorce, education, and economic independence.

Whatever the argument is, what is clear is that the colonial intervention had a profound effect on precolonial economies and women's roles
in it. Colonial rulers shifted subsistence agriculture to a system of cash

cropping in agricultural raw materials such as cocoa, cotton, and coffee. In this endeavor, African women bore the greater share of the labor burden of growing the new crops because in eastern, central, and southern Africa, in particular, colonial rulers methodically withheld agricultural supplies and access to markets in an effort to force men to work in European mines and plantations. Not only were women forced to divert their attention from food cultivation to cash cropping, they could no longer depend on their husbands and male members of their families to clear the land for farming. The emigration of men into European mining and plantation areas left many women to take responsibility for both domestic duties and the farming activities alone. Adding to the absence of male labor, the majority of women in eastern, central, and southern Africa had to contend with lack of financial resources and lack of access to land and credit to facilitate their farming activities.[12]

Ultimately, many rural women and their children faced increased hunger and impoverishment. However, in some areas such as among the Beti of Cameroon, women responded to the colonial restructuring of agricultural production by expanding their involvement in farming activities that required the least help from men.[13] As will be discussed later on, some women reacted to the emigration of their husbands into the urban centers by accompanying them to the urban centers or by migration there themselves. This caused many urban populations to swell dramatically during the colonial period as compared to the precolonial era. Yet, as contemporary population trends indicates, the majority of African women lived, and continued to live, in the rural areas and worked in the agricultural sector. To maximize agricultural output and to entice people to shift from subsistence farming to cash cropping, colonial rulers introduced new agricultural technologies with adverse effects on women's roles in agriculture. For instance, the introduction of the plow increased men's food production output among the Tswana, which inadvertently expanded their socioeconomic importance and their control over women's labor.[14] Adding to the situation was colonial rulers' gender ideology that the woman's place was being a good wife and a good mother. As a result, colonial rulers readily granted male farmers financial assistance and access to international markets and new agricultural technologies as opposed to women farmers even though women were the majority group in farming activities.

WOMEN'S ROLE IN THE MARKET ECONOMY

African women have been involved in market economies since the exchange of commodities began on the African continent. Although their level of involvement has been subjected to debates and interpretations, many researchers agree that since the precolonial era, women have traded handicrafts, cooked and uncooked food items, cloth, and other supplies on both small-scale and large-scale and in local and long-distance trade. For example, researchers have reported of Kikuyu women participating in large-scale long-distance trade and controlling the wealth they gained in as far back as the early 19th century. Even in cases where African women's participation in trade was restricted to the local level and was small-scale trade, their trading activities were very significant to the expansion of large-scale trade and of towns and cities in Africa. Before the establishment of formal colonial rule, many states along the West African coast and in East Africa participated in exchanging goods among themselves and with North Africa and later in the slave trade with Europeans. The development of the Asante kingdom in the Gold Coast was based in part on their participation in trade, as was the case among the Oyo in Yorubaland. The market centers that developed in these places expanded to support a growing urban population, and women involved in the market economy played essential roles in these expansions.

As demonstrated among the Oyo, men traded the more luxurious items while women traded foodstuffs, cloth, and other essentials needed to support the growing number of people who trouped to these areas.[15] Early European accounts of trading activities in the Gold Coast suggests women's participation in the market economy—selling foodstuffs, crafts, mats, and cloths—was vital for the expansion of the coastal towns and the trade between the coast and the hinterlands. In addition, women in the Gold Coast, particularly those of mixed African and European parenthood, worked as cultural intermediaries and as translators between Europeans and Africans, and through their work connections, many were able to become successful traders.[16] When the exchange of goods and services between Africans and Europeans extended to the realm of trading humans, astonishingly, women participated in this market economy, not as victims of slave catchers as has been generally espoused in literature but as active beneficiaries in the trade.

It has also been pointed out how prior to the 19th century most Senegambians could not participate in the slave trade because they lacked the resources needed for such an endeavor. Slave catchers had to be provided with the proper equipment and paid, and the slaves had to be fed before being sold. Consequently, men had more direct involvement in the trade than women did, but a surprising number of women also participated indirectly as intermediaries, cooks, and in some cases as prostitutes for the slave catchers and the Europeans. Some scholars have thus discounted the predominant idea that women only participated as hapless victims of the slave trade. When the slave trade reached its peak, some of the women who participated had gained enough wealth to become important traders. Accordingly, their wealth allowed them to acquire domestic servants, houses, jewelry, trading ships, houses, gold, silver, and fashionable clothes, which also translated into higher socioeconomic status for these women.[17] They gained the respect of their male counterparts and exerted influence in their communities. For example, Senhora Philippa, who in the mid-1630s, controlled the trading post at Rufisque in Western Senegal, and Senhora Catti, the commercial agent of the ruler of Cayor, in the Wolof state in 1965 were among some of the more prominent women who benefited as a result of the slave trade in the Senegambia region.[18]

With the end of the slave trade and the formal establishment of colonial rule, the socioeconomic sectors of African societies became fundamentally changed with significant consequences for both African women and men. As with many of the changes that Africans experienced, the introduction of colonial capitalist economy adversely affected women's work. As discussed above, the colonial capitalist mode of production forced Africans to shift from subsistence agriculture to cash cropping, which demanded the most labor input; yet, at the same time, it systematically forced African men to move into urban areas to work in colonial plantations, mines, and clerical jobs. The ripple effect was that many African women were left alone to bear the burden of farming. Rural women responded by either migrating with their husbands to urban centers or adopting strategies to meet the labor demands imposed on them as a result of the absence of their male relatives.

Women in the work place. (Courtesy of Toyin Falola)

Many rural women shifted their focus from farming activities to petty trading in their locality, while others migrated either with their male relatives or alone to towns and cities. Some of the women who moved to the towns and cities sought trading opportunities as most had little or no educational backgrounds to enter into skilled wage labor, and the job opportunities for unskilled labor was limited for women.[19] Indeed, during the colonial period, few avenues in the wage economy opened up for women in towns and cities. Wage employment was almost exclusively limited to men, particularly in government agencies and industries. In places where European plantations existed, women were seasonally employed to help in the harvesting and processing of crops. However, only women living within immediate environs could take advantage of these few opportunities. White has indicated that the vast majority of women who migrated to southern and eastern African towns and cities worked as petty traders, beer brewers, and as prostitutes: all in peril of running afoul of the authorities.

In South Africa, for example, when caught, such women could face a jail sentence; and in Mozambique, they could get a jail sentence of up to a year of forced labor. In some areas, women's only avenue to wage employment was working as domestic servants. These women received the lowest pay and were often exploited. In South Africa, Kenya, and Mozambique, selling food items, tobacco, and a limited number of manufacturing industries provided opportunities for women to earn income.[20] The negative impact of the colonial intervention in African economic structures on women was demonstrated among the Baule of the Ivory Coast. The Baule, since the precolonial era, had been participating in regional trade with cloth as their major trade item. Baule women and men cooperated to jointly produce this trade item, although the women were considered the ultimate owners of the cloth. However, when European colonizers intervened in this arrangement, it destabilized the balance in gender relations established among the Baule and eroded women's economic autonomy and control.

Within the Baule agricultural setup, women were responsible for growing the cotton, harvesting, and processing it into dyed threads. The part played by men in the process was clearing the land, weaving, and sewing the prepared threads into strips of cloth. To expand cotton production, the French colonial rulers insisted that Baule men should plant cotton as a cash crop by taking over the production of cotton from women. To facilitate the process, they opened the Gonfrevile textile factory near Bouak in 1923 and provided men with financial resources and agricultural technology to the detriment of women cotton farmers. As a result, Baule women not only lost their roles in the production of cloth but also of the income generated through the sale of this trade item.[21] In spite of the negative consequences that the colonial capitalist mode of production visited on African women, many women managed to create spaces of agency within the commodity market by exploiting any available avenue to engage in trading activities.

Many historians agree that the colonial period was, perhaps, the worst period of gendering in African societies; yet, a critical analysis reveals that it had unintended implications for women's roles in colonial market economies. This was exemplified among the Sefwi Wiawso in the Gold Coast where between 1925 and 1932, the colonial government passed a number of amendments to existing customary laws in order to "properly" structure gender relations in the area. As with the Baule example, before the colonial introduction of cocoa as a cash crop, men and women in Sefwi Wiawso in the Gold Coast cooperated in their agricultural production, although each had a separate sphere of influence and control. Men were responsible for clearing the land while women took charge of farming the land to feed the family. The production of cocoa as a cash crop disrupted the balance in the work responsibilities between men and women and tilted it in the favor of men when colonial rulers instigated men to take control of cocoa production.

The regional amendments passed between 1925 and 1932 in the region intended for women to stay in their marriages, remain the wards of their husbands, and assist them on their cocoa farms. However, when the cocoa market shrunk in the late 1920s, Sefwi Wiawso women took advantage of the growing mining and transportation business in the area by shifting their energies from helping their husbands on their cocoa farms to marketing foodstuffs to the many man (and women) that came to the region to look for wage employment. For many of these women, participating in trading activities not only gave them control over their incomes and physical labor, but it also granted them the opportunity to decide whether to remain in a marriage or to seek divorce.[22] Colonial authorities, however, viewed women's increased autonomy and social mobility with disdain. They associated women with prostitution, venereal diseases, adultery, and divorce—and in many instances, increased the number of legislations intended to confine women to their "proper" place in society.

Akin to the laws passed to regulate gender roles in Sefwi Wiawso, the colonial authorities in northern Rhodesia passed legislations that required Africans to legally register their marriage before they could occupy a household. This was intended to limit women's access to divorce and to curb the increasing number of independent women in the urban centers. As discussed previously, African women have not been acquiescent or victims in every situation, be it instigated by colonial rulers or by African patriarchal institutions. For instance, Kenyan women have publicly attacked and objected to "traditional" women's roles, the arduous physical labor imposed on them, and the deference toward men. In other instances, women—particularly market women—organized themselves into associations and

networks to assist themselves and to change their situations.[23] In the case
of how, for example, Yoruba women engendered for themselves spaces of
autonomy and control in the market economy in the early postcolonial period, it has been argued that they appropriated the marketplace and used
their control of this space to persuade influential men in the Yoruba society
who also wanted financial assistance from the women. The exchange of favors between the Yoruba market women and the prominent political actors
allowed the women to extend their field of influence and control beyond
the market space into the sociopolitical realm.[24]

NEW CAREERS AND NEGOTIATING
GENDERED WORK

African market women were not the only group of women in African societies who found ways to break the cycle of poverty colonialism visited on
them, and to enter into spaces previously restricted to them to gain fame,
fortune, and influence. Toward the end of colonial rule in Africa in the
mid-20th century, a small but significant number of African women had
managed to attain higher levels of Western education and begun working
in the public sector. The majority of these women, however, worked in professions attached with femininity such as teaching and nursing fields. With
the formal end of colonial rule on the continent, things started to improve,
but the improvements as they related to women's work have been tempered
with varying degrees of success and failures across the board. Many African nations made concerted efforts to improve education, create jobs, and
better the life of its citizens. But conflicts, droughts, poor economic strategies, and political instabilities thwarted their efforts.

Added to the above, the few jobs that opened in the early postcolonial
period were highly gendered such that women's access to them was limited. Jobs were labeled by sex—teaching and nursing for women, law and
the medical profession for men—meaning that even when a woman managed to acquire, for instance, a law degree, getting employment could be
daunting. Lack of educational opportunities for women also added to the
disparity between women and men in the job market. In their 1990 *African Employment Report,* Jobs and Skills Program for Africa (JASPA) noted
that contemporary African governments have been taking significant steps
toward promoting the formal education of girls in an effort to decrease
the gap between men and women in the socioeconomic sphere. In addition, activist groups and nongovernmental organizations have increased
awareness to the socioeconomic inequities women face in many African
societies.

Yet, in spite of these measures, women continue to constitute a vulnerable group as compared to men in the labor market. The educational

enrollment ratio for women remains lower than that of men, with women tending to concentrate overwhelmingly in fields that offer low pay and fewer opportunities to reach a higher level. Women's concentration in low-paying jobs, it must be pointed out, has not been out of choice: rather such areas are usually the only avenues of employment open to women. Furthermore, many African countries have not changed the obsolete colonial laws that prevented women from working in such masculine occupations as the mining and transportation sectors. Consequently, African women have had to redouble their economic and educational efforts to help feed, clothe, and provide shelter for their families. Many turned to the informal sector by engaging in self-employment businesses. For example, women in Brazzaville and Kinshasa carved out a niche for themselves in the informal sector by entering into the food distribution trade. Soon, the supply of fish and market produce to the growing urban centers was entirely under their control.[25]

The JASPA report shows that between 1970 and 1985, women's involvement in this sector rose from 29 percent to 35 percent. As many as 7 million women entered the informal sector; and when coupled with the 10 percent increase in women in the formal sector, African women's unemployment dropped from 6 percent of the total female labor force in 1980 to a mere 1.2 percent in 1985. Unfortunately, the growth in women's employment in both the formal and the informal sectors could not be sustained. Between 1985 and 1990, female unemployment began to rise due to such factors as the collapse of African economies. This resulted from ineffective stabilization and structural adjustment programs, the lack of political expediency, retrenchment policies, and the oversaturation of the informal sector, especially by retrenched and civil service employees seeking additional incomes. Thus, in the period after 1985, the percentage of the female labor force in Africa dropped from 6 percent to a current 5 percent, suggesting a loss of 2.5 million jobs for women.[26]

The above notwithstanding, the 21st century has brought significant changes to African women and their work responsibilities. Everywhere on the continent, women have moved beyond the domestic realm into the public arena, or have combined their domestic responsibilities with their public roles and have been competitive—even if it is not head-to-head—with their male counterparts in all spheres of the job market. African women have now taken the lead in engendering discourses on the dangers of "gendered work" not just for women but also for the society in general. More than ever before, women have attained higher education and can be found working in previously labeled "male jobs" as physicians, college professors, lawyers, engineers, writers, police officers, and political actors and leaders. Africa can now even boast of a number of female heads of state and government.

Self employment is common, with a strong informal sector everywhere. Here a woman trader in Cameroon stands by her wares. (Courtesy of Toyin Falola)

Perhaps, the most substantial change in women's employment in contemporary Africa was the large-scale progression of women into clerical work. In the colonial years, leading up to the early postcolonial periods, secretarial work was fundamentally the work of African men who had middle-level educational backgrounds. However, in recent years, women have filled the majority of secretarial jobs. Admittedly, such jobs offered women little or no opportunities to advance; nonetheless, it has come to have some degree of acceptance among women since it offered those with minimal educational backgrounds the opportunity to move out of jobs associated with domesticity and hard labor. The expansion of the information technology in many African countries has permitted many women in clerical jobs to improve their level of education through virtual colleges and long-distance learning, which allows them to enter into higher-income professions. A number of women have also entered the military and the armed services and have been fighting side-by-side with their male colleagues.

The new roles African women have taken on have also shaped their family relationships and arrangements. Increasingly, husbands can no longer hide behind the traditional ideal of being sole breadwinners. In families where both parents are working, husbands have to participate in sharing the domestic responsibilities and in caring for their children. In the same vein, children's previous unlimited access to their mothers has declined, and older children may be required to help look after their younger siblings while their parents are at work. In this formulation, the gendered delineation of work between women and men and family duties has been redefined to be more fluid to accommodate African women's new socioeconomic development. The dynamics of the changes, which have occurred in the urban African family as a result of women entering the contemporary job market, is our next focus.

WOMEN AND WORK IN THE URBAN FAMILY

The history of African women as part of the African urban scene has been as long as the emergence of the urban centers themselves. They have lived and worked in a variety of employment avenues in order to provide food and shelter for themselves and their families. Irrespective of the family structure that women establish for themselves in the cities—whether conjugal family household or single-headed family household—their family life and work activities are the key mediums through which we can understand the effects of continuity of African traditional family arrangements and the socioeconomic changes that have occurred in contemporary Africa. The productive roles African women play in the urban family have been analyzed from various angles and perspectives. Feminist scholars have argued that based on the myriad of activities women are engaged in at the domestic level, a substantive degree of actual productive work occurs within the household usually unaccounted for as actual work and equally unremunerated. These involve all the various processes that go into food processing for consumption as well as processing food items and other consumer goods for longer shelf life.

In fact, it has been suggested that even the act of consumption in itself constitutes some form of work. That is, mundane activities such as queuing to buy food, arranging for transportation, scheduling and attending medical appointments, and deciding the amount of money to spend and when to spend it, all count for the daily productive work women undertake within the family.[27] In hopes of broadening the discourse and definition of what is considered work and nonwork carried out by women in the families, some researchers have employed the theoretical framework of status production of work. In one such study, the author points to the numerous avenues of work women undertake, which generally go unnoticed, but the expectation is that married women must be vigilant in keeping up with these "invisible" tasks in order to safeguard the social status of their family. They, for instance, must ensure that their spouses keep appropriate work clothes, they must occasionally entertain their husbands' friends, train their children to behave morally and to speak appropriately in public, and concern themselves with the general appearance of their children in public.[28]

By instilling these values into their children, women ensure the security of their family's social status as well as its hopes of moving up the social ladder. In addition, in undertaking these responsibilities, particularly those regarding the social training of their children, women effectively shape, and probably enhance, their children's occupational and marital future. Within the urban family, women continue to exhibit characteristics of family arrangements usually associated with rural African families, but as some point out, the work of women in middle-class income families, including cooking, shopping, and childcare has not decreased or changed as much as is commonly perceived as a result of their urban living or change in social status. In some regards, the work of women in the middle-income urban household has actually increased because of their adoption of Western lifestyles and higher standards of living.[29] With limited and, in some cases, complete lack of assistance from family members for domestic chores, women now have to devote a great deal of labor time to domestic responsibilities, added to the fact that most of these women are also working outside the home in high demanding jobs.

Added to the above is the fact that most urban families strive for lifestyles and social statuses that demand the acquisition of such material items as private cars; expensive furniture; home appliances; clothing and above all, one's own house. As previously discussed in chapter 2, in some urban families, women have used their educational and financial resources as an advantage in getting their husbands to participate in domestic duties. Nonetheless, in the vast majority of urban families, women continue to constitute the main body responsible for household chores. With the acquisition of cars, home appliances, and the like, women's work in the home doubles, if not triples, when you factor in caring for children and the husband, which in themselves can be full-time jobs. Women of both rural and urban middle-class families carry out their household duties dealing with different impediments and in different mediums, but on some level, the challenges are the same. That is, even though middle-class women do not spend long hours as rural women do hauling water, making charcoal, pounding grain, or fetching firewood, nonetheless, they do spend equal amounts of time at shopping centers and marketplaces, in traffic, preparing a more varied number of meals, and cleaning the increased number of dishes and utensils after meals.

Undoubtedly, the major area of domestic work in household for urban women who have children is providing sufficient care for their children. Besides the fact that many do not have access to childcare support usually abundant to rural women, contemporary developments in educational and social values have increased the amount of time mothers (and fathers) have

to put into taking care of their children. Women who hold outside employments have to combine their working schedules with their children's socialization and education—doing homework, school projects, extracurricular
activities, sports, and so on—as well as making sure that their children are
safe at all times in the neighborhood. For some women, having fewer children may be the solution, but fewer children, in itself, does not completely
alleviate the problem. To combine a full-time or even part-time job with
motherhood, many women rely on house girls. The effects of this arrangement is that the children grow knowing the house girl more so than the
parents, and they may in fact acquire many of their social skill and values
from what she teaches them.[30] Added to the complexity of women's family life is the broadly accepted view that a woman's primary role lay within
the domestic sphere, tempered sparingly by socioeconomic and political
hierarchy some few women manage to achieve. Hence, the idea of a woman
working and leaving her children to the care of others appears completely
unacceptable to some Africans.

The general assumption associated with the above view is that women
do not have the ability to combine effectively their outside employments
with their domestic responsibilities. In other words, a woman's ability to

Women play leadership position. Bisola Falola introducing speakers at a
conference. (Courtesy of Toyin Falola)

perform her family roles is greatly undermined by her work outside the home. Many gender and feminist scholars have engendered new ways of envisioning women's work roles and have, to some degree, been successful in undercutting the strength in the view that domesticity is the domain of women, in many African societies this view still persist. Women essentially face what has been commonly referred to as "the double burden," which is also seen as an exclusive women's problem. The obvious solution—men participating in domestic responsibilities—has not only failed to gained major acceptance among many African men, but even the most avid women supporters and radical gender feminist scholars have yet to instigate any substantive changes. Whatever changes we see in recent years have been what women themselves who go through the complexities of managing work and family roles have engendered. In many Western countries, some women deal with the double burden by entering into part-time employment, which could be regarded as the ideal solution for married women who want or need to work but have family responsibilities that require their increased presence in the home.

Some women have demanded wages for domestic work while others wanted nursery assistance, which would relieve them of the burdens of childcare. For women in Western societies, many of these demands have been met either by their governments or by their spouses. The United States government, for example, provided nursery assistance for low-income mothers to be able to go to work or seek higher education. Increasingly, more and more men are staying home as "stay at home fathers" to take care of their children while their wives are at work and many more men are sharing domestic responsibilities, even if not on equal basis. Some of these dynamics, such as husbands helping their wives with domestic responsibilities have been achieved in some urban African families, but other aspects such as governmental assistance for working mothers and husbands staying home to be the primary caretakers of their children have yet to be realized. In recent years, the question of women combining family and work has drawn heated debates in feminist circles, and in everyday conversations, but as the following discourse shows, the challenges that face women in the urban family are here to stay. The question, then, is how women can combine their work and family life effectively.

BALANCING WORK AND FAMILY

Many scholars who do research on the family systems and work agree on the interconnectedness of these two structures. The family not only socializes a person and serves as a support network for people, but it is also closely intertwined with work roles that it is sometimes difficult to distinguish between the two roles. In precolonial African societies, there was hardly any delineation between women's family and work roles since many women engaged in trading and other businesses conducted their activities from the homestead. For example, as discussed in chapter 5, women who made pottery, basketry, did calabash decorating, and the rest, carried out their artistic production in their homes side by side with their other domestic chores. Some market women cooked their family meals at their stalls at the marketplace, and indeed, it is a common sight in many marketplaces across West Africa in contemporary times. Recently socioeconomic developments have demarcated the work place from the home without much of a success and compounding the challenges people face in their work and family relations.

For the contemporary urban women, in particular, family and work roles are not just intertwined, but very challenging to combine. Indeed, for both women and men and regardless of whether they are working for someone, working for themselves, or working in a family business, combining work and family is not an easy task. Numerous studies have found how people transfer their work-related stresses and emotions to their home environment or transfer their home-related stresses and emotions to their work environment in what researchers refer to as "work-to-family spillover/family-to-work."[31] The spillover could be positive or negative, and both women and men could be at the giving or the receiving end. Negative spillover occurs when people verbally or physically abuse or ignore their spouses and children as a result of events that happened at their work or as a result of the stress they are experiencing because of the demands of the work. On the other hand, when work-related experiences make couples more tolerant of each other and kind to their children and those around them, the work-to-home spillover is considered a positive one. For instance, when spillover emotions in a woman's role as a mother strengthen her role as a worker, a positive spillover has occurred. The reverse is the same of home-to-work spillover.

Some scholars have suggested that the general assumption of children has not been compatible with high-level success at work and is flawed for it ignores the retreat that a loving family provides people with; and how having children especially can be a source of positive home-to-work spillover. For the majority of African women, while they enjoy the social benefit of having children, the need to be successful in their careers means that they have to come out with effective ways of marrying the two together. Time conflict is one of the common stress factors that the urban working mother has to contend with almost on a daily basis. On many occasions, a working mother may have a work-related meeting at the same time as her child's doctor's appointment, or she may be called from a meeting because of an emergency involving her child. If married and the husband is a compromiser, then the woman may be able to alleviate the problem. If not married, she may rely on childcare, which can equally be stressful for some mothers for their inability to be there for their child at all times.

Childcare, whether provided by family or nonfamily members, can be unreliable at times causing added stress for many working mothers. Of course, having children and a career is not the only source of stress for working mothers. Some husbands can be demanding of the wives, and as already discussed above, social changes in the African family structure has not only changed the dynamics of urban family households but also in many instances it has added onto the work responsibilities of women. While the conflict of time contributes to spillovers, some scholars have asserted that the real culprit of spillovers is not the amount of time a job may demand of a person; rather, it is the severe devotion to work that interferes into the quality of family life.[32] In other words, for both women and men, the anxieties associated with completing work-related tasks when added to the lack of participation in family activities results in discontent and frustration.

To manage the demands of family and work, some women, especially those with high-income careers, rely on their financial resources to employ house girls to take care of cooking, cleaning, and washing and house boys to do the gardening, washing the car, and driving. Women in middle-income and low-income families usually have to take care of their domestic responsibilities themselves. Many working mothers have also identified individual choice as essential in balancing work and family. Here, a mother may consider her family obligations before choosing the type of work environment she wants to enter into or she may consider her work before choosing to have children or not to have children. Individual choice is also important in a woman's decision to forgo a work meeting or party in order to spend time with her family or vice versa. Increasingly, many career women are effectively balancing their family and work roles and are rejecting the traditional model of housewife.

In a study by Michael Ford and his colleagues on work and family they found that the experiences, skills, and opportunities women acquire at either their workplace or at home augments their ability to perform their roles at their work and at home. The women interviewed cited their ability to multitask at work as emanating from the fact that they multitask at home. In the same vein, their work experiences and skills allows them to be resourceful in managing their family's budgets and other activities.[33] The same can be said of women in the African context. Throughout their history, African women have had very little time to perform their roles; yet, they have had to deal with an overwhelming number of responsibilities. Thus, multitasking, perhaps, has become second nature to most women. Their ability to perform multiple duties at home has enabled women to do the same in their careers, which in turn reinforces their chances of succeeding at their jobs and inversely improves their lives and family relations.

Women continue to be active, even in manual labor. (Courtesy of Toyin Falola)

Other areas of contention about women's outside employment and their family responsibilities have been the notions of women not being the primary breadwinners of their families, women do not need to earn as much income as men, and that women's participation in the labor market has always been tempered by marriage. Regarding the latter, the assumption is that the vast majority of African women look forward to getting married and settling into their marital responsibilities; and hence, once they do get married, they would no longer be interested in pursuing their professional careers. This assumption not only persists in recent years, but it has also informed many of the gendered notions about professional women; resulted in the low pay of women; limited the career and promotion opportunities available to women; and increased work-related violence against women. However, many women are combining work and family rather than giving up work for family or for marriage.

Indeed, African women have come a long way since the colonial period when few employment opportunities were available to them, and access to education was a luxury to a selected few. Now, we can reasonably say that women's access to education, training in career fields, and employment opportunities have increased tremendously. However, it is still fair to interject that in many African societies, men continue to hold an advantage in

education and at the job market because of the persistence of colonial legacies, patriarchal structures, and the ways we continue to think of the roles
of women in society. Thus, in the world of public production and private
reproduction, women continue to face disadvantages even though women
activism and public awareness has increased the recognition that action
needs to be taken to bridge the disparity between women and men in the
job market and in domestic responsibilities. Perhaps, equilibrium will be
reached when both women and men receive fair treatment in reaching
their full potential at work and when every girl has access to quality education. Furthermore, the balance will be achieved when family responsibility
and work is no longer a "double burden" for women and when they can play
their roles in the public and domestic spheres without the fear of having to
give one up in order to perform well at the other.

African women, since precolonial periods, have worked inside and outside the home in a variety of areas. They have been responsible for domestic and reproductive duties, agricultural production, and the distribution
of commercial goods and services. Many African societies determined the
specificity of women's work and their sphere of influence based on the gender division of labor although, in most cases, enough flexibility and fluidity
existed to allow both women and men to cross the gender barrier. In agricultural societies, just as in pastoral ones, women and men cooperated in
farming, trading, and in the rearing of livestock in order to provide food,
clothes, and shelter for their families. With the formal introduction of European colonialism and imperialism beginning in the 19th century, African
societies began to experience dramatic transformations that have affected,
and continue to affect, the sociocultural, economic, and political life of
Africans.

These transformations have also had significant impact on the economic
roles African women have performed over the course of Africa's history. In
particular, colonial gender ideologies regarding the "proper" place of women
in a society not only restricted African women to the domestic roles of
wifehood and motherhood, but also, it stripped them of any socioeconomic
autonomy and control they previously enjoyed. African women responded
to these changes and challenges by creating, and sometimes appropriating, for themselves new spaces of control and influence. In contemporary
Africa, while the majority of African women, especially those residing in
rural Africa, continue to work as subsistence farmers and in domestic roles,
many women have now transcended the domestic sphere into the public
domain and enjoy expanded opportunities in education and in the modern job market. The life of women in the urban family exhibits change and
continuity. Change in the sense that education has afforded many women
professional careers, and continuity because much of the work required of
women in the traditional setup has not changed that much.

Indeed, the history of African women and their work responsibilities is intrinsically linked to their struggle for social, economic, and political equality and a voice to chart their own paths. As the above discussions show, there have been many impediments, but progress has also been made, and there are challenges that still need to be surmounted. In all this, some women based on social class, ethnicity, race, and even nationality have been more advantaged at the contemporary work environment than others have. But in some cases, the changes have not meant much for the domestic responsibilities of women, especially to ones in rural areas.

Women's roles outside the domestic sphere have also raised important questions regarding the effects of globalization and women's exploitation, poverty and the sex industry, and the effects of HIV/AIDS and women's work. We are left to question how the African strive for industrialization and capitalization would affect women's work and family relations in the near future. Would African men be content in sharing on equal basis the domestic responsibilities of women? Would African women refuse to be consigned to the sphere of domestic roles, or would they ask to be paid for their domestic labor as their Western counterparts? Would women continue the dialogue around whether they want to be given the same treatment as men in the workplace? Would they be willing to demand new working conditions that attend to their broader roles as mothers, workers, and equal contributors to socioeconomic growth in their societies, or would they settle to following the usual male-defined working protocols so prevalent in many workplaces in African countries.

Of course, we can speculate that African women have shown great resilience in other aspects of their lives, and charting their own course in the working environment is no different. In addition, as many would agree, the course set by colonialism and its resultant Western impositions have come to stay in African societies; and globalization and industrialization, coupled with the rise of capitalist market ideas, would modify, over time, the working landscape in Africa and women's roles in it. With the westernization of African countries and capital market growth, the need for more labor force than what the male workforce could provide would obviously ensure that women would not be entirely restricted to the roles of domesticity.

The challenges that African women face at the work environment in contemporary times are in some ways the same as the challenges that women faced in during the colonial era or even that of the precolonial period; but in many ways, the challenges are also different. As with the previous eras, women contend with gender discrimination, unequal pay, sexual harassment, lack of promotion, lack of work-related protection, and lack of opportunities at the workforce in addition to dealing with the daily challenges of domestic management. In some countries, legislative regulations have done well in addressing some of the injustices in women's employment; however, women themselves have initiated the mass majority of changes at the workplace and in their homes. Some have depended on other women to help with childcare and domestic responsibilities while they work; some have been able to get their spouses to help them manage family and outside employment; and some have giving up family roles so they could focus on their professional careers. Yet many African women have been able to combine their domestic roles with their career responsibilities on their own. With all these changes, continuities, and challenges, one thing that has held still is that African families have depended on women throughout the course of history, and they will continue to depend on their work.

NOTES

1. Jeanne Koopman, "Women in the Rural Economy: Past, Present, and Future," in Margaret Jean Hay and Sharon Stichter (eds.), *African Women South of the Sahara* (New York: Longman Group Limited, 1995), 4.

2. Iris Berger and E. Frances White, *Women in Sub-Saharan Africa: Restoring Women to History* (Bloomington: Indiana University Press, 1999), 27.

3. Margaret Kinsman, "'Beast of Burden': the Subordination of Southern Tswana Women, ca. 1800–1840," *Journal of Southern African Studies*, Vol. 10 (1983): 39–54.

4. J. D. Krige and E. J. Krige, *The Realm of a Rain Queen* (London: Oxford University Press, 1943).

5. Marguerite Dupire, "The Position of Women in a Pastoral Society (The Fulani WoDaaBe, Nomads of the Niger)," in Denise Paulme (ed.), trans. H. M. Wright, *Women of Tropical Africa* (Berkeley: University of California Press, 1963), 75.

6. Ibid., 75–91.

7. Ibid., 77.

8. Enid Schildkroudt, "Dependence and Autonomy: The Economic Activities of Secluded Hausa Women in Kano, Nigeria," in Edna G. Bay (ed.), *Women and Work in Africa* (Boulder, CO: Westview Press, 1982), 60–65.

9. Ibid., 60–65.

10. Margaret Jean Hay, and Sharon Stichter (eds.), *African Women South of the Sahara* (New York: Longman Group, 1995), 13.

11. Ester Boserup, *Women's Role in Economic Development* (Oxford, UK: Earthscan, 1970).

12. Jane Guyer, "Women in the Rural Economy: Contemporary Variations," in Hay and Stichter (eds.), *African Women South of the Sahara* (New York: Longman Group, 1995), 23–43.

13. Ibid., "Female Farming in Anthropology and African History," in Micaela di Leonardo (ed.), *Gender at the Crossroads of Knowledge: Feminist Anthropology in the Postmodern Era* (Berkeley: University of California Press, 1991), 236–257.

14. Elias Mandala, "Capitalism, Kinship and Gender in Lower Tchiri (Shire) Valley of Malawi, 1860–1960: An Alternative Theoretical Framework," *African Economic History*, Vol. 13 (1984): 137–169.

15. Berger and White, 68.

16. Daniel McCall, "Trade and the Role of Wife in a Modern West African Town," in Aidan William Southall (eds.), *Social Change in Modern Africa: Studies Presented and Discussed* (Oxford: Oxford University Press, 1963).

17. Berger and White, 68–77.

18. George E. Brooks Jr., "The Signares of Saint-Louis and Goree: Women Entrepreneurs in Eighteenth Century Senegal," in Nancy J. Hafkin and Edna G. Bay (eds.), *Women in Africa: Studies in Social and Economic Change* (Stanford, CA: Stanford University Press, 1976), 19–44.

19. Niara Sudarkasa, "Women and Migration in Contemporary West Africa," in Wellesley Editorial Committee (ed.), *Women and National Development: the Complexities of Change* (Chicago, IL: University of Chicago Press, 1977).

20. Berger and White, 46.

21. Mona Eteinne, "Women and Men, Cloth and Colonization: The Transformation of Production-Distribution Relations among the Baule (Ivory Coast)," in Mona Etienne and Eleanor Burke Leacock (eds.), *Women and Colonization: Anthropological Perspectives* (New York: Praeger, 1980).

22. Penelope A. Roberts, "The State and the Regulation of Marriage: Sefwi Wiawso (Ghana), 1900–1940," in Haleh Afshar (ed.), *Women, State and Ideology: Studies from Africa and Asia* (Albany: State University of New York Press, 1987), 48–69.

23. Berger and White, 47–55.

24. Toyin Falola, "Gender, Business, and Space Control: Yoruba Market Women and Power," in Bessie House-Midamba, and Felix K. Ekechi (eds.), *African Market Women and Economic Power: The Role of Women in African Development* (Westport, CT: Greenwood Press, 1995), 23–40.

25. Catherine Coquery-Vidrovitch, *African Women: A Modern History* (Boulder, CO: Westview Press, 1994), 104–105.

26. Jobs and Skills Program for Africa (JASPA), *African Employment Report 1990* (Addis Ababa: International Labor Organization, 1991).

27. Batya Weinbaum, "The Other Side of the Paycheck," in Zillah R. Eisenstein (ed.), *Capitalist Patriarchy and the Case for Socialist Feminism* (New York: Monthly Review Press, 1979), 190–205.

28. Hanna Papanek, "Family Status Production: The 'Work' and 'Non-Work' of Women," *Signs*, Vol. 4 (1979): 775–781.

29. Sharon B. Stichter, "The Middle-Class Family in Kenya: Changes in Gender Relations," in Sharon B. Stichter and Jane L. Parpart (eds.), *Patriarchy and Class: African Women in the Home and the Workforce* (Boulder, CO: Westview Press, 1988), 199–200.

30. Ibid.

31. Stewart D. Friedman and Jeffrey Greenhaus in *Work and Family—Allies or Enemies? What Happens When Business Professionals Confront Life Choices* (New York: Oxford University Press, 2000), 138.

32. Ibid., 138–140.

33. Cited in Diane F. Halpern and Fanny M. Cheung, *Women at the Top: Powerful Leaders Tell Us how to Combine Work and Family* (Malden, MA: Wiley-Blackwell, 2008), 134–135.

SUGGESTED READING

Aderanti, Adepoju, Christine Oppong, and International Labor Office. *Gender, Work and Population in Sub-Saharan Africa*. Portsmouth, NH: Heinemann, 1994.

Bay, Edna G. (ed.). *Women and Work in Africa.* Boulder, CO: Westview Press, 1982.

Boserup, Ester. *Women's Role in Economic Development.* Sterling, VA: Earthscan, 2007.

Hansen, Karen T. *Urban Women and Work in Africa: A Zambian Case.* New Brunswick, NJ: Transafrica Forum, 1987.

Kevane, Michael. *Women and Development in Africa: How Gender Works.* Boulder, CO: Lynne Rienner Publishers, 2004.

Kyomuhendo, Grace B. and Marjorie Keniston McIntosh. *Women, Work and Domestic Virtue in Uganda, 1900–2003.* Athens: Ohio University Press, 2006.

McIntosh, Marjorie K. (ed.). *Yoruba Women, Work, and Social Change.* Bloomington: Indiana University Press, 2009.

Tsikata, D. and Kerr, J. (eds.). *Demanding Dignity: Women Confronting Economic Reforms in Africa.* Ottawa, Canada: The North-South Institute, 2000.

5

---∞∞∞---

Women and the Arts
and Literature

In almost every society in Africa, art forms convey messages encoded in expressions that may invoke a sense of ambiguity and mystery to outsiders. Arts are also important media in studying culture and history because through them societies communicate their values; attitudes; experiences; challenges; worldviews; and sometimes, their sense of humor. At the same time, they offer avenues for understanding gender constructions in a society and the way women and men negotiate their social, economic, political, and religious roles within gendered spaces. More importantly, as societies undergo changes in their social, economic, political, and religious structures, such changes are reflected in the arts through the changes in techniques, availability of resources and materials, mode of production and distribution, and the intended audience. Historical and archeological records reveal that African women, although not equally represented on the same level as men, have played significant roles in constructing and conveying social and cultural meanings through their arts. In this chapter, we focus on such roles, detailing how African women through art and literature have addressed gender issues, captivated our attention, and controlled their spaces.

The majority of women's work in art and literature is oriented toward the domestic, reflecting in part, the amount of time women spend within this space and their control of it. Various scholars have provided different perspectives of pottery, in particular, in the life of African women and perhaps why women who produce them are tied to the domestic space. For instance, in rural West Africa, pottery is, more or less, synonymous with life. As rural women carry out their daily activities including fetching water for drinking, cooking, bathing, washing, and the rest, they depend on clay pots, which seem as though they are themselves part of the women's bodies.[1] Women's arts, however, is not restricted to the domestic field. To the contrary, many of women's artworks, including pottery, embroidery, basketry, beadwork, and weaving are highly professionalized, especially in contemporary Africa, and have significant social and economic value in both national and international markets and in the African public life. This chapter explores women's arts within the domestic space, the gendered spaces in arts production, the social and economic changes as reflected in women's arts, and the social and economic importance of arts to women. We analyze the ways through which women collaborate with one another to protect their craft skills and marketing channels. The chapter also discusses themes, trends, and contestations in women's narratives, songs, poems, and poetry, stressing the point that women's production in literature reveals a lot about changes in the African social life. First, we discuss women's roles in the arts, followed by their roles in literary production.

WOMEN'S ARTS WITHIN THE DOMESTIC SPACE

A number of researchers have discussed African women's roles in the production of arts within the domestic space. Some have argued that women's domestic roles have been influential in moving women toward the production of certain artworks including pottery, beadwork, calabash decorating, and basketry, while others have suggested that women's arts are not necessarily restricted to the boundaries of the domestic space.[2] In essence, African women's domestic responsibilities, including childcare and meal preparation, have directed where women perform their artistic works, how they organize their artworks socially and economically, and how they transmit their artistic knowledge from one generation to the next. In addition, the domestic space, for the most part, has determined the type of artworks women produce.[3] The same argument has been made about Weh women of Cameroon. These women have historically been the predominant producers of basketry. Basket making has been an activity that fits into their daily patterns of agricultural and domestic work.[4] Another argument is that women engage in arts such as wall painting, body decoration, cloth dyeing, and pottery because these activities are closely connected with their domestic duties of child rearing, preparing meals, overseeing general compound activities, and participating in farming activities.[5] These assessments are perhaps true of African women's arts production within the domestic space; however, there is no indication that women cannot cross from their domestic production into public production or that only women, and not men, undertake domestic art production.

When we insist on such rigidly divided spaces, we run the risk of ignoring the links between the ordinary and the sacred or the domestic and the public in African life and thought; for although two pottery vessels may be made in an identical way, possibly within the domestic space, their intended use will connect the domestic and public spheres. That is, one may be used for cooking while the other may be for ritual purposes of public nature.[6] Indeed, many African societies affirm the reverse side of things such as the public/private, mundane/sacred, and women/men's spheres, but enough social rules exist to allow flexibility between these realms brought on by social, cultural, and economic necessities. As indicated above, a number of African women's arts such as beadworks, pottery, and basketry could be made within the household and used for domestic purposes; nonetheless, many of these products could also be used in the public space especially for ritual and ceremonial purposes and during public displays.

For instance, in southern Ghana, the majority of beads produced by Krobo men and women are used within the domestic sphere, particularly in rituals of birth, to track the growth of infants, and in marriage. And these same beads are used extensively during public rituals and festivals such as during the *Dipo* ceremony (female initiation rite). A similar instance can be found among the Asante of Ghana where bead production is limited to one space, but its usage bridges the gap between two spaces. The phenomena has been studied among the Kpeenbele Senufo of the northern Ivory Coast, where women potters make about 29 different forms of pottery, some of which are for ritual purposes of the public nature.[7]

Weighing in on how women's art production in the domestic space transcends into other realms, some researchers have argued that calabash decorations produced by women of northeastern Nigeria in the Benue Valley have both domestic and sacred functions. It is noted that the use of the Benue Valley women's calabashes for ritual purposes occur only because of its connection with the domestic realm. In other words, it draws on the symbolism of women's domestic and reproductive roles as well as on values connected with African womanhood and femininity to reinforce the sacred.[8] Many of these instances have been studied in other societies. For example, in the Aghem-Fungom region of the Cameroon grassfields, basketry remains within the female domestic sphere, and women dominate in its production. Yet, in spite of being part of women's domestic repertoires, this art form has significant social and political meanings for the peoples of this region.[9]

Insights into the work of Ilorin women weavers provide further understanding into women's art within the domestic space. Unlike Ilorin men, who also engage in weaving, Ilorin women confine their weaving activities to their living quarters. Working at home allows them to combine weaving with their other domestic responsibilities. The same observation has been made among women weavers in the Igbo village of Akwete in Nigeria, among the Shai women potters in southern Ghana, and among the Gurensi women wall decorators in northeastern Ghana. In the case of the Gurensi, men take charge of putting up the mud buildings, but the responsibility of painting the walls falls on the women within the household. Gurensi women integrate this activity with their other domestic duties because the walls are part of their compound. The types of pattern a woman selects for her wall painting often reflects her daily experiences and/or her social identity, and they are often objects commonly found in her immediate environment.

In general, Gurensi women undertake much of their wall painting during the dry season when agricultural work requires minimal time. Within the social organization of a household, it is usually the responsibility of the senior wife to organize her co-wives to resurface an old wall or to paint a newly made wall. The women collaborate in choosing the motifs and in deciding the arrangements. Wall painting for the Gurensi, thus, represents a

An old woman weaving a basket in Accra, Ghana, 1996. (Courtesy of A. Olusegun Fayemi)

collective effort that allows the women to form and cement the social identity of their group. In other words, because the paintings are open to the
public view and criticisms, Gurensi women take great efforts in ensuring
that the designs are properly made to reflect upon the status of man of the
household and on their own social status.[10] Besides wall painting, Gurensi
women also participate in basketry and pottery work and in the production of other crafts such as large twined bags, wide-brimmed hats, conical
rattles, and semicircular fans, although on a smaller scale as compared to
their production in basketry and pottery.

Much of the designs employed in Gurensi women's pottery, basketry,
bags, hats, and fans relate to those they already utilize in their wall paintings, although in the case of the pottery and the rest, the designs are intended to attract commercial clients and not to communicate a social
status as in the case of the wall paintings.[11] Wall painting is not unique to
this West African group nor is the ability to employ art forms to communicate social statuses. In Kenya's Western Province, Baluyia women decorate
their houses with murals. The women rely on flower motifs for their murals, which they belief expresses beauty, happiness, and renewal.[12] In South
Africa, Sotho, Xhosa, and Ndebele women also engage in mural painting.
It has been pointed out that mural painting in this region is a domestic art
identified with a particular dwelling, and the women who inhabit that particular dwelling are responsible for the design.[13]

The following quote about mural painting shows how significant art is in
African women's life:

> Wall painting is an accepted activity, a way of life, a joy of life. For women,
> the art is a natural gesture, as necessary and incorporated in the lifestyle of
> these people as is walking, eating, sleeping. Foremost, the art form is a means
> of beautifying the space in which they and their families spend a great deal of
> time, enhancing an otherwise harsh environment. It is also a magical form
> of creativity, the magic coming not from its meaning or intent, but from the
> actual act of applying paint to the wall.[14]

In a similar observation, Betty LaDuke, describing her exploration of Tiebele (Burkina Faso) women's wall painting writes:

> It was fascinating to observe these women painting, as they physically seemed
> to enjoy each stage of the process, from the preparation of the pigments and
> the wall surface, to the actual painting process. whether with bold strokes of
> the hand, with the delicate tip of the guinea fowl brushes, or with flat white
> rocks burnishing around each shape between black forms.[15]

To produce their wall paintings, Tiebele women go through a series of
steps. They start a new wall painting whenever there is the need to resurface an old painting, or a new wall is erected and it needs to be decorated.

They begin by scraping smooth the old surface of a wall with a garden hoe to prepare it for the new painting. The women then prepare the basic color palette by mixing a pail of cow dung with water and earth, which they apply to the wall with their hands as a gesso or first undercoat. The art of producing the wall painting also involve several women working and coordinating their efforts together. While a number of women work to get the wall ready for the painting, another woman prepares the basic color by pounding hard red rock and soil in a wooden mortar until it become a fine, red sand. She then sifts the red sand through a strainer into a large calabash and adds water until she gets a thick, creamy consistency out of the solution.

Working together, several women apply this mixture over the wall to cover the darker brown cow dung that they had applied earlier. They then smooth the surface of the wall with flat river stones and allow it to dry for several hours before they begin painting the final design on the prepared wall. Meanwhile, another woman prepares a black pigment from pounded rock, which the women would use to make the designs over the red paint. Another woman has the responsibility to make the paintbrushes from the

Hairstyle is part of African artistic creations. (Courtesy of Toyin Falola)

feathers of a small chicken for the group to use for the painting. Through-out the whole process, the women consult each other about the type of de-sign to apply and direction of the application. Once that decision is made, the final painting begins. The women would finish the entire process by repeatedly polishing the surface with short, circular strokes in order to highlight the contrast in the designs applied, after which they would cover the entire wall with a glutinous liquid made from locust bean pods from the dawa tree.

This last step—repeated three times—is crucial and it is intended to pro-tect the wall and the painting from heavy rains; guaranteeing a life span of about four years before the women would need to repaint the wall again.[16] While the above description does not tell us whether Tiebele women's wall painting represents social status other than, perhaps, its intent to make the compound beautiful, we can deduce that a connection almost always ex-ists between women's domestic responsibilities and their artistic instincts. Not only do African women concern themselves with providing food for their families, but they also provide their families with complete care and comfortable environments, even if such activities do not bring them any economic, social, or political benefits.

GENDERED ARTS AND WOMEN'S SPACES OF CONTROL

As with other aspects of the African social and cultural life, gender rules regulate a person's participation in one role or the other depend-ing on their sex. Therefore, gender constructions influence the roles both African women and men play in the arts. Yet in their separate spheres of influence, African women and men collaborate, more often than not, in their artistic enterprises. Both women and men may work with different materials in their respective crafts or with the same materials but utilize different methods. Women have been noted to work generally with clay and with other natural substances, while men commonly use wood and metals. In instances where both participate in the same craft and use the same material such as in weaving, they may employ different techniques.[17] The point here is that while many African societies may stress distinct so-cial, cultural, economic, and political differentiation between women and men, they equally acknowledge and accept the reality and necessity that women and men must sometimes depend and cooperate with one another.

For example, among the Hausa of northern Nigeria, men and women combine their artistic skills to produce aluminum spoons normally given to women as gifts. Hausa men make the spoons, but women are in charge of the decoration.[18] The same instance is true among the Kuba of the Demo-cratic Republic of Congo (Zaire) where male and female artists cooperate in creating the popular embroidered raffia cloth of the region.[19] In another example in Benin society, the gender barrier between women and men dissolves in one significant area of artistic production: that is, in the area of creating arts for the religious activities relating to Olokun (the Bini god of the sea and the most widely worshipped) and his pantheon of river deities. In conjunction with the male priests of Olokun, Bini women, usually wives of brass casters, make the large ritual vessels, which illustrate male and female members in Olokun ceremonies as well as the anthropomorphic (human-like) clay figures, which are central objects at Olokun shrines.[20]

Besides being gendered, African art, whether produced by women or men, could also stimulate racial tensions. For example, until recently, Zimbabwean sculptures produced by the Shona received little or no internal support at the national level. Racial discrimination was essentially not limited to the economic and political spheres but transcended into the world of artistic production. Aside from the struggle to get their productions sold, African artists in Zimbabwe could not get the recognition they minimally deserved. These artists had to fight their own way into the international scene, and it was only when they began to gain international acclaim that the public and the national press reconsidered their position on Shona sculptures. For Zimbabwean women sculptors, they had to deal with a double jeopardy, for not only were they confronting racial discrimination, but also they had to struggle to gain access into a space controlled by men. Nonetheless, they found a way to create spaces of autonomy for themselves within the changes that have taken place in Zimbabwean society. Furthermore, contemporary social and economic changes have caused Shona women sculptors to move away from the domestic scene. They are now producing a number of stone sculptures and self-portraits to honor women's maternal roles in society, their emerging creativity, and their achievements in breaking into the sculpturing profession, which men have dominated for decades.[21]

Sometimes, women artists may not control the contexts within which people use their artworks. However, their roles as producers afford them the opportunity to not only engage in the processes in which material symbols aid in negotiating and constructing social meanings, but also art allows women to dialogue with the men who control the contexts, especially in religious activities, where the artifacts are used. This is best illustrated among the Rugange Bata of northeastern Nigeria, who in the past maintained an ancestral cult where people annually petitioned the ancestors for their well-being, or during periods of misfortune. Some women artists played important roles in this cult by being responsible for making the vessels used for containing the spirits of deceased male chiefs, although the responsibility for maintaining the shrine, making offerings and other rituals lay with men.[22] Among the Senufo, women, through their artworks, play significant roles in the Poro secret society although it is regarded as a male society. In particular, in the dramatic contexts of the arts, such as masquerade performances, men dominate. But in the area of spectacle and aesthetic display, women generally take center stage—especially during the Fodonon funeral performances.

Like their male counterparts, Senufo women have created spaces of control for themselves by maintaining their own secret society, the Sandogo, where they exercise power and influence through their artistic and ritual performances and arts production. The Sandogo secret society, which includes a branch of divination specialists, has the primary responsibility of safeguarding family relationships and lineage. In particular, they have the duty to protect the purity of the matrilineage and to punish men from other lineages who commit adultery and other unsanctioned premarital sexual behaviors.[23] In the Senufo system, while Poro men may have control over the social and political order and control over masks, women have the ultimate responsibility in ensuring the goodwill and blessings of the supernatural world, deities, and the ancestors are on the people as well as the control over sculptural arts use in ritual performances. Yet, within these two spheres of power, there exists a complementary relationship that allows both women and men in Poro and Sandogo to go beyond the gender divide to become recognized members of the other group and to work jointly to ensure the safety and continuity of the group.

For example, postmenopausal women who have undergone special initiation rites can attain full Poro membership, and under certain circumstances, men could be trained as diviners in the Sandogo society. Therefore, while gender rules may work to create separate spaces of control and roles, the Senufo example shows that interactions between women and men in both the Poro and the Sandogo allow the Senufo to connect at the realm of the physical and the metaphysical, which is important in the social and religious life of Africans. To put into context the collaborations between the Poro and Sandogo, some researchers have pointed out that aesthetic form and performance become part of the vital process whereby conflicts and tensions, which can threaten harmony and balance, are resolved.[24] Women also create spaces of power by controlling the mode through which they transmit their artistic knowledge from one generation to the next. In most instances, the transmission of artistic knowledge is from mother to daughter and from the elderly to the young.

Although this mode of transmission may limit individual creativity and ingenuity, it allows artistic designs and techniques to be preserved within a household or a lineage, making the decorative designs of mothers to become that of their daughters and granddaughters. In Kpeenbele women's ceramic production, for instance, the type of materials available could have caused the ceramic technology to develop in different directions, yet what developed reflects the "age-class system," which Senufo society is based on. In other words, Kpeenbele women's ceramic technology is essentially that of aesthetic replication and continuity of the older generation. That is, contemporary pottery is built upon those of older generations.[25] For example, there is a contention regarding the origin of wall painting; nonetheless, many scholars agree that it is a tradition that mothers have passed onto their daughters, and this has been done from one generation to the next for ages. It has also been argued that among the different forms of artwork that African women produce, wall painting has been the most ignored, and least understood, yet in spite of the many odds of this art form completely disappearing from the art scene, women have found ways to ensure its survival. Essentially, wall painting has survived, although sporadically, through peoples' belief in their societies' values. In polygynous societies, social interactions among the women, especially ones that exist between co-wives and the need of married women to please their husbands as well as express themselves, account for the survival of wall painting in contemporary times.[26]

There is the need to point out that contemporary social and economic changes have caused some artists to balance long-standing techniques and designs with new ones, and in some cases, to retire old traditions in order to meet the new market demands. For instance, among the Tera of the northeast state of Nigeria, the decorative motifs women use in their calabash decorations have been passed down from one generation to the next, but recent studies show that the styles have been changing to meet market trends and demands. According to accounts, the calabash decorations of a Tera woman known as Kakuhawa, who was considered to be among the finest artists in the region, have been retired and preserved. Calabash decorators in Tera no longer copy her designs because they have fallen out of style even though they still admire her creations. The reason given for this development is that women, in recent years, demand modern designs, and styles in general have changed.[27] The Tera instance is not unique. Since the 1970s, African societies have endured many changes, and outside influences have affected almost every aspect of the African experience. Therefore, African women's arts will undoubtedly be affected. Among the Bemba of Zambia, increased urbanization has not only allowed men to enter the female-dominated art of pottery making, but also, it has caused women pottery makers to adopt new strategies in their production of pottery.

Among the Bemba of Zambia, the transmission of pottery techniques continue to follow the mother-to-daughter apprenticeship model, and women still depend on the simple traditional pottery designs and shapes. However, changes in demand in the new market economy have caused Bemba women to decrease the number of traditional beer pots they used to make and to instead create a new space in the economy for themselves by brewing and selling the beer they use the pots to carry.[28] These changes notwithstanding, African women artists, in many instances, have been able to maintain the specificity of their artistic knowledge, which has allowed them to earn power and to control and maintain their spaces as well as express symbolically their values and worldviews.

THE ECONOMIC DIMENSIONS OF WOMEN'S ARTS

In their capacity as artists, African women have historically served as architects and transmitters of Africa's social and cultural symbolism and ritual meanings, but more importantly, their artistic performance has had significant economic impact not only in their lives and in the lives of their families but also in their communities as well. Indeed, the economic aspects of arts have significant influence on how women perform it and how they control their performance. Arts have also allowed most women to earn some form of income independent of the financial resources of their husbands' and if they are not married, an income to sustain themselves. A study among Akwete weavers reveals that women can generate substantial income from their arts to support themselves and their children. Furthermore, the need to maximize the economic benefits of a craft can sometimes prompt women artists to institutionalize strategically certain norms and practices to keep others out of their profession or to increase their own level of mastery of the craft in order to stamp out competition.

Various examples from a significant number of studies reemphasize the above point. Akwete women weavers, for instance, have created a myth that restricts the origins of weaving to their village in an effort to hold onto the market and maintain control. Essentially, the myth affirms the "Akwete's ownership of weaving and prevents neighboring villagers from capitalizing on what has become a lucrative industry"[29] in Nigeria's contemporary market economy. The same is the case among the Shai of southern Ghana where the pottery industry has flourished for women involved in pottery production. The force behind the industry comes from the fact that Shai clay-pit priestesses ritually control access to the clay deposits in the region, and there are taboos that prohibit outsiders—all men and non-Shai women—from participating in the production of pots. This not only safeguards the overexploitation of the clay beds, but also it ensures Shai women's monopoly of the trade in pots.[30] Many of these examples can be found elsewhere in Africa where women claim exclusive rights to their crafts to prevent others from accessing any of its economic benefits.

Contemporary market forces and the need to stamp out competition also influence some women artists to improve upon their skills and the quality of their works. It has been pointed out that in the Umuahia region of Igboland, Nigeria, what motivate potters to change their designs and

Traditional fashion is commonly used to celebrate
all major functions. (Courtesy of Toyin Falola)

patterns are economic pressures rather than traditional habits. The Umuhunta of this region produces plain and small quantities of pottery because
of the fact that the Umuhunta have fertile farmlands from which they get
sufficient income from farming. In contrast, the farmlands of the villages
of the Ndume Ibeku are not as productive and, as such, they depend on
pottery. As a result, their pottery has a lot more elaborate designs to ensure
a good market value.[31] Among the different groups of the northeast State of
Nigeria, the techniques of pyro-engraving and pressure-engraving[32] calabashes are not easy to master. It takes several years of practice before one
can master the skill; however, because calabash decoration is one of the
few avenues through which women are able to earn both prestige and cash,
they have a strong incentive to become skillful.[33] Besides applying complex
designs to make the calabashes marketable, some women artists have been
reported signing their artworks as a way of guaranteeing the quality of their
products and marketing themselves as the best in the business.

   In some systems, as among Kpeenbele potters, the economic benefits of
the industry are based on an apprenticeship system. Here, women potters
start their apprenticeship at a young age, but they only become true ap-
prentices after they have married since it is the responsibility of the older
women in the husbands' family to teach such skills. During the period of

apprenticeship, which may take up to a period of about five years, a young woman is completely dependent on her husband's family. The Kpeenbele apprenticeship system guarantees that older women would maintain the control of the economic benefits from pottery since they provide the fundamental teaching instructions to the younger generations. Older women are also the ones who have mastered the art and have the highest production output. And as some scholars have pointed out, "If young girls were to be allowed to make pots before marriage, it is possible that a skillful young potter might be able to earn an 'independent income'. This would go against the values of traditional Senufo society, which is based on an age-class hierarchy in which elders rule juniors."[34] In other cases, women take control of the economic importance of their arts by being responsible for all the processes of production and distribution and by determining the monetary value of their productions.

Another way women take control of their artistic production is through the creation of cooperative unions and organizations. Such organizations represent both the economic and social interests of women artists and give them a sense of communal security. For example, in Timbuktu, the Women's Federation of Artisans of Timbuktu is responsible for organizing and regulating the commercial displays of women's artworks in Timbuktu and their participation in national artisan festivals. Sometimes, the protection women seek for their productions goes beyond the realm of preventing outsiders from gaining access or from enjoying some of the benefits of a particular craft or artwork. In recent years, in particular, the majority of African women are responsible for financially supporting their children with or without the presence of a male partner. As a result, women sometimes prioritize where they feel it is necessary to invest the income from their trade. When a woman decides on how she wants to spend her income from her artistic productions, her decision has the potential of changing the relationship within her family, especially if she places her children's education above all other needs.[35]

AFRICAN WOMEN ARTISTS

It is a popular opinion that every African woman is an artist. This perception is, indeed, true when we understand African women's artistic roles as those that involve the lullabies they sing for their children; the stories they tell to the youth; the dirges they sing to the dead; the pots, baskets, mats, and beads they make for domestic use; and the decorations they adorn their homes to make them visually appealing. Yet the majority of women who engage in these activities, even for commercial purposes, do not think of themselves as artists. This is not to suggest that there are no professional African women artists. On the contrary, Africa has a significant number of contemporary female artists such as Tracey Rose, Princess Elizabeth Olowu, Fatimah Tuggar, and Wangechi Mutu who have achieved both national and international acclaim for their artistic performances. Their works have invigorated art conversations across the continent and ignited questions about the roles and responsibilities of African women artists in highlighting some of the social, cultural, economic, and political challenges that Africans, particularly African women, encounter in contemporary times.

For example, Tracey Rose, a mixed-race South African feminist artist uses her artistic production to reflect on the various aspects of social, economic, cultural, and political challenges of today's world, along with the politics of sexual- and identity-related issues. Sexual and identity issues, in particular, have been prominently featured in Rose's work for she uses the majority of her works to respond to the restrictions of belief systems and the problems associated with cultural norms. Typical of Rose's work is the ways in which she situates herself in her performances in order to bridge the abstract with the concrete as well as to put a human/woman face on some of the issues African women confront on daily bases. Since the late 1990s, Rose has produced a variety of artworks and film productions including the *Hitchhiker* and the *Cross/ings* exhibited at the Generator Art Space, Johannesburg; and at the University of South Florida Contemporary Art Museum respectfully. She also presented her film *Sin Título* at the South Florida Contemporary Art Museum, which showed herself shaving the hair on her body with an electric razor. This film reflects on identity politics and the cultural norms to which a person's life is usually subjected.

Besides these early works, some of Rose's other publicly recognized works include *Venus Baartman, Cicciolina, Lolita,* and *Mami.* These four photographic works act as examples of sexualized black femininity. For instance, in *Cicciolina* Rose is featured as a caricature porn star on a sports car. She is wearing cheap heavy makeup and a leather gear, invoking an image of a drag queen and the low-priced nature of pornographic movies. Unlike *Cicciolina, Venus Baartman,* and *Lolita,* which all reflect on the sexualized female body, *Mami* tells the story of a woman effectively desexualized and normalized into the mainstream expectation of someone working as a governess or housekeeper. She is a middle-aged woman wearing nothing on her face except for plain spectacles and who is greeting someone coming home off camera.[36] Here, Rose is wrestling with the limitations of sexual and gender constructions for while she is desexualizing the character, she still has to confront gender notions of women's domestic roles. The photograph is meaningful and ambiguous at the same time for it speaks to women's presumed roles as caretakers although there is a strong possibility that the woman could be the owner of the house rather than the housekeeper or the governess.

African women artists have also demonstrated that their artworks are not restricted to the conventional pots and pans. Even in areas where cultural notions have prevented women from participating in certain artistic productions, they have found ways to break such barriers and to produce engaging masterpieces that rival the works of their male colleagues. One such woman is the Nigerian female artist, Princess Elizabeth Olowu, whose sculptures marries tradition and modernity along with feminist perspectives. Olowu produces a variety of sculptures ranging from figurative ceremonial vases and portraits of gods to life-sized representations of the themes of birth and death as exemplified in her work *Zero Hour,* depicting a pregnant woman in labor, and *Soldiers of the Biafra War,* showing a soldier carrying a wounded warrior and stepping over the dead. Olowu's feminist perspective is especially influenced by her own personal experiences. In developing her talent, she had to overcome cultural taboos that prohibited women from sculpting. Her own royal background probably helped her in overcoming this restriction, and she recognizes the fact that such cultural taboos have prevented many African women from been able to develop their artistic abilities as well.[37]

Some of her works include *Ovbiekpo* or Young Masquerader (a granite and cement image of a young prince), *Oba* or King (a bronze image of her father, Oba Akenzua), and *Acada* (a cement image of a young girl studying). According to Olowu, her inspiration for *Ovbiekpo* was an ancient Benin legend about the romantic adventures of a young prince. The image itself represents the transitional sphere where man and spirit encounter each other. The image is a vertical form of over seven feet tall and contains four carved faces to allow *Ovbiekpo,* who is an ancestor spirit, to see the whole world from different directions.[38] *Acada* is one of Olowu's works that confronts the challenges of tradition and modernity. It is a realistic sculpture cast in white cement that depicts a young student seated at a desk, absorbed by a book. This piece is autobiographical as it reflects on the challenges Olowu had to endure as a young girl keenly interested in Western education. In fact, *Acada,* or bookworm, was a nickname her peers used in teasing her. Olowu, like most African women, have had to find ways of integrating tradition and modernity into their lives.[39] Like Olowu, Fatimah Tuggar of Nigeria also combines imagery of both personal and the collective to explore the ways in which tradition and modernity could be constructed or deconstructed.

One of Tuggar's visually most arresting works is *The Cake People* in which she features a young black woman wearing a homemade fuchsia dress (a vividly red or pinkish purple dress named after the fuchsia flower) decorated with frills at the shoulders and hem. In a smiling posture, the woman presents a cake with an awkward image of a thatched hut and an African female form perched on top of it. The background of the image

Dr. Aderonke Adesanya of the University of Ibadan, a notable artist and art historian, relaxing at a warm water spring in Nigeria. (Courtesy of Toyin Falola)

portrays a domestic Western kitchen with tiled walls, utensils, pots, kettle, and excessively huge oven appliances. To the right of the woman rests a cake decorated as a patch of green land on which stands an African-styled hut with its occupants staring inquisitively at the viewer. Although depicted in a domestic setting, the images reflect on the effects of globalization and the influence of Western culture on African cultures. Another prominent African female artist is Wangechi Mutu from Kenya. Mutu uses Technicolor to create critical masterpieces that reference history, fashion, race, class, beauty, and the coalition of Western and African cultures. Some of her most important works include the *Pin-Up Series, Soul on a Peg-Leg, Riding with Death in My Sleep,* and *Queen Ugly.* In these works, Mutu appears to have erased all visions that negatively portray womanhood, especially black womanhood.

In each of these works, Mutu features a central female character expressed in watercolor and collage and reflecting ideas of femininity, culture, beauty, and change. For example, in *Soul on a Peg-Leg,* Mutu presents an extraordinary woman in a scene with mushrooms floating in the background. The woman is wearing an elaborate headdress of butterflies and an abstract African mask. As with her other female figures, the woman in *Soul on a Peg-Leg* represents the legacy of violence piled on the black female body through rape and degradation, coupled with the social negation of the black female body and the internalized self-dislike many black women experience as a result of the idealized Western notions of beauty. Mutu, through her female characters, further challenges our assumptions about the sexuality and identity of African women.[40] Besides the aforementioned African women artists, there are others such as Adérónké Adésolá Adésànyà of Nigeria, Candice Breitz of South Africa, and Sokari Douglas Camp of Nigeria. Like the others discussed above, Camp is not only among the first African female artists to have gained entrance into the international art market with her expressive sculptural masterpieces, but she also utilizes masks and ritual clothing as themes to reflect on the cultural and political relations between Africa and the Western world. What all these women, together with countless others, have shown is the talent and the creativity of African women artists as well as the diverse artistic mediums through which they engage the social, cultural, economic, and the political challenges of their time.

WOMEN'S ROLES IN AFRICAN LITERATURE

Literature, as one form of cultural reflection, reveals an author's preoccupation with recounting and defining the relations between a society's culture and its people, particularly in terms of such issues as identity, gender, and politics. Just as they have done in the visual arts, African women have played, and continue to play, significant roles in African literature, recounting social and cultural issues through a variety of literary media. In Africa's literary productions, women perform in two contexts—one, which is not professionalized where every woman, in one way or the other, is a vessel for the creation and transmission of oral traditional literature; and another, which is professionalized where a few women engage oral traditional literature and social issues and transform them for future generations. The centrality of women's oral performance in the life cycle—birth, puberty, marriage, death—of Africans cannot be overemphasized. From lullabies that soothe newborns to praise and love tunes for the young and dirges for the dead, African women use poetic expressions to convey social values, cultural beliefs, and bring attention to women-centered issues.

In the context of professionalized literary production, Africa now boasts of an unprecedented wave of highly recognized women writers who have given form and shape to issues women care about and which society generally ignores. In the decades of colonial rule and a few years afterward, male authors whose treatment of women's issues hinges on objectifying women, and sometimes patronizing women's experiences, dominated the African

Women dressed for a social party, wearing the same attire. (Courtesy of Toyin Falola)

publishing scene. Indeed, the majority of male writers who included female characters in their writings could not envision a distinctive female
perspective, or the multiplicity of women's experiences and interactions,
or the power that women willed. From the mid-1960s, African women
writers gradually emerged from the backgrounds with an engaging voice
that delivered brilliant and enticing stories for all ages and focusing on a variety of social and cultural issues that are important to women in particular
and to the public in general.

    With the pioneering works by writers such as Flora Nwapa, Bessie Head,
Ama Ata Aidoo, Grace Ogot, and Buchi Emecheta, countless others have
joined their ranks in bringing attention to what has been called the "women's
condition" as a reflection of social health. In which case, motherhood represented Africa's efforts against the corroding influence of Western culture; a
wife's servile state symbolized the lack of harmony in polygynous homes; and
prostitution denoted defiant behavior brought on by social exploitation.[41]
As storytellers, singers, writers, critics, and activists, African women have
created literary works on social problems, female leadership and politics,
womanhood and motherhood, as well as on nature, love, and sex, proving
just how engaged they have been in every aspect of private and public life.

WOMEN AND NONPROFESSIONALIZED
LITERARY PRODUCTION

African women have historically been producers, performers, and transmitters of the various forms of Africa's oral literary genres. From birth to death, women use lullabies, poems, songs, dirges, lamentations, and poetry to give meaning to the demands these events bestow on society. Just as the majority of women's visual arts are produced within the domestic space, many researchers have noted that women's oral genres are largely produced and learned within the homestead and as part of women's daily activities. Ordinary events such as food preparation, sitting around the fire, and comforting a child could ignite in a woman "the spontaneous sweetness of song," storytelling, and the recitation of poems.[42] Married Hausa women, often in *purdah,* have been noted singing while grinding corn and playing several kinds of calabash "drums" in the privacy of the inner compound where they reside. Indeed, from the very beginning of life, children are welcomed with songs and praises.[43] Newborns are both soothed and socialized with praise names and catchy tunes. An example of a rhythmic lullaby frequently used by mothers among the Akan is:

> Whose baby is this?
> It is mother Akosua's baby
> Where should the baby be laid?
> Go and lay it under the cotton tree
> The cotton tree will fall on my baby
> Go and lay it under the palm tree
> The palm tree has a lot of air
> The palm tree has a lot of shade.[44]

In various societies in Africa, women also utilize poetry, in the form of love poems or songs, as an instrument in courtship rituals. As discussed in chapter 1, among the Zulu, a tradition existed, and continues to exist to some degree, whereby young unmarried women performed love poems/songs at informal gatherings to attract potential future partners. The young girls relied on a bow instrument called an *umakhweyana* to communicate their feelings of love. In addition, when couples settled on one another, they were required to remain separate from each other during the period of courtship, and the longing experienced by the girl for her prospective husband found continued expression and release in the singing of love songs.[45] Among the Luo of Kenya, girls of marriageable age sing special love songs called *oigo* to court young men. The girls utilize traditional motifs in composing their love songs, which anticipates marriage in its subtle references to physical love.[46] Women also play significant roles in using different forms of poetic expressions either to praise people of their group or family or to conduct social gatherings. Yoruba women use panegyric poetry, known as *oriki,* to praise a person for making the family or group proud. Tonga women of Zambia also excel in elegiac poetry called *zitengulo.*[47] The *zitengulo* is a sad mourning song women compose and perform as solos when death occurs in the family. During these performances, people who pay any attention to the singers would be the nonrelatives of the dead person who have come to comfort the mourners. The *zitengulo* is a simple short composition done exclusively for a particular person. The women base their songs on the life's work of the deceased, and they work alone in coming up with the lyrics and melody to complete the song.[48]

Unlike the *zitengulo,* which women perform without any special training, some forms of poetic genres such as mastering the Zulu bow instrument, *umakhweyana,* and its accompanying love poems; performing the Akan funeral dirges; and singing the *impango* among the Tonga of Zambia require skills even when these genres are universally known. Some women acquire the necessary skills and therefore play important roles in performing these arts. At the same time, these oral traditions are flexible enough to allow women to reconstitute them with their individuality. It has been noted that "every Akan woman is expected to have some competence in singing a dirge, and though some singers are considered more accomplished than others, nevertheless, every woman mourner at a funeral is expected to sing—or run the risk of strong criticism, possibly even suspicion of complicity in the death."[49] Indeed, usually women who have distinguished themselves in performing the dirges lead the singing during funerals.

In recent years, some women may be contracted to perform at funerals, in which case they have the chance to show their own individual creativity. For example, Akan dirges are generally fixed because they follow "specific thematic, formal, and linguistic patterns." However, they are also "flexible in the sense that they can be accommodated to the performer's individuality and creativity."[50] In the following example, a woman uses her individual sense of loss to compose a dirge to mourn her mother:

> Mother, who did you leave to take care of me?
> What will your children eat?
> Your children will eat spider!
> Getting a mouse to eat would be a luxury!
> Where will your children sleep?
> Mother, you have made me an orphan
> You have taken away my sense of security
> Mother, I will go with you to the ancestral world.[51]

As with the Akan dirges, almost every woman in Tonga and Ila societies of Zambia knows how to develop a personal repertoire of the *impango* (poem/

praise song), yet only a small number of women develop high expertise in this art. Individual creativity is again stressed in this performance since the composer of a song retained ownership though she may use the help of her friends to perfect the song.[52] Individuality often leads to personal statements, and women have been found to sometimes use their songs as tools to establish social influence.

Such songs could be used to lampoon or ridicule people who exhibit deviant and socially unacceptable behaviors. The songs could also be used to target individuals or the collective enemies of a group.[53] Khoisan women, for example, utilize sarcasm in their songs as a censorship against deviant behaviors.[54] The use of songs and poems as a means of censorship is common in various regions across Africa. For instance, a popular Nigerian poet, Hajiya 'Yar Shehu, uses her poems as a political tool. In one of her poems, she writes about the Nigerian census conveying the wastefulness in resources when Nigerian citizens are inaccurately accounted.[55] In the same vein, women sometimes use their songs and poems to praise others. Among the Hausa of northern Nigeria, women use praise epithets (*kirari*) or praise song (*wa'karyabo*), to praise a person, usually a royalty. The praise epithet or praise song lists a person's royal titles, skills, accomplishments, and may allude to parentage or children. It has been noted that a praise epithet functions by connecting two images. The composer calls a person by a nickname that indicates something about that individual, and there-

A woman in Calabar, Nigeria works on an oil painting, 2001. (Courtesy of A. Olusegun Fayemi)

fore, implying a metaphoric connection between that person's character and the nickname. For instance, "Bull elephant" (*toron giwa*) is a common nickname for an emir. It implies his position as the mightiest, the most impressive, and most powerful man among men.[56] There are other cases where praise songs focus on honorable women. Among the Hausa of Nigeria, *roko* (praise song) is practiced by both women and men praise singers/eulogists (*maroka*). Yet with the exception of female eulogists, whose praise songs are exclusively performed for kings, female *maroka* focuses on poetic artistry that pays tribute to only women.[57] As seen from the above, women's roles in Africa's oral literary productions transcend the domestic sphere where they perform for their children, their families, and entertain others into a realm where they exercise their privileges as artists to influence the spaces around them.

WOMEN AND PROFESSIONALIZED LITERARY PRODUCTION

The transition of African women from their roles as nonprofessionalized literary producers to their roles in professionalized literature was slow in coming since colonial education and the mastery of colonial languages—English, French, German, and Portuguese—privileged the African man. Nonetheless, African women had something that men did not have—they have been *the* main medium for the performance of oral literature, which offered them a natural starting point. African women writers have creatively depended on tradition in their theatrical performances to reflect on problems women face in literary representations. Women have used the theater to contest and subvert abusive forms of (mis)representation.[58] By the 1970s, more and more women had entered the field as professional writers and were using their space to change perceptions about and toward women.

For instance, a powerful Yoruba market trader, Alice Oyedola, is noted to have given a feminist interpretation to a female character from a story a man had earlier told in her village. In the man's account, there was once a young, passive girl, whose beauty consumed an elderly man to such an extent that he started a relentless campaign to win the girl. In the end, he did not win the girl's heart, but he covered his failure by insisting that the girl's passive character and witless indifference dissolved his burning desire for her. In the version told by Alice Oyedola, the image of the girl was that of a shrewd and a successful independent trader. The girl rejected the elderly man's proposal in preference for the freedom her business offered her. In another example, the feminist prose writer, Mazithathu Zenani, in creating the Mityi's adventure puts women in a favorable light by overpopulating her narratives with men with undesirable characteristics.[59]

Flora Nwapa's *Efuru*, the first published novel by an African woman, was particularly important for women's roles in literature. This is because it broke grounds for writers such as Mariama Bâ, Zulu Sofola, Efua Sutherland, Tess Onwueme, Ama Ata Aidoo, and Werewere Liking to be able to confront gendered notions about the proper place of women and the conduct acceptable of their sex. In *Efuru*, the female figure subverted the African belief that a woman's ability to bear children is not only her fundamental reproductive role but also the main source of her happiness and self-fulfillment. By seeking happiness in spite of her failure to bear children, refusing to accept prescribed feminine responsibilities, living with a man without the payment of a dowry, and going through a string of unsuccessful marriages, *Efuru* illustrated Nwapa's efforts to create a representation in which women acted independently of their ascribed roles.[60]

Like Nwapa's *Efuru*, Emecheta's *In the Ditch*, Sutherland's *Foriwa*, Grace Ogot's *The Rain Came*, and Aidoo's *Anowa* all configured and reconfigured women's roles in a male-dominated literary space and disrupted the master narratives that have portrayed the female figure as voiceless and hapless victims of societal regulations. Moreover, in writing as they did, African women writers have challenged the orthodoxies that place literary production in the male domain and define female creativity as inherent in their reproductive roles. It has been argued that although African women writers occupy a marginal place in a tradition of masculine literary culture, these women have developed a variety of strategies to (re)present their views and positions.[61] All across Africa, south of the Sahara, women writers are confronting changes and challenges of their time and summoning the courage to claim for themselves the rights and privileges that society did not freely grant them. In particular, Emecheta's work *In the Ditch* unleashed a series of feminist writings in which she draws on her own life experiences to portray the resilience of women as well as to engage African leaders' social, economic, and political ineffectiveness that have been the sources of women's suffering in recent years.

Writers such as Zoe Wicomb, Aidoo, and Amina Sow Fall have taken the discourse beyond the confines of autobiography by exploring feminist themes against the background of national and international scene. In Wicomb's *You Can't Get Lost in Cape Town*, the author engages South Africa's racial and gender disparities in a story in which a black woman, Sally Smit, had to undergo a clandestine abortion because she found herself in a double jeopardy where she could not access safe health care and could not marry her white boyfriend. Aidoo, in *Someone Talking to Sometime*, uses the death of an infant to challenge the focus of Ghana's policy on family health care. Likewise, Amina Sow Fall in *The Beggars' Strike* takes on political leaders caught between the values of tradition and the demands of modernity. She satirizes a health minister whose ambitions caused him to clear the city streets of beggars in an effort to promote tourism and to further his career. Ironically, the minister's promotion came to depend on the beggars who had decided to go on strike by refusing the minister's gifts.[62]

As nonprofessional and professional literary producers, African women have in multivoiced, multicreative ways stimulated discussions about women's roles, statuses, challenges, and societal responsibilities. In their daily activities, women have utilized oral traditions to recreate and transmit social and cultural values, notions, and aspirations; and throughout the human life cycle, they have provided expressive artistry to entertain, praise, and mourn human losses and achievements. The transition to professional literary artists was delayed, but it could not be denied to African women. When African women writers began publishing their works in the mid-'60s, they had to contend with the problems associated with speaking about the experience of women, in general, and fighting against the gendered conventions of colonial and anticolonial writings.[63] But as the above discussions indicate, African women writers have succeeded in their response and have earned their rightful place in Africa's literary history.

Until recently, African art, particularly that of the south of the Sahara, was considered by many as "primitive." That it lacked technological background and techniques and that it was dependent on mythical and animalistic beliefs and practices. However, as scholars have succinctly pointed out, African art has always combined the social, cultural, economic, religious, and the political facts of life in an effort to portray African cultures, power, values, and belief systems.[64] Furthermore, Africans use art and other literary productions to express aesthetic beauty, humor, joy, sarcasm, frustration; and to console, mourn, warn, encourage, hope, and offer outsiders both visual and nonvisual windows into their world and worldviews. African art also combines elements of both the physical world and that of the spiritual world, which symbolizes how Africans view their world. Indeed, many forms of African arts have religious significance, and they communicate the essence of religion in the life of Africans to outsiders.

As Africans themselves know, and as almost every visitor to the continent would attest to, African art and African life are but one and the same. African women have been at the forefront of artistic and literary productions both in the private and public spaces. African women have combined their artistic sense and material world to produce not only "ordinary"— everyday pots and pans—and extraordinary designs and artifacts, but they have also through their work, revealed some of their innermost feelings about their personal lives and their societies. More importantly, women's arts essentially functions by connecting chains that bind the society together and reinforcing the collective sense of the community. African women's passion for art is evident in their zeal to produce artistic works at all times and in all circumstances—even in the most dire and unimaginable circumstance. In times of peace, you will find women's artworks, just as you will find them in times of war and other calamities.[65]

Throughout the "African continent from Timbuktu in Mali to Asmara in Eritrea, women work creatively—weaving; working with leather, straw, beads, or clay; painting with mud, sadza, oil, acrylic; sewing fabric appliqué; or sculpting monumental stone."[66] Decorative art is African women's most vividly expressed art forms: found in the smallest clay bowls to the brightly painted walls of their homes.[67] African art is also gendered, not just in terms of its producers, but also in terms of its uses. There are specific instances where both women and men have been restricted to the production of certain artifacts because of their sex as well as instances where either a woman or a man is the only one allowed to handle certain artifacts for a particular purpose because of religious beliefs associated with the gender implications of such artifacts. Yet, in spite of any restrictive measures that keep both sexes from certain activities in their artistic productions, women and men have always cooperated in undertaken certain artistic works; and in fact, in some cases, one cannot work without the other. The flexibility of the African gendered division of labor, together with the pressures of contemporary market forces, has allowed both women and men to cross the gender barrier and to participate in each other's workspace.

As we have seen from our discussions, African women's art, and indeed, African art in general, has been under attacks to change and to modernize to meet Western market standards. In many instances, such changes occur radically, forcing the cessation of certain arts and crafts and forcing women who have depended on the production of these artworks as their main source of livelihood, to look elsewhere for sustenance. At other times, the change has been gradual enough that it goes almost unnoticed either by the producers or the consumers. However, for the most part, African traditional arts such as women's wall painting in Burkina Faso and South Africa; pottery making in Ghana, Togo, and Cameroon; calabash decorating and weaving in Nigeria; and women's sculpturing in Zimbabwe have persisted and continue to strengthen the cultural values and history of African societies.

The production of artifacts and crafts are not the only works in the repertoire of African women when it comes to their artistic roles. Literature, which also reveals how people define and portray their societies to others, has been one of the many preoccupations of African women. Akin to what woman have done, and continue to do in the visual arts, they have depended on the spoken arts to recount social, cultural, economic, and political issues using different literary media. From both the domestic and the public/professional realms, African women have utilized oral traditions to perform the cycle of life—birth, childhood, adolescence, adulthood, and death. From singing lullabies to soothe newborns, to praising the young

Headgear is part of creativity, an aspect of fashion.
(Courtesy of Toyin Falola)

and bold, and singing dirges for the dead, African women have used oral literary expressions to communicate their personal views, societal values, cultural beliefs, and to engage women-centered issues.

For African women engaged in literary production at the professional level, male domination from the colonial period through to the postcolonial period, almost nearly excluded them from having their voices heard. Taking up the struggles (and victories) of their predecessors, contemporary African women writers have ensured that there is a continual expression of African traditional values from the female perspective, and that through the verbal arts, Africans would find ways to stimulate avenues of social and economic development and political progress. Indeed, women's knowledge about African cultures and their very essence as the transmitters of cultural values from generation to generation requires that they remain at the helm of African arts and literature.

NOTES

1. Betty LaDuke, *Africa: Women's Art, Women's Lives* (Trenton, NJ: Africa World Press, 1997), 41.

2. For discussions on women's art and domesticity, see William Dewey, "Shona Male and Female Artistry," *African Arts,* Vol. 19 (1986): 64–67; Carol Spindel, "Kpeenbele Senufo Potters," *African Arts,* Vol. 22 (1989): 66–73.

3. Lisa Aronson, "Women in the Arts," in Margaret Jean Hay and Sharon Stichter (eds.), *African Women South of the Sahara* (New York: Longman Group, 1992), 123.

4. Christraud Geary, "Basketry in the Aghem-Fungom Area of the Cameroon Grassfields," *African Arts*, Vol. 20, No. 3 (1987): 42–53, 89–90.

5. Margaret Courtney-Clarke, *African Canvas: The Arts of West African Women* (New York: Rizzoli, 1990), 70.

6. Spindel, 66–73.

7. Ibid.

8. Maria C. Berns and Barbara Rubin Hudson, *The Essential Gourd: Art and History in Northeastern Nigeria* (Los Angeles: University of California, 1986), 26–27.

9. For discussions on sociopolitical importance of basketry, see Christraud Geary, "Basketry in the Aghem-Fungom Area of the Cameroon Grassfields."

10. Fred T. Smith, "Gurensi Wall Decoration," *African Arts*, Vol. 11, No. 4 (1978): 36–41.

11. Smith, "Gurensi Basketry and Pottery," *African Arts*, Vol. 12, No. 1 (1978): 78–81.

12. Eugene C. Burt, "Mural Painting in Western Kenya," *African Arts*, Vol. 16, No. 3 (1983): 60–63.

13. Thomas Matthews, "Mural Painting in South Africa," *African Arts*, Vol. 10, No. 2 (1977): 28–33.

14. Courtney-Clarke, 70.

15. LaDuke, 11.

16. LaDuke, 11–12.

17. Aronson, 120–121.

18. Norma Wolff, "A Hausa Aluminum Spoon Industry," *African Arts*, Vol. 19, No. 3 (1986): 40–44.

19. Patricia Darish, "Dressing for the Next Life: Raffia Textile Production and Use among the Kuba of Zaire," in Annett B. Weiner and Jane Scheneider (eds.), *Cloth and Human Experience* (Washington, DC: Smithsonian Inst. Press, 1997), 117–140.

20. Paula Ben-Amos, "Artistic creativity in Benin Kingdom," *African Arts*, Vol. 19, No. 3 (1986): 60–63, 83.

21. LaDuke, 13–15.

22. Chappel, "The Death of a Cult in Northern Nigeria," *African Arts*, Vol. 6, No. 4 (1973): 70–74.

23. Anita J. Glaze, "Woman Power and Art in a Senufo Village," *African Arts*, Vol. 8, No. 3 (1975): 24–29, 64–68.

24. Glaze, 24–29, 64–68.

25. Spindel, 66–73.

26. Courtney-Clarke, 70.

27. Barbara Rubin, "Calabash Decoration in North East State, Nigeria," *African Arts*, Vol. 4, No. 1 (1970): 20–25.

28. Benetta Jules-Rosette, *The Messages of Tourist Art: An African Semiotic System in Comparative Perspective* (New York: Plenum, 1984).

29. Lisa Aronson, "African Women in the Visual Arts," *Signs*, Vol. 16, No. 3 (1991): 550–574.

30. A. K. Quarcoo and M. Johnson, "The Pottery Industry of the Shai People of Southern Ghana," *Baessler-Arch*, Vol. 16 (1968): 47–88.

31. Kenneth C. Murray, "Pottery of the Ibo of Ohuhu-Ngwa," *Nigerian Field*, Vol. 37, No. 4 (1972): 148–175.

32. In pyro-engraving, the artist uses fire or heat to make incised or raised patterns, characters, lines, and the like on the surface of the calabash. In pressure-engraving, on the other hand, rather than using heat or fire to make the decorations, the artist applies force or pressure to make the imprint.

33. Rubin, "Calabash Decoration in North East State, Nigeria," *African Arts*, Vol. 4, No. 1 (1970): 20–25.

34. Spindel, 71.

35. LaDuke, xvi, 39.

36. S. Murray, "Africa: Candice Breitz, Wangechi Mutu, Tracey Rose, and Fatimah Tuggar," *Nka, Journal of Contemporary African Art*, Special Issue, (2003). The works of these women were showed in an exhibition titled AFRICAINE at the Studio Museum in Harlem, New York, from January 24, 2002 through March 31, 2002.

37. LaDuke, *Africa through the Eyes of Women Artists* (Trenton, NJ: Africa World Press, 1991), 22–31.

38. Ibid.

39. Ibid.

40. Murray.

41. Deirdre LaPin, "Women in African Literature," in Hay and Stichter, 143–163.

42. Ibid.

43. David W. Ames, "Igbo and Hausa Musicians: A Comparative Examination," *Ethnomusicology*, Vol. 17, No. 2 (1973): 250–278.

44. This lullaby is commonly used among the Akan of Ghana. The translation is the author's own.

45. Joseph, "Zulu Women's Bow Songs: Ruminations on Love," 107.

46. LaPin, 143–163.

47. Obioma Nnaemeka, "From Orality to Writing: African Women Writers and the (Re) Inscription of Womanhood," *Research in African Literature*, Vol. 25, No. 4 (1994): 137–157.

48. A. M. Jones, "African Music in Northern Rhodesia and some other Places," in Bronislaw Stefaniszyn (ed.), *The Material Culture of the Ambo of Northern Rhodesia* (United Kingdom: Manchester University Press, 1974), 84.

49. Ruth H. Finnegan, *Oral Literature in Africa* (Oxford: The Oxford Library of African Literature, 1970), 103.

50. Nnaemeka, 137–157.

51. The translation is the author's own.

52. Finnegan, 103.

53. Nnaemeka, 137–157.

54. Finnegan, 98.

55. Beverly B. Mack, "Metaphor Is a Bridge to Ultimate Reality: Metaphor in Hausa Women's Poetry," *Research in African Literatures*, Vol. 37, No. 2 (2006): 43–60.

56. Ibid.

57. M. G. Smith, "The Social Functions and Meaning of Hausa Praise-Singing," *Journal of the International African Institute*, Vol. 27, No. 1 (1957): 26–45.

58. Thérèse Migraine-George, *African Women and Representation: From Performance to Politics* (Trenton, NJ: Africa World Press, 2008), 5.

59. LaPin, 148.

60. Flora Nwapa, *Efuru* (London: Heinemann, 1966).

61. Nnaemeka, 137–157.

62. See discussion in LaPin, 154–162.
63. Kathleen McLuskie and Lynn Innes, "Women and African Literature," *Wasafiri*, Vol. 8, 1988): 3–7.
64. Courtney-Clarke, 70.
65. LaDuke, 39–40.
66. Ibid.
67. Ibid.

SUGGESTED READING

Adeola, James (ed.). *In their Own Voices: African Women Writers Talk.* Portsmouth, NH: Heinemann, 1990.

Aronson, Lisa. "African Women in the Visual Arts." *Signs: Journal of Women in Culture and Society.* Vol. 16 (1991): 550–574.

Berns, Marla. "Ga'anda Scarification: A Model for Art and Identity." In Arnold Robin (ed.), *Marks of Civilization: Artistic Transformations of the Human Body.* Los Angeles: The University of California Press, 1988.

Courtney-Clake, Margaret. *African Canvas: The Art of West African Women.* New York: Rizzoli, 1990.

LaDuke, Betty. *Africa: Women's Art, Women's Lives.* Trenton, NJ: African World Press, 1997.

Newell, Stephanie. *Writing African Women: Gender, Popular Culture, and Literature in West Africa.* Atlantic Highlands, NJ: Zed Books, 1997.

Noy, Ilse. *Weya Women's Art.* Harare, Zimbabwe: Baobab Books, 1992.

Perkins, Kathy A. (ed.). *African Women Playwrights.* Urbana: University of Illinois Press, 2009.

Spring, Christopher. *African Art in Detail.* Cambridge, MA: Harvard University Press, 2009.

6

⸺∞⸺

Women and Government

As with all the various forms of social and economic structures exhibited in African societies, political organizations have been both diverse and significant in the performance of governance in African societies. Africa's political structures ranged from aristocracy to democracy, from large states to small villages, and from centralized to decentralized forms where families or lineages exercise the power of authority. The multifaceted nature of political institutions on the continent has often been demonstrated in other structures whereby the tools of governance were inherent in social, economic, and religious roles and, hence, availing to both women and men various opportunities to participate in the political life of their societies. As already discussed in earlier chapters, the colonial invasion disrupted almost every institution in Africa with political ones being no exception. At the same time, women experienced the worst of the colonial encounter. Not only were their roles in the social, economic, and religious fabric of the African life undermined, they were methodically excluded from participating in the new form of government. Alas, postcolonial governments were built upon the structures and systems of the previous order and consequently limited the avenues for women to participate actively and fully in the activities of government.

This chapter examines women's roles as political actors by looking at their experiences, statuses, and exercise of power in governance or in other forms of authority from the precolonial period through colonial to the postcolonial era. It highlights colonial rulers' imposition of gender ideologies on African political institutions and its resulting alienation of African women from the activities of government. In contemporary Africa, women seeking equality in governmental institutions have found the task most daunting. Indeed, a number of researchers have suggested that regardless of the position of a country, whether poor or rich, small or large, and developed or underdeveloped, women have had minimal access to decision-making positions such as heads of governments, leaders of political parties, members of parliaments and cabinets, and the rest. In certain circumstances, political environments remain hostile to the idea of equal power sharing between men and women. This chapter also analyzes the historical and ideological basis for women's exclusion in government and efforts made by women to surmount this inequality and the niches they have found in this unwelcoming milieu to have a presence and play a role in government.

WOMEN'S POLITICAL ROLES IN PRECOLONIAL AFRICAN SOCIETIES

In many precolonial societies, a number of avenues were available for women to exercise some form of political authority, usually through the essential roles they played in family and domestic affairs, and in agricultural and economic production and distribution. However, their political roles often depended on the type of economic structure and the social stratification of their societies. Women's statuses and positions differed in centralized and decentralized states. States, characterized by complex hierarchical structures, provided women who either belonged to, or had familial ties with, the royal family the opportunity to enjoy authoritative power through the various political offices they held. Such women frequently held positions of territorial authority over one or several villages or may have had full powers over a whole district. In some cases, the sociopolitical positioning of these women would grant them rights and privileges distinct from the rest of the female population, even before they gained the ability to exercise their special roles. The distinguishing feature in the centralized system was that very few women participated in the activities of governance.

The roles royal women played in centralized states also enabled their actions to be comparable to that of men, rather than to the actions and behaviors of their own sex. In addition, through their marriages and childbearing roles, they provided the basis for the solidification of political power. In contrast, political authority was dispersed in decentralized societies and not clearly divided between women and men. Participation in the affairs of public nature extended to a larger number of women; however, economic and historical factors usually determined their level of participation. In these societies, women's authoritative control could be comparable to that of men, and women generally had control over their own activities.

The essential point in both systems is that women, in one form or the other, participated in the political administrations of their societies. In almost every society in Africa, south of the Sahara, stories and myths exist about women who founded cities, led migrations, and conquered kingdoms.

For example, the Songhai groups in the Niger region continue to remember and celebrate women who in the past governed them. Queen Amina of Katsina is celebrated as having conquered vast territories. In West Africa, the Akan of southern Ghana have oral traditions in which women founded small states such as that of Mampong, Wenchi, and Juaben. The So in northern Cameroon also tells of myths in which women often selected the site where a settlement would be established. They held important political positions and could be responsible for the governance of a district. Many more of these accounts of women's political leadership exist in other regions of Africa in such places as among the Gezo, Glegle, and Behanzin. Early travelers such as Ibn Batuta have provided accounts of the political roles women played in their societies in the 12th century. For example, Queen Kassa, as a wife of Mansa Suleyman (ruler of the Mali Empire from 1341 to 1360), participated with the king in the affairs of government.[1]

Women have also participated in government in complementary positions in many African societies. Most commonly, women complemented the leadership roles of their sons, or they acted in a capacity that balanced the powers vested in male rulers. Among the Swazi, the mother of the king, known as *indlovukati,* shared political authority with her son. They collaborated in resource allocation, dispensed justice, and presided over religious ceremonies. Frances White has indicated that the share of power between mother and son balanced the power of the other. White discusses women wielding equal political power as their male counterparts in Lunda society and among the Bamileke of southern Cameroon. In the Lunda society, a woman (*Lukonkeketha*) ruled alongside the king (*Mwata Yamvo*). She participated in the general political administration of the society, but she also exercised separate control over the affairs of her own court, officials, and the collection of taxes. In the case of the Bamileke, the *Mafo* (mother) of the *Fong* (chief) was equal to the chief in terms of governance and had superiority over him in the administrative council. She held control over women's affairs, and since women predominated in agricultural production, the *Mafo* essentially controlled the work of the entire community.

Many of these instances have been found among the Chamba of Donga in the Benue region of Nigeria, among the Bemba in northeastern Rhodesia (Zimbabwe), and in groups in the Great Lakes region of East Africa.[2] In the Buganda kingdom (present-day Uganda), the political structure was such that the power of the king was balanced off with the power of the queen mother. They both exercised equal powers in terms of appointment of ministers, allocation of land, and the collection of taxes.[3] In some cases, the women exerted more influence in public affairs and on their male counterparts, particularly if the king was her son, in private than that portrayed in public. In fact, it might have been this very recognition that caused the British colonial government to exile the queen mother of the Asante, Yaa Akyiaa, when they were exiling her son, Prempeh I, ruler of the Asante kingdom from 1870 to 1931, to the Seychelles Islands where they both died. In all the Akan groups, which the Asante are part of, female stools complemented the male stools in the political organization of the society.[4] Although it is reasonable to think that in most cases, male stool holders wielded more power than the female stool holder did, nonetheless, Akan queen mothers (obaa hemaa or ohemaa) took part in the legislative and judicial processes and in other important decisions such as the decision to make war or peace and in allocating land to individuals and families.[5] Queen mothers also had their own courts and oaths of office and though their jurisprudence usually covered feminine issues, male litigants could transfer their civil cases from the chief's court to queen mothers' courts for lower fees and fines.[6]

Among the many political roles that the queen mothers performed, they were the official authority on the genealogy of the royal matrilineage, and therefore, had the first and final say on who was the rightful successor to a male stool. As has been pointed out by some researchers, while the Akan vested in the royal matrilineage the right of political leadership, they did not categorically indicate who an actual successor might be among the eligible males. This decision was left to the ohemaa and members of the governing council. During consultations with the other members of the governing council, the queen mother held the key to operating and manipulating the rules to ensure a successful succession. Her role in this process meant that social, economic, and political stability, to a degree, depended on her. The society could end up with an able leader or with bad one based on the choices and machinations of the queen mother.

The role played by Yaa Akyiaa during the succession crisis to the stool of the Asantehene (Asante king) from 1885 to 1888 best illustrates the critical role played by a queen mother in a contested election. Although it was highly uncommon for both mother and son to occupy the highest office in Asante society at the same time, Yaa Akyiaa ensured that her own son Kwaku Duah III (later Prempeh I) ascended the Asante throne amid protest from a segment of the ruling council. Her actions caused the Asante Kingdom to split into two factions as well as initiating a civil war, which weakened the state and made it an easy target for the British colonial conquest in 1896.[7] The downside to the queen mother's political powers was that she did not have the collective solidarity of all women in the society and, hence, could not count on women's collective bargaining power. In contrast, a female Mende chief in the Sierra Leone hinterlands, known as Madame Yoko, effectively captured state power from 1885 to 1905 by depending on the collective solidarity of women through a system known as *Bundu*.

However, it has been suggested that Madame Yoko's political power was a bit unconventional in the sense that she utilized slave raiding and military offenses to expand her empire. Nonetheless, Mende women have always been at the helm of political activity in Mende's history and were sometimes even chiefs of towns. Through the *Bundu* initiation system, Madam Yoko not only controlled the marriage arrangements of young girls under her training, but she also formed alliances with influential families to further her political career. Apparently, Madame Yoko utilized the institution of polygynous marriage in ways men could not in the sense that she established significant political alliances in two directions. One, when she took the girls into her Bundu bush and wardship, and two, when she married the girls off to prospective men.[8] Parents became indebted to her for ensuring that the girls got good husbands, and husbands became indebted to her because she found them good wives. Furthermore, when the British colonial power established itself in Sierra Leone, she manipulated them to help consolidate her political power.

In some instances, as among the Lovedu of South Africa, women have been found to exercise power superior or equal to that of men. In her capacity as the spiritual leader, the Lovedu queen mother's supernatural ability to "make rain" for her own people while preventing the enemies of her people from receiving any rains for their farming activities allowed her to lead both the judicial and political systems of the Lovedu. Accordingly, the queen mother carried her administrative responsibilities by appointing other females known as "mothers of the kingdom" to represent the various districts and to act as the link between her office and the public.[9] In the empires of Oyo and Edo among the Yoruba and Edo, women, referred to as "ladies of the palace," played significant roles in the political life of these empires. They formed effective groups that ensured there was political stability and humane rule, and the interests of women were attended to at the highest political level.

In Igbo society, the institution of Omu allowed a woman, acting as the official mother of the society, to control women's affairs. The Omu's political role was comparable to that of the Obi (king) in the governance of the society.[10] The above examples indicate that African women exerted political influence in a variety of ways. In the kingdoms of Asante, Dahomey, Oyo, Edo, and the rest, queen mothers forged alliances, which ensured the succession of their sons to power and the cementation of their own rule. Women in authoritative positions helped societies balance the powers vested in male leaders. In societies with less centralized and hierarchical

Three African Women Leaders at a Reception in their honor. (Courtesy of Toyin Falola)

governing structures, a large number of women participated in political roles and in public affairs through their roles in social, economic, and religious affairs.

WOMEN'S POLITICAL ROLES IN COLONIAL AFRICA

In line with their ideological notion that women are only good for marital and reproductive purposes, colonial rulers made all the necessary attempts to erode women's participation in politics and in the affairs of government. The colonial administrative machinery depended on male authority, and as suggested by Okonjo, they formalized male institutions but ignored their female equivalents. For example, among the Igbo of Nigeria, British colonial government made the traditional male office of the obi into a salaried position but ignored its female counterpart position of the Omu. Okonjo adds that "the British colonial administration either failed to see or, having seen, refused to recognize, the political institutions evolved by Igbo women of their governance."[11] On the Gold Coast, as elsewhere in the British colonies in Africa, the British employed indirect rule to govern through chiefs and other male leaders, ignoring the fact that African societies had always had female political structures, and women had played important political roles in their various societies. Colonial rule submerged the office of the

Akan female stool and its supporting institutions as well as the important political roles of its occupants. The British colonial authorities refused to include female chiefs on the list of chiefs recognized as members of the Native Authority councils and courts. In effect, the British could not conceive of any woman as having the capacity to hold a significant political position or to play advisory roles in public governance.[12]

In response to the colonial pejorative imposition, African women participated vigorously in anticolonial resistance and in the wave of nationalist and liberation movements that occurred on the continent in the period after World War II. A good example of anticolonial protests was the 1929 Aba riots (women's war) in which Igbo women utilized the traditional institution of "sitting on a man," which humiliated men who violated women's rights as a collective political tool against the British colonial authorities. It has been shown that the Aba Riots were a direct response of women to the colonial introduction of taxes in 1927 and 1928 in the five southern provinces of eastern Nigeria. Fearing that the impending taxes would affect them, women demonstrated against colonially created native courts as well as warrant chiefs who represented the colonial administration in the region. The women continued their demonstrations and attacks until the administration assured them that the taxes only affected men.[13]

Various accounts have been reported of women participating in anticolonial protests and in public roles in Tanzania, Kenya, and Cameroon resulting from colonial imposition of taxes and their interference in the socioeconomic life of women. For example, among the Kom of Cameroon, women rioted in reaction to the colonial government's insistence that they adopt vertical contour farming rather than the horizontal contour farming they relied on and rumors of the sale of Kom lands to Igbos of Nigeria. In the ensuing three-year conflict, known as the *Anlu* Rebellion (1958–1961), Kom women seized political power from men. As with the tactics adopted by the Igbo women in the Aba riots, the Kom women utilized the traditional practice of *lu* in which women would use public displays and demonstrate to shame social offenders into repentance. In its three-year "reign of terror," the women demanded the closing of schools and markets, interfered with rituals of the dead, set up roadblocks, heaped insults on men in public, destroyed and burned property, and defied both traditional and colonial authorities.[14]

Similar to the above political agitations, women in the Pare District in Tanzania in the1940s politically demonstrated against colonial taxation. Some researchers have argued that the riot was perhaps the first active role in modern politics for many Pare women.[15] Arising out of complicated methods that the colonial government adopted for assessing and collecting taxes and their refusal to modify the procedures in spite of the public objection, the Pare District riots initially involved thousands of men who, in early 1945, marched to the district headquarters to demand the abolishment of the taxes. Unable to make any headway with their demands, the men continued to remain at the headquarters for several months. The impact of their absence caused many women, mostly the female relatives of the men, to organize and march on the district headquarters to show their support for the cause of the men. The contention of the women was that the continued absence of their men was disrupting the patterns of their lives and livelihoods and would thus stay in Same (the location of the district headquarters) with their husbands, fathers, and brothers until the tax issue was resolved.

The local officer at Same could not contain the angry women and therefore sought help from the colonial government at both the provincial and national levels. The women responded to the presence of the colonial officials in Pare in 1946 by stoning them. The women's actions eventually caused the colonial officials to agree to establish new ways to assess tax liability. Nonetheless, they could not completely resolve the tension until the following year when they finally decided to drop the idea of a graduated tax and instead to raise the existing poll tax.[16] Muslim women of Usumbura, (present-day Bujumbura, Burundi), reportedly organized an effective revolt in the late 1950s against a special tax the colonial government levied on single women. The "women were incensed at the implication that all widowed, divorced, and polygynous women were *malaya* (prostitutes)," and therefore, refused to pay the tax for several years.[17]

Besides protesting against colonial taxes and other social impositions, women's roles in nationalist and liberation movements significantly influenced the end of colonial rule in many places on the continent. In places like Sierra Leone, Guinea-Bissau, Nigeria, Angola, Tanzania, Mozambique, Zimbabwe, and Namibia, women actively participated in colonial struggles. Some women became prominent and emerged as leaders of liberation movements. Examples of such women included Muhumusa of northern Rwanda, Nehanda Charwe of Rhodesia (Zimbabwe), and the Empress T'aitu Bitoul of Ethiopia. These women's claims to spiritual and political authority allowed them to engage in resistance activities against colonial rule. According to reports, the empress participated in armed battle against Italian troops.[18] In some places, the struggles were violent while others had no violent elements. Nigeria has been cited as one of the few places where the nationalist movement was less violent and utilized the electoral processes. Here, market women, through their financial resources, politically influenced the outcome of elections, and in some cases, a political party's ability to control an area depended on the endorsement or participation of these market women in their activities.[19]

On the Ivory Coast, women's participation in nationalist activities was challenging because unlike in other West African countries where men al-

lowed minimal levels of tolerance for women, men of the Ivorian independence party, the Parti Démocratique de la Côte d'Ivoire-Rassemblement
Démocratique Africain (PDCI-RDA) hardly tolerated Ivorian women in
politics. This was a challenge for women because the PDCI-RDA in the
1940s was the main voice of political activism in the country. Nonetheless,
women found ways, as they always do, to organize, and by 1949, Abidjan
women had organized a women's wing of PDCI-RDA. These women set
bold objectives, which included holding a congress and a nationwide literacy campaign for the benefit of other women. They called on women
to organize and participate in public affairs and even though their activities were limited by the French colonial administration, they managed to
play a leading role in the demonstration against the colonial government
in 1949. The demonstrations were ignited when the government arrested
Marcelline Sibo, a market woman and leader of the Agni women activists,
and negotiations for her release had failed.[20] This demonstration became
a milestone for the subsequent political encounters "ordinary" Ivorian
women had with the French colonial government.

In South Africa, women took part and led in the demonstrations against
passes, which required women to carry reference documentation already
carried by men. In fear that their life and family structures would come
under the same severe regulations that controlled the lives of men, South
African women took to the streets in protest to protect their way of life and
family values. The intensity of the demonstrations across the country was
typified in Pretoria when on August 9, 1956, 22,000 women took part in
the demonstrations. Not only did the demonstrations increase in its mili-
tancy, but it also spread to the countryside. The Bafarutshe reserve near the
Botswana border, for example, was engulfed nearly in a "virtual civil war
against anyone who cooperated in the distribution of passes."[21] In the end,
South African women failed to win in the struggle against the passes, but
they inadvertently won for the struggle, becoming a vital political learning experience for women and Nelson Mandela, for instance, was quick
to understand that if the ANC was to win political power, women must be
encouraged to enter into the struggle against apartheid.

Individual women also exemplified themselves by spearheading political
agitations or engaging in political activities to encourage other women to
participate in the affairs of government and in public life. One such woman
was Mrs. Elizabeth Adeyemi Adekogbe of Ibadan, Nigeria, who was one
of the few women to become a member of the colonial administration as
well as to create a movement for women's participation in public affairs.
The Women's Movement, which Adekogbe created in 1952, later became
incorporated into the National Council of Women's Societies (NCWS). Officially, the NCWS portrayed itself as not politically motivated; yet, it had
connections with the action group, that was involved in lobbying political

Professor Bolanle Awe, noted African woman, administrator and cabinet minister in two governments. (Courtesy of Toyin Falola)

leaders.[22] Perhaps the quintessential story of women's political participation during the colonial period was the case of Constance Cummings-John of Sierra Leone. Cummings-John developed her political interest early in life from her family background and from personal experiences.

She embarked on a political journey that sought to unravel the hold of colonialism in Sierra Leone and to gain political acceptance in a system where women were not expected to participate in politics. Working with market women and encouraging them to fight for self-actualization and self-government, Cummings-John became an effective political leader. In 1938, she was elected to the municipal council of Freetown and by this achievement became the first African woman to hold this position. Her political activities resulted in the birth of two women's unions: the Sierra Leone Market Women's Union and the Washerwomen's Union. After her mayoral duties in Freetown in 1966 ended, Cummings-John left politics, but through her efforts, others were encouraged to continue the course for women's participation in government and public affairs. Following in her wake, women such as Nancy Koromah became involved in politics in the period after Sierra Leone's independence.[23]

On the Gold Coast (Ghana), women's role in political activities was both important for the nationalist struggles against colonialism and pioneering for women's political development in West Africa. Women on the Gold Coast had, by 1951, attained the right to vote, and soon afterwards, the first female candidates began standing for elections in municipal assemblies. In September of 1953, Mrs. H. Evans Lutterodt and Stella Dorothy Lokko on the ticket of the Ghana Congress Party (GCP) and Mabel Dove on the ticket of the Convention People's Party (CPP) stood for election in the Accra Town Council elections. although none of them won, their involvement set precedent for others. Dove (later Mrs. Danquah) would go on to become the first woman in West Africa to be elected by popular vote to the national council in the Gold Coast in 1954. Dove's political participation began in 1950 when she joined the Convention People's Party (CPP). For the CPP, Dove devoted her columns in the *Accra Evening News* to espouse the objectives and ideologies of the party, Nkrumah's heroism, agitated for "self-government now" and brought attention to the injustices of colonial rule.

For her constituency, Dove worked for the provision of clean water, good roads, dispensaries, legalization of distilling the local gin (akpeteshie), and the promotion of women's education. Of equal importance were the political activities of Aoua Keita of Mali and Wuraola Adepeju Esan of Nigeria. Both women were significant in the early stages of African women's nationalist and political activities. Keita became the first woman to be elected a deputy to a national assembly in French-speaking West Africa. She was also one of the first women to be elected to the national political bureau of the Rassemblement Démocratique Africain (the African Democratic Assembly). Esan was also the first woman to serve on the federal legislative council of Nigeria as well as the first to be on the federal executive committee of the action group.[24]

In East Africa, women like Rebecca Njeri played an important political leadership role in Kikuyu society. She was famous for her nationalist activities, and between 1947 and 1948, she helped organized the "women's war" in which Kikuyu women demonstrated against the British colonial government's insistence that the women use antierosion contouring in their farming practices. For her roles in political agitation in Kenya, the British colonial administration imprisoned Njeri in 1952 at the same time they imprisoned Jomo Kenyatta. Indeed, the colonizers, vividly perceptive of the role women played in what they called the "passive wing," initiated their own strategies of propaganda and social measures to counteract them.[25] From the above, it is reasonable to assume that women's active participation of colonial resistance and in nationalist activities would help forge their political consciousness in the period after the end of colonial rule on the continent.

WOMEN'S ROLES IN GOVERNMENT IN POSTCOLONIAL AFRICA

African women fought their way through colonial ignorance, degradation, and manipulations and supported their male counterparts to achieve independence, but when they arrived at the theater of the succeeding political arena, society was ill prepared or reluctant to welcome their roles. In contemporary Africa, women play minimal roles in government and in politics and have been underrepresented in these areas, evident by the few positions they hold. The early years after independence were perhaps the hardest period for a woman to gain access to a political position. In Nigeria, for instance, Yoruba women became politically active in the 1950s and help organized women's wings of political parties, yet between 1950 and 1960 not a single women was elected as a representative in the Nigerian national legislative council.[26]

In 1986, when the United Nations surveyed the number of women who occupied seats in their country's national legislature, they found that an average of only 7.1 percent of women held positions. Among the reasons attributed to women's underrepresentation in the political arena is the commonly held view that politics is the quintessential male sphere of influence and action and one in which women are considered ineffective and generally not welcomed. Furthermore, the women who enter politics are usually far removed from other women by class, and as such, pursue interest that have little or no relevance to the interest and needs of "ordinary" women.[27] The effect of the latter is that through the actions of elite women in politics, other women are less encouraged to join and play roles in government. For instance, elite women campaigned vigorously for changes in the divorce laws in Uganda and Kenya and the National Council of Ghanaian Women pressured the Ghana government to incorporate nursery school into its educational system.

Although both reforms would have been significant for women's political achievements, practically, only elite women in the urban centers would have felt their effects[28]; leaving the rural areas where the vast majority of African women live and with daily concerns that have everything to do with food and health security and little to do with divorce laws and nursery schools. In spite of this observation, the divide between elite women and "ordinary" women has been quickly closing in recent years as a greater number of women are getting educated, and many more are becoming conscious of the power of their electoral vote and voice. African women are gradually increasing their participation in government and in other political capacities as prime ministers, cabinet members, ministers, legislative representatives, and even as presidents, and playing significant roles in national and international politics.

Indeed, it is not only in African countries that women's participation in government and national decision making have been growing. Since the 1990s, women's participation in government and politics steadily rose around the world. Some researchers have suggested that for many decades now, women have enjoyed some form of formal equality, including the right to vote, to stand for elections, and to compete for offices—although not religious—in countries that claim to be democratic. During the 1990s, women in Australia (1903), the United States (1920), West Germany (1919), the United Kingdom (1928), and in Switzerland (1971) had fought and won their right to vote and to participate in their country's national decision-making processes. With the exception of the Nordic countries, where the figures of women's participation in politics were higher, women's involvement in national politics in Western countries stood somewhere between 2 and 10 percent, with women in Britain and the United States hardly breaking the 5 percent mark. Since then, women in these countries have experienced an increased participation in national and local politics.

By the end of the decade, many of the countries had caught up with the Nordic countries, where the figures stood between 36.4 and 42.7 percent, with percentage increases ranging between 1 and 36 percent.[29] When the map is extended worldwide, only the Arab states, with 3.6 percent of women participating in politics and government, fell below the standard 10 percent for this time frame.[30] In Africa, the 1980s and early 1990s were a slow pace for women's participation in politics and other governmental activities. Colonial political legacies, African patriarchal structures, gender notions, and lack of education, among many other reasons, which we will discuss later on, accounted for the slow entry of women into the national political scene. As indicated above, by 1986, African women who were actively participating in their country's legislative bodies, accounted for an average of about 7.1 percent; in countries south of the Sahara, those who held ministerial positions was about 4 percent, and a huge 60 percent of all countries in the region had no women ministers.[31]

In a little over 10 years, African women managed to change their representational figures in many countries. According to the 1999 Inter-parliamentary Union report on women in national parliaments, women's representation in parliament south of the Sahara had risen to an average of 11.5 percent with four countries in southern Africa showing an average of 20 percent or more. Some countries in the region have made impressive gains while others have lagged behind. For instances, in countries such as Mozambique, Namibia, Seychelles, South Africa, and Tanzania, women hold more than 20 percent of parliamentary seats; but in others such as Djibouti, Lesotho, Niger, Nigeria, and Togo, they account for less than 5 percent of parliamentary seats.[32] What the above suggests is that on the one hand, women have been underrepresented throughout the history of political participation and to an extent continue to be underrepresented in their country's national politics. However, on the other hand, they have never rested on their oars and have engendered spaces of agency for themselves where none existed.

The political achievements that African women have gained since the colonial days emanated from a variety of sources and grievances including economic and social struggles, involvement in independence and colonial resistance struggles—particularly in eastern and southern Africa—and their general efforts to bring the plight of women and children to the fore-front of national discourses. Their steps were slow and fraught with many challenges, but pioneers such as Mabel Dove, Wuraola Adepeju Esan, and Aoua Keita never gave up. Their struggles and successes encouraged those who came after them to work harder to engage the general public and political leaders about the importance of not just women's participation in politics, but also their participation in the general activities of public life for the betterment of society. Although their success stories in Africa were minimal and far in-between, African women were not discouraged by either colonial governments' gendered restrictions or postcolonial male appropriation of political power and their neglect of women who fought side-by-side with them in the struggles for independence.

African women's participation in politics and governmental issues was not limited to their countries' political spaces. They took major steps in the international scene and made significant impact in redirecting Western feminist focus on women and political power. African women leaders who participated in the 1975 and 1980 United Nations Decade of Women Conferences in Mexico City and Copenhagen respectfully played significant roles in instigating changes in the views and position of women in the international women's movement. These changes would eventually lead Western women to recognize that involvement in formal politics was as valid as any feminist agenda.[33] The conferences sought to bring women from both the Western and non-Western worlds in a collective way to engage the challenges and problems that face women around the world and to find effective solutions to alleviate such problems. From the onset, both conferences were plagued by conflict of interest and ideological positions between women of the Western countries and those of the non-Western countries.

The conflict in the Mexico City conference was based on the insistence of Western feminist participants who wanted to focus on the disparities and inequality between women and men, while women participants from the non-Western countries prioritized the socioeconomic disparities between the developed and the developing countries and on issues relating to racial and class discrimination. During the Copenhagen conference in 1980, women of the Western world saw themselves as champions of other women's burden by insisting that the issue of clitoridectomy—the removal of the clitoris practiced in some African countries—must be the priority of the conference and were, perhaps, shocked when they received no support from the African women participants. African women, on their part, were not only infuriated over the pretence of Western women to care about their sexuality, but also the fact they found the position of Western women patronizing, racist, debasing, and insulting. The African women were of the view that Western women know nothing of their needs and struggles, and hence, could not possibly begin to understand their position.[34] The Western feminist participants, on their part, deemed the African women's position as "reactionary conservatism." In other words, African women were willing to ignore any discourse on the issue of clitoridectomy, which Western women viewed as demeaning and oppressive—and instead focus on dealing with political issues, such as racism, apartheid, colonialism, and liberation struggles.[35] The Western feminists saw the African women's action as a betrayal of the cause of women, particularly since the intent of the conference was to dialogue women's issues and not general political struggles.[36] One Ruth Mompati of the African National Congress (ANC) countered the Western feminist accusations by reiterating that for African women, all the basic sociocultural, economic, and political components of life must be instituted if they were to achieve equality and equity in society. In other words, for African women, "all issues were women's issues," and they must all be addressed in unison if poverty and other social discrimination against women were to end. Mompati sums the position of African women by questioning how anyone could ask them to discuss equality between women and men, when they are yet to receive recognition as human beings.[37] Essentially, the catch-22 insinuated by these women is that women must first have access to the political process and a space of agency in their country's national decision-making processes in order to be able to talk about and effect any change.

The significance of the above conflicts of interest was not because they occurred and that African women took their position and stood their ground. Rather it was because the dialogue between the two sides initiated changed in Western feminists' thought and the development of "global feminism," which was certainly more inclusive and broadly based than the Western feminism. The reassessment of the effects of social, economic, and political factors in advancing women's lives together with the activities of the Development Alternatives with Women for a New Era (DAWN) on women's empowerment agendas worldwide produced the changes. To DAWN, women's political empowerment was twofold: one that insisted on a new trend in which development would be characterized by the redistribution of wealth from rich countries to poor countries, and another in which women have a greater role in the sharing of political power.

Many scholars have indicated that DAWN's reimagination of women's empowerment and their stand against all forms of oppression against women allowed Western feminist scholars to reenvision a new core stand from "victim feminism" to "power feminism." It has again been pointed out that there was a new dawn of thinking, and envisioning women's issues around the world and Western feminism had to change to ensure

Oluyemisi Bamgbose, famous attorney, professor and Dean of the School of Law, Univeristy of Ibadan, Nigeria. (Courtesy of Toyin Falola)

their own dialectical survival. The ironic significance of the contributions African women made toward the changes in global feminism discourses was not driven by a need to challenge African patriarchal structures and gendered notions that sought to subjugate them. Rather, it was based on their need to resist Western leadership control. For the case in many southern African countries, the majority of women entered the political arena not to fight against the social imposition of motherhood roles but to guard against it. For these women, the fight against racism held more currency for it impinged on many issues that affected them, even more so then the disparity between women and men in the political sphere. The merit of this focus was that it profoundly empowered women to seek strategically other rights and privileges denied them because of gendered inequity.[38]

While women in other places on the continent may not have necessarily been as antagonized socially, economically, and politically by racism as women in southern and eastern African countries have been, their struggles against structural inequities and discrimination have not been any less. In a milieu of poverty, colonial-engineered invisibility, and African patriarchal and gender notions that kept the vast majority of women restricted to the domestic space, a significant number of women rose to meet the challenges of their time and to perform exceptionally well in their country's political scene. This is not to suggest that every woman who entered politics did so with the broader aim of alleviating the problem of the masses. As the example of the elite Ghanaian women who entered politics in the early postcolonial period shows, not all the agitations of the elite class suited or were needed by the "ordinary" Ghanaian woman trying to make ends meet in an environment of economic hardships.

Some women politicians either had to give up their "noble" goals of bringing economic relief to others as a result of being rendered tangential by their male colleagues in the political parties or in government. Some entered into deals their ensured their own political careers, rather than carrying out their goals; or they simply forgot about their platforms and promises to better the lot of women's (and men's) lives. These scenarios notwithstanding, the roles African women leaders played in their national politics and what they were able to produce during the two UN Decade of Women Conferences shows their zeal and determination to ensure women's active participation in decision-making processes, particularly those that directly affected their lives. They took advantage of the conference marking the End of Decade, which was held in Nairobi in 1985. The conference afforded the African women participants a platform to "refocus energies, build alliances across the continent, and lobby governments,"[39] and to engage women in finding solutions to the many socioeconomic problems women face and to improve the general conditions of women in their countries.

Undoubtedly, the roles African women have played, and continue to play at the local, national, and international scene brought significant rewards in the electoral and democratic processes in many countries on the continent, especially in countries south of the Sahara. In almost every country in the region, there was a marked increase in women's representation in government and in national politics. Reports on West Africa suggest that many West African countries have recently been experiencing an increase in the number of women in their national legislative bodies, and many more hold ministerial positions. The Southern African Development Community Gender Monitor similarly reported that many of SADC member countries have achieved a greater representation of women in their national politics. Women made substantial gains in countries such as Botswana, Malawi, Mozambique, Namibia, and South Africa, which held elections in the late 1990s. While the situation was not a repeat in every election held on the continent, because in places like Zimbabwe and South Africa women in fact lost some of their previously held parliamentary seats, current statistics give a hopeful improvement in the general number of women in African legislative bodies.

Indeed, since the 1980s, women's participation in national politics and in government has steadily increased across the continent with some women playing major roles in the highest office of their land. For instance, one of Africa's politically powerful women, Luisa Diogo, who served as prime minister of Mozambique from February 2004 until January 2010, was herald by the female Prime Minister Elisabeth Domitien from the Central African Republic. Others included Mame Madior Boye in Senegal, Agathe Uwilingiyimana in Rwanda, Maria das Neves Ceita Baptista de Sousa in Sao Tome and Principe, and Sylvie Kinigi in Burundi. A few women have had the privilege of serving heads of state or interim heads of state. These included Carmen Pereira who served as the interim president of Guinea-Bissau for three days (May 14, 1984–May 16, 1984); Ruth Sando Perry, interim president of Liberia (1996–1997); Rose Francine Rogombé, interim president of Gabon (June 2009–October 2009); and of course, Africa's first elected female president, Ellen Johnson-Sirleaf of Liberia (2006–present).[40] The roles these women have played, and continue to play, have been generally at the high end of the political spectrum. At the local and grassroot levels, many women—some whose work history may never record—are bringing the government to the people and working in less-recognizable governmental and political roles. The success of their work signifies what is politically possible for all women.

CHALLENGES WOMEN ENCOUNTER IN THEIR POLITICAL ROLES

In their work, African women politicians have had to deal with a variety of challenges since their entrance into the political scene from the colonial period to contemporary times. The origins of these challenges could be from the women's personal family relationships where spouses and family members object to their participation in politics because of the dangers associated with offices. The challenges could equally be from the women's political party affiliations and their roles in government where ideological pressures force them to kowtow to certain norms, or the challenges could be in how they relate with people in their electoral constituencies and with their male counterparts. One of the ironic sources of challenge to women's political roles is other women. In this regard, women have utilized the platform of activist movements to serve as not only watchdogs on the activities of women political leaders, but also to ensure that they stay focused and committed to the course as guardians of women's rights in the government.

Admittedly, many of the women's movements and women's lobby groups scattered across Africa have worked extremely hard to ensure that women have equal representation in political affairs and in government, and hence would expect that those who get the opportunity to get elected or be appointed into the government would advance the course of women. Many researchers have pointed out how some of these groups have stated their disenchantment with some female political leaders who have failed to speak for their agendas or have adopted strategies considered detrimental to the improvement of women's lives. Furthermore, female leaders in politics and in government have had to work in a male-structured environment and from within the context of rules, values, and expectations established by the male order. While we are not insinuating that male political figures have an easy go in their political careers, the challenges women politicians encounter are generally those that have nothing to do with their ability to perform their public responsibilities.

Rather, the challenges women politicians face are social impositions that view women as incapable of performing public roles even before women political figures have the chance to prove themselves otherwise. Because of these social impositions and gendered notions, women in politics and government, unlike their male counterparts, have had to go the extra mile in carrying out their public responsibilities. The increased empowerment agendas in many African countries have resulted in an increased women's participation in politics, but their arrival at the political scene was met with a rude awakening of the not-so-changed ideological underpinnings of Africa's political spectrum. Maverick women politicians have been mocked, insulted, branded as un-African, and queried about their capabilities to deal with the functions of political offices, and criticized as having rejected their roles as wives and as mothers. They have had to contend with "powerful male gatekeepers"[41] who, for all intent and purpose, want these women to remain in the sphere of domesticity or, at best, limit their activities to women's leagues and not mainstream political activities.

In South Africa, where women's participation in governmental affairs and in politics have increased tremendously since the mid-1990s, with the women coming from diverse backgrounds and of different age groups, simple stereotyping of women politicians is no longer possible. Hence, the public, and even male political figures, have had to focus on caricaturing the way female politicians appear in public. For example, one Jessie Duarte, who was a member of the Gauteng provincial legislature, had claimed that the South African media had resorted to focusing on the appearance of women politicians for ridicule. Duarte stated that the media judges women on "their sexuality and morality rather than their intellect, journalists, she claimed, got distracted from political achievements 'by the size of my feet and the color of my toenail polish.'"[42] In another example, Inonge Lewanika, a member of the Zambian parliament, in 1995 had to endure humiliation in parliament at the hands of her male colleagues by the mere wearing of attire that exposed her bare arms—Zambia as well as Zimbabwe had dress codes for women parliamentary members.

Apparently, a male colleague made Lewanika's bare arms the subject of an order, to which the Speaker interjected that "'arms are all right. What we are concerned about are the legs.'" Interestingly, this same body, and its male members, takes exception to women hiding the legs the speaker was concerned about in pants because pants are male clothing.[43] In other parts of Africa, south of the Sahara, where parliamentary bodies do not have dress regulations for women members, the public steps in to provide one. Judging them mainly through the lens of African motherhood values and ideals, women politicians who especially dress in Western-style clothing are sometimes considered as "flirts" and unfit to lead. Some women cabinet ministers have reported been mistaken for secretaries, and even worse, endured sexual harassment from their male counterparts.[44]

Besides the sexual harassments, insinuations, and sarcastic comments made about the appearance of women political leaders, they have had to contend with the general lack of trust that they are as capable and as qualified as their male counterparts to get their jobs done effectively and efficiently. More often than not, women politicians find their performances downplayed or regarded as inadequate. Ironically, when women show traits of determination, straightforwardness, and no-nonsense attributes in carrying out their responsibilities, they are "characterized as 'ruthless, belligerent, and doggedly determined,'" regardless of whether they are doing an excellent job. When men show the same traits, their attributes are the complete opposite.[45] It seems that African women in politics and in government face a vicious cycle of unending and unwinnable challenges. From left and right, they have had to deal with patriarchal structures, gendered normative practices and role expectations, conform to certain prescribed behaviors, combine their public and private roles without any hiccups, follow party directives, and satisfy the demands of their constituencies.

Any action contrary to the above expectations and directives, attracted severe criticisms and translated into incompetence. Yet, as with the many constraints placed in their way, African women have not been agreeable to their lot nor have they played the trump card of victimhood. Rather, they have faced the challenges head on. All around Africa, south of the Sahara, women, whether in politics already or wanting to enter into politics, are gaining in confidence and engaging and challenging political processes, patriarchal values, and gender notions intended to restrict their public roles. As the cases in Rwanda, Burundi, Liberia, South Africa, Guinea Bissau, and Gabon show, women are now serving Africa in various political capacities such as prime ministers, presidents, vice presidents, and in other important governmental positions. A component of the success of women in politics has been the ability of individual women to become a part of the political process and to forge a niche for themselves.

The other component has been the dynamics of the regions or countries in which the women serve. That is, the societies had to be willing and ready to front and accept women as prime ministers/presidents/heads of government ministries, and the women themselves had to be ready for such positions. This notwithstanding, we cannot lose sight of the fact that the African women politicians who have broken the gender barrier, and become somewhat of a beacon for other women are not "images of perfections." Many have had to deal with charges of corruption and inappropriate behavior in office. For instance, Agathe Uwilingiyimana of Rwanda was accused of being a "political trickster" while in office, and Africa's first female president, Ellen Johnson-Sirleaf, had to deal with questionable election meanderings.[46] While the above clearly shows that African female political leaders have dealt with, and in many cases, continue to deal with a myriad of constraints in carrying out their political roles, the vast majority of African women never get the opportunity to play any role in politics or in government, to which we now turn our attention.

FACTORS THAT HINDER WOMEN'S ROLES IN POLITICS AND GOVERNMENT

Existing scholarships on factors that hinder African women's political participation point to the lack of women's access to educational opportunities, women's minimal participation in general public roles, socioeconomic and cultural conditions of a country, and cumbersome electoral processes as the major factors that prevents women's adequate representation in politics and government. A number of scholars have suggested that when women have access to adequate education, it not only facilitates their interest in seeking political offices, but it also enhances their competence and success in office.[47] The ripple effect of this is that more and more women will be willing to stand for elections at the local and at the national levels. Until recently, the majority of African governments did not prioritize the education of women as an important component of socioeconomic development. Even with the increased focus on educating girls, the enrollment rate of females as compared to those of males is abysmal in many countries.

As the 2000 United Nations Development Program report on *Human Development* shows, female enrollment rate south of the Sahara is the lowest in the world; and in nearly a decade since the report, there has not been any significant improvement in their position when compared with the rest of the world.[48] Many researchers have contended that the gap between women and men in education has been responsible for not only the limited number of women qualified for certain legislative and governmental offices, but also, it is the course of women's underrepresentation in the national decision-making processes in many African countries.[49] Another area of concern has been the economic conditions and cultural structures that exist in African countries. Poor economic performances that many African governments have exhibited have meant that the condition of women has steadily deteriorated since the end of colonial rule.

As many researchers agree, African women have been the ones who suffer the most because they bear the largest responsibilities in the maintenance of the African family. Others have argued that economic hardships negatively affect women's participation of national politics because making ends meet consumes the majority of their time and reduces their interest in standing for elective offices.[50] As has been alluded to in our discussions above, cultural values and gender notions influence how society perceives of women's roles. Because of the social expectation of women to act and behave in certain ways, it influences the willingness of many women to put themselves up for societal scrutiny. In particular, African patriarchal structures, reemphasized by colonial gender legacies, have consigned women to domestic roles and have prevented their active participation in political activities.

Electoral processes in many African countries have equally been blamed as being unfavorable to women and restricting their ability to stand for

Omotayo Ikotun, Registrar and third person in control, the University of Ibadan, Nigeria. (Courtesy of Toyin Falola)

elections or even vote in one. Very few countries devote resources to educating the populace about voting rights, political issues, and the right of
every citizen to stand for elections regardless of background, educational
level, sexual orientation, and the rest. African women, with the numerous responsibilities on their shoulders, usually have very limited time to
educate themselves on public issues or get involved in one. Thus, African
governments, nongovernmental agencies, women's movements, and all the
various agencies interested in women's issues must make conscientious
efforts to bring women into the fold of the political discourse and consciousness. Already, some organizations such as the Namibian Women's
Manifesto Network, the Gender and Development Action, the Women
Empowerment Movement, and the National Council for Women's Societies, all in Nigeria, as well as the Southern African Development Community among others have achieved some level of success in increasing
women's representation in politics and in government. Undoubtedly, the
task of ensuring that the gender gap between women and men in the national decision-making process close will not be easy or straightforward
for either side; nonetheless, it will ensure that African women assume their
rightful share of public responsibilities.

From precolonial through colonial to postcolonial periods, the roles African women have played, and continue to play, in government and politics
have been both dynamic and real. African societies provided various avenues for women to participate in power, particularly in terms of ensuring
male authoritative figures do not abuse their powers as well as ensuring
that the interests of women were catered for and the values of society maintained. Commenting on women's political roles in Africa, south of the Sahara, Sandra Barnes writes that African women are among history's most
viable populations for political engagement.[51] Colonialism created for African women a contested site of social, economic, and political struggles.
Colonial rulers erased the balance that women provided in the political
structures of African societies by systematically preventing them from any
active participation in the new political order.

Nonetheless, women were not agreeable to what colonialism dished
them; they not only fought for their right to survive, but also for the maintenance of the values of their societies and for their freedoms. Postcolonial African governments have not created the environments for an equal
participation of women in the affairs of government. African women have
had to struggle to create their own spaces of empowerments and create
for themselves avenues of political participation. Those who have had the
opportunity to participate in politics and in government have found the environment unwelcoming and steep in patriarchal ideologies and the populace unwilling to accept and judge them on their own merits. However,
and as always, African women have risen to the challenge; gradually, many

African women are becoming politically active at the local, national, and international levels. They are voicing their opinions on how the governance of their societies affects their lives and the life of their families and communities.

NOTES

1. Annie M. D. Lebeuf, "The Role of Women in the Political Organization of African Societies," in Denise Paulme (ed.), *Women of Tropical Africa* (Berkeley and Los Angeles: University of California Press, 1963), 93–114.

2. Iris Berger and E. Frances White, *Women in Sub-Saharan Africa: Restoring Women to History* (Bloomington: Indiana University Press, 1999), 99.

3. Holly Hanson, "Queen Mothers and Good Government in Buganda," in Jean Allman, Susan Geiger, and Nakanyike Musisi (eds.), *Women in Colonial Histories* (Bloomington: Indiana University Press, 2002), 221.

4. In the Akan political setup, occupation of a stool is the same as having ascended a throne from which the occupant exerts his or her political authority.

5. Kwame Arhin, "The Political and Military Roles of Akan Women," in Christine Oppong (ed.), *Female and Male in West Africa* (London: George Allen and Unwin, 1983), 91–95.

6. Agnes Akosua Aidoo, "Asante Queen Mothers in Government and Politics in the Nineteenth Century," in Filomina Chioma Steady (ed.), *The Black Woman Cross-Culturally* (Rochester: Schenkman Books, 1981), 66.

7. Arhin, 91–95.

8. Carol Hoffer, "Mende and Sherbro Women in High Offices," *Canadian Journal of African Studies*, Vol. 6, No. 2 (1972): 151–164.

9. Lebeuf, 98–99.

10. Kamene Okonjo, "Women's Political Participation in Nigeria," in Oppong, *Female and Male in West Africa*, 214–215.

11. Ibid., 219.

12. Arhin, 93–97.

13. Catherine Coquery-Vidrovitch, *African Women: A Modern History* (Boulder, CO: Westview Press, 1997), 163–164.

14. Eugenia Shanklin, "*Anlu* Remembered: The Kom Women's Rebellion of 1958–1961," *Dialectical Anthropology*, Vol. 15, No. 2–3 (1990): 159–181.

15. Jean O'Barr and Kathryn Firmin-Sellers, "African Women in Politics," in Margaret Jean Hay and Sharon Stichter (eds.), *African Women South of the Sahara* (New York: Longman Group, 1995), 198.

16. Ibid.

17. Berger, 48; See Nancy Rose Hunt, "Domesticity and Colonialism in Belgian Africa: Usumbura's *Foyer Social*, 1946–1960," *Signs*, Vol. 15, No. 3 (1990): 447–474.

18. Berger, 35; See Chris Prouty Rosenfeld, *Empress Taytu and Menilek II: Ethiopia, 1883–1910* (Trenton, NJ: Red Sea Press, 1986).

19. Coquery-Vidrovitch, 176–177.

20. Ibid., 177–179.

21. Berger, 49.

22. Coquery-Vidrovitch, 173, 195.

23. Ibid., 176.

24. LaRay Denzer, "Gender and Decolonization: A Study of Three Women in West African Public Life," in Andrea Cornwall (ed.), *Readings in Gender in Africa* (Bloomington: Indiana University Press, 2005), 217–220.

25. Coquery-Vidrovitch, 196.

26. Okonjo, 216.

27. Coquery-Vidrovitch, 196.

28. Kathleen Staudt, "Class Stratification and its Implication for Women's Politics," Claire Robertson and Iris Berger (eds.), *Women and Class in Africa* (New York: Africana Publishing Co., 1986), 203.

29. Anne Philips. *Engendering Democracy* (University Park: Pennsylvania State University Press, 1991), 60.

30. Inter-Parliamentary Union, *Women in National Parliaments* (Geneva: Inter-Parliamentary Union, 1999).

31. United Nations, *World's Women: Trends and Statistics, 1970–1990* (New York: United Nations, 1991), 39–40.

32. Gisela Geisler, *Women and the Remaking of Politics in Southern Africa: Negotiating Autonomy, Incorporation and Representation* (Uppsala, Sweden: Nordiska Africkainstitutet, 2004), 9–14.

33. Ibid., 10–14.

34. Ayesha Imam M. "Engendering African Social Sciences: An Introductory Essay," in Ayesha Imam M., Amina Mama, and Fatou Sow (eds.), *Engendering African Social Sciences* (Dakar, Senegal: CODESRIA, 1997), 17.

35. Geisler, 11.

36. Abena Florence Dolphyne, *The Emancipation of Women: An African Perspective* (Accra: Ghana Universities Press, 1991), xi. Cited in Geisler, 11.

37. International Feminist Collective, *Sammen er vi stærke—før den alternative kvindekonference 1980* (Copenhagen, 1981), 53. Cited in and translated from Danish to English by Geisler, 11.

38. Geisler, 13.

39. Ibid.

40. Gunhild Hoogensen and Bruce Solheim, *Women in Power: World Leaders Since 1960* (Westport, CT: Praeger Publishers, 2006), 44. For a detailed look at African women in politics and government, see Book LLC, *African Women in Politics: Simone Gbagbo, Djoueria Abdallah* (Memphis, TN: General Books, 2010); Anne Marie Goetz and Shireen Hassim, *No Shortcuts to Power: African Women in Politics and Policy Making* (New York: Zed Books, 2003); Emmanuel Konde, *African Women and Politics: Knowledge, Gender, and Power in Male Dominated Cameroon* (New York: Mellen, 2005).

41. Geisler, 173–190.

42. Ibid.

43. Monde Sifuniso, "Zambian Women in Parliament," in Mbuyu Nalumango and Monde Sifuniso (eds.), *Woman Power in Politics* (Lusaka, Zambia: Zambia Women Writers Association, 1998), 213. Cited in Geisler, 173–190.

44. Anne Ferguson and Kimberly Ludwig, "Zambian Women in Politics: An Assessment of Changes Resulting from the 1991 Political Transition," *MSU Working Papers on Political Reform in Africa*, No. 13 (East Lansing: Michigan State University, 1995), 17.

45. Media Monitoring Project, "Biased? Gender, Politics, and the Media," Commission for Gender Equality, *Redefining Politics: South African Women and Democracy* (Braamfontein, South Africa: Commission for Gender Equality, 1999), 164–166. Cited in Geisler, 177.

46. Gunhild Hoogensen, and Bruce O. Solheim, *Women in Power: World Leaders since 1960* (Westport, CT: Praeger, 2006), 60.

47. For a detailed discussion on women's participation in political processes see Richard E. Matland, "Women's Representation in National Legislatures: Developed and Developing Countries," *Legislative Studies Quarterly*, Vol. 23 (1998): 109–125; Carol A. Christy, *Sex Differences in Political Participation: Processes of Change in Fourteen Nations* (New York: Praeger, 1987).

48. United Nations Development Program (UNDP), Human Development Report (New York: Oxford University Press, 2000), 164.

49. Annie Foster, "Development and Women's Political Leadership: The Missing Link in Sub-Saharan Africa," *Flecher Forum of World Affairs*, Vol. 17 (1993): 101–116; Titi Ufomata, "Linguistic Images, Socialization, and Gender in Education," *Africa Development*, Vol. 23 (1998): 61–75.

50. Maria Nzomo, "The Gender Dimension of Democratization in Kenya: Some International Linkages," *Alternatives*, Vol. 18 (1993): 61–73.

51. Sandra T. Barnes, "Gender and the Politics of Support and Protection in Precolonial West Africa," in Flora Edouwaye Kaplan (ed.), *Queens, Queen Mothers, Priestesses, and Power: Case Studies in African Gender* (New York: New York Academy of Sciences, 1997), 2.

SUGGESTED READING

Hoogensen, Gunhild and Bruce O. Solheim. *Women in Power: World Leaders since 1960.* Westport, CT: Praeger, 2006.

Kasfir, Nelson (ed.). *Civil Society and Democracy in Africa: Critical Perspectives.* London: Frank Cass, 1988.

Saidi, Christine. *Women's Authority and Society in Early East-Central Africa.* Rochester, NY: University of Rochester Press, 2010.

Tordoff, William. *Government and Politics in Africa.* Bloomington: Indiana University Press, 2002.

Young, Tom. *Readings in African Politics.* Bloomington: Indiana University Press, 2003.

7

Women and Education

The history of women and education in Africa is one subject that scholars, government agencies, activist organizations, and nongovernmental bodies have debated and dissected for decades in an effort to understand women's roles in education, the impact of education in women's lives, women's lack of access to educational opportunities, and the solutions to making education equal between women and men. The emerging dialogue reveals the important educational roles African women have played in their various societies and the disparaging trend of governmental neglect of women's education by both colonial and postcolonial governments. More importantly, the discussions show that African women themselves, more so than any other body and in spite of the mountain of obstacles they encounter, have been actively pursuing various avenues to improve their educational backgrounds in order to take advantage of contemporary economic and political opportunities. It has been argued that the inroads African women have made into formal education and professions have not necessarily been the result of social policies that contemporary African governments have designed specifically to enhance women's advancements or to address their underrepresentation. Rather, women have themselves taken advantage of whatever periodic expansion made it to the educational system in their countries.[1] In this chapter, we trace African women's roles in education in the precolonial, colonial, and postcolonial eras. We also look at the gendered dimensions of women and education and how gendering has negatively affected women's access to education.

Anyone taking a cursory look at the abundance of scholarships on African women and education would find that for the longest period, girls' access to formal education was not the priority of both parents and governments in many African societies and, indeed, in many parts of the world. Hence, a great disparity existed in the educational levels of girls and boys and between women and men. However, in the last few decades, changes in the educational policies of many African countries as well as the funding of education by international and nongovernmental agencies have caused some level of gains in bridging the educational gap between girls and boys of school age, particularly at the primary level. The literature also reveals that although much of the progress that has been made in education is at the primary, elementary, and secondary levels, the percentage of women in higher education is gradually increasing.

In the 1990s, the total literacy rate for women between 15 and 24 years of age south of the Sahara was 58 percent. By 2008, the figure had slowly increased to 67 percent. From a very negligible figure, the enrollment of African women at the tertiary level rose to 35 percent in 1993, and by 2006, it had risen to 40 percent.[2] Some African countries have registered substantial increases for the number of women who continue their education to the college level. For example, in South Africa in 1975, black women made up of about 21 percent of the students' population at the university level while that of white women was around 33 percent. Just a decade later, the percentage for black women had risen to 44 percent and that of white women had gone up to 36 percent.[3] By 2006, the percentage for both black and white women at the tertiary level in South Africa had increased to 55 percent.[4]

Although the above figures seem insignificant especially when compared to the figures of the male population, it is still substantial when viewed from the perspective of where women have come from in the educational scheme of colonial and postcolonial governments. Perhaps the downside to the increase in women's educational levels has been the lack of economic avenues for them to express fully their potentials. Put differently, women's educational input has not been corelated to, or reflective of, their educational output. In essence, an inverse relationship exists between the level of education women achieve and her involvement in the labor market, which in part is the result of educational policies that encourage women to specialize in areas that are traditionally noncompetitive, provides low pay, and offers little opportunities for improvement. The other part involves gender notions that persuade women to accept traditional domestic roles even when they have the educational background to be competitive in the labor force.

While our discussions in chapter 4 clearly indicate that African women's domestic role is indispensable to the well-being and the very survival of the African family, any measure that systematically restricts women with formal education to the domestic domain and impedes their role in the public space appears counterproductive to national development considering the length of time and financial resources both women themselves and governments devote to education. The above is in no way a suggestion that once women acquire formal education, they have limited roles in the domestic sphere or that when they play public roles based on their educational backgrounds, they would be liberated from all their problems. As some researchers have argued, while formal education has the potential to alleviate women from the constraints of poverty and inequality, it could equally surrender women to public reproach for rejecting their African cultural values for values of the Western world.[5] Our suggestion is that in the 21st century in which every African society is chasing after Western ideals generally attain through formal education, women must have the right to choose where they want to invest their human resource and the equal chance to access both nonformal and formal education.

In the African context, both forms of education are particularly important if women are to achieve the equal access and quality of education available to the male population. As it has been argued, the achievement of a complete parity of education for African women includes combining the home environment, which fundamentally sets their roles in society, with the school environment, which prepares them to express their roles in the public domain. The issue is that on the one hand, the African home remains the unit where children acquire their basic social and cultural values, including gender identity and notions of gendered division of labor. On the other hand, the contemporary school system, more or less, extends social values children receive at home. Combining the two would not only allow the roles, activities, and goals set in the home to be reinforced, but it would also ensure that the demands of institutional change exerted on the female child as a result of being introduced to formal education would be eliminated.

The resulting outcome is one in which the "new African woman" emerges from the milieu of the home and school, which collaboratively prepares her to play her roles in the emerging technologically oriented world order where the division of labor is based on ability, skill, and interest and not on one's sex or on gender notions.[6] Many researchers hold this view. Some have made more compelling arguments for the incorporation of traditional forms of education and the Western-style education now offered to Africans. Many have suggested measures such as expanding the number of schools, increasing female teachers, broadening the educational curricula, and reducing child labor and the domestic duties of girls. In addition, they have called for the incorporation of traditional education as a vital step in promoting women's education with the view that educational projects and policies implemented without the acceptance of the people are bound to fail.[7] In 1988, Bolanle Awe argued that for women's education to achieve its desired objectives, "it must be life-long, community-based, and oriented to the real-life experiences of the students."[8] The need for both parents and governments to focus on both nonformal and formal education is imperative. This is because if African societies are to continue to depend on and benefit from the role of women as the transmitters of sociocultural values and their position as the foundation of socioeconomic development, then ensuring that the girl-child receives institutionalized support in the nonformal setting is equally as important as any support she would get in the formal setting.

Undoubtedly, the two forms of education are important for the development of women, but regrettably, the discourse on the factors that have accounted for the high rates of illiteracy among African women and their lack of educational opportunities have often overlooked nonformal education as a means of knowledge transmission and the essential roles women play in this area of education. All over Africa, women's secret associations and the homestead were the means through which societies ensured the successful transmission of its values and traditions to girls and young women, and graduation was almost nearly a guarantee. In the next section, we discuss the roles women played in precolonial societies as educators; the advantages, disadvantages, and gendered dimensions of traditional nonformal education; the various aspects of nonformal education that have persisted in spite of the colonial onslaught and those that could still be useful for the education of girls and the empowerment of women in contemporary times.

EDUCATION IN THE PRECOLONIAL PERIOD

In many precolonial African societies, the education of girls was primarily the responsibility of mothers, grandmothers, sisters, aunts, and indeed, in the hands of the entire community of women. These women provided sociocultural, economic, religious, and sometimes, political knowledge through institutionalized structures such as secret societies and women's organizations and through everyday living situations. Education was a vital component of most precolonial African societies regardless of whether it was carried out in a "school" setting or not, yet, Western observers as late as the 1970s continued to contend that African societies lacked any tradition of education. It has been pointed out that those who hold this view argue from the perspective that in the African context, any indigenous form of education, if it existed, was intended purely for socialization purposes and thus cannot qualify as a structured education. In Europe and in the Islamic world, the same process of imparting knowledge from the older generation to the younger generation has been, as expected, accepted as "education" because it took place in a school environment.[9]

An excellent illustration is Herbert M. Philip's observation about indigenous African education, which underscores how outsiders often fail to conceptualize the core essence of Africa social structures and their value systems. Philips writes:

> In Africa, education was extremely limited and associated with the very small numbers who were in contact with Islam over the land routes and later with Europeans in the ports or administrative centers already starting to be set up in those parts of Africa, which were colonized. But basically the continent as a whole was still completely underdeveloped and tribal. African potential, though great, was late in being mobilized.[10]

African educational systems, particularly those of precolonial societies, may not have conformed to what the European colonizers envisioned education to be, yet there is no doubt of its existence and the central roles women played in it. A number of researchers have established that outside of the home environment, traditional education during the precolonial period was transmitted through such structures as age-grade groups, secret societies, and other women's organizations.

While many of the above societies are no longer functioning in many places in Africa because of the colonial assault, a number of them still exist in some societies and continue to provide valuable skills for the social, cultural, and economic development of their communities. For instance, among the Gbandes of the Liberian, hinterlands education was not only a continuous process for all members of the society, but also it was through structured school systems with compulsory attendance policy and curriculum. This feature undoubtedly made them "examples of formal education par excellence and formally recognized as such within the communities."[11] The schools had the responsibility of instructing both girls and boys in practical life skills and social values as well as transforming immature children into matured members of the adult community. Such structured education has been found among other societies. Perhaps the most studied among the extant ones are that of the Bundu society found in the countries of Guinea, Sierra Leone, and Liberia.

The Bunda society educational system fundamentally transformed girls into women through such curriculum activities as circumcising the girls; instructing them in various subject areas such as cleaning rituals, singing, feasting, and gift giving; and instructing them to be of service to both the society officials and to the entire community. At a young age, girls left their parents' homes for a period of time to attend the Bundu society's school.[12] Once girls had been admitted to start their training, they received instructions relating to female sexuality, childbirth, prenatal and postnatal nutrition, breastfeeding, birth control, acceptable female sexual behavior, marital responsibility, and the act of being a good mother and a good wife. The basic medium of instruction was through practical observation such as observing and perhaps assisting in an actual childbirth or circumcision.[13]

The benefit of this educational system for women was twofold. First, they played the essential role as instructors of this educational system, and second, it prepared them from a young age for societal responsibilities. Their roles as the guardians of reproduction, fertility, and sexual health not only allowed the women of Bundu society the opportunity to regulate women's reproduction and to control male fertility and regulate their sexual behavior, but it also empowered them and elevated them to a status of reverence. For example, men who committed acts of sexual misconduct could be severely punished by the high Bundu officials, and wives and mothers could stand in the authority of the Bundu society to mete out their own form of punishments when the men in their lives went astray.[14] They also had control over medicinal knowledge that cured the reproductive diseases of men. Beyond their instructional responsibilities to young girls about reproduction, the Bundu society members also provided midwifery services to the entire community. It has been suggested that in order to maintain control over their reproductive knowledge and the mystery of their rituals and to probably keep the community dependent on their skills, the Bundu society kept to themselves the core essence of their reproductive knowledge. Nonetheless, the society was noted as being flexible enough to allow specially selected women to acquire their skills by paying fees and after performing certain rituals.[15]

Besides reproductive education, Bundu education also equipped girls and women with knowledge in general social values and competence in traditional songs and dance. For the Bundu society, their fundamental goal was to preserve the traditions and values of the society by passing them onto the younger generations. It was through the teaching of social values to the initiates that accepted principles of social conduct were directed and regulated.[16] Like in many African societies, songs and dances provided a vital medium through which social values and cultural traditions were transmitted from one generation to the next. Among the Akan of Ghana, young girls learned dirges from older women to mourn and honor the departed. More importantly, they learned through the dirges, the importance of living a righteous life for a person's entire life could be played to the public through such songs.

Similarly, among the Bundu, dance and songs formed an important medium for social learning. In other words, songs and dances formed a significant part of the corpus of knowledge that older women passed onto younger women. This helped to shape women's consciousness of themselves as a corporate group. The songs and dance constituted the core of the national folk culture and helped shape national self-consciousness and cohesion.[17] While contemporary changes have affected the length of time girls spent learning the songs and dances, in recent years, women have found ways to continue carrying on this educational tradition by reinforcing their knowledge of songs and dance through communal singing and dancing. Some women have even taken a step further by forming "semiprofessional 'folk-singing' groups" and singing the songs they learned at the Bundu school.[18] In the case of the Akan, the practice of older women actively teaching young girls how to sing the dirges has significantly died out in many places. Now young girls generally learn how to sing the dirges by just watching others perform it during funerals, especially in the rural areas.

The Bundu educational system represented one set of ways Africans imparted knowledge from one generation to the next during the precolonial period. We must point out that the application of the term "precolonial" does not necessarily denote that a particular educational practice is no longer in use in the contemporary period. Rather, it is intended to demarcate time and space and to also distinguish the changes that have occurred as a result of outside contact. As the Bundu example shows, officials of the society had their own secret way of providing midwifery services, and for generations they depended on their methods to render them. In the 1970s, the Sierra Leonean government enrolled the Bundu midwives in training courses in Western biomedical management of childbirth, which allowed them to incorporate scientific methods into their practices.[19] It is reasonable to suggest that while the Bundu society have maintained some aspects of their practices, a great number of them is no longer applied, and it would be confusing not to specify them under time frames.

In other African societies, a less institutionalized system of education was utilized to transmit knowledge to the younger generation. As with other sectors of the social setup, occupational and social training were segregated based on sex, and women took responsibility for the training aimed at the girl-child. Here, women transmitted knowledge regarding domestic duties such as cooking, cleaning, washing, and the rest by encouraging young girls to participate in these activities or watching as their mothers, sisters, and other female relatives performed them. Through active participation, listening, and watching, girls also learned about farming practices and techniques, reproductive health, customs and taboos, acceptable social behavior, and social values. In some cases, training was provided in a semistructured environment through apprenticeship arrangements. For example, a young girl may have served as an apprentice to a midwife, trader, healer, or artisan. When such occupations were within a family, girls may not have formally entered into apprenticeship, although they may have studied for years under the directions of their parents.

A kindergarten class in Nairobi, Kenya, 1994. (Courtesy of A. Olusegun Fayemi)

Initiation ceremonies were also occasions for girls to be educated in reproductive and social values. However, unlike the Bundu society system, initiates did not have to leave their homes for extended periods. The elderly women in the community may have set up special times to educate the initiates and usher them into womanhood, or parents may have provided the education. Among the Krobo of southern Ghana, initiation of young girls into womanhood took place after their first menstruation. It was only when a collection of young girls had undergone the biological change that they were brought together for a short duration to receive reproductive knowledge and to undergo the initiation rite. In the meantime, the parents of these girls were responsible for ensuring that the girls had been adequately schooled in female sexuality, sexual behavior, and in other reproductive knowledge: for any girl found to have had sexual contact or to be pregnant at the time of the initiation brought shame not only to themselves but also to their entire family. In African precolonial societies, opportunities for education were practically endless. It involved both specialized training and nonspecialized training, and both women and men received education according to their roles in society.

As Jomo Kenyatta wrote about the Kikuyu in Kenya, education was both general and specific, and they were oriented toward the realities of daily living.[20] The above suggests that educational opportunities have existed and, indeed, abound in precolonial African societies. They were pragmatic and attuned to the social, cultural, economic, religious, and political needs of the African people, and women played significant roles in it both in the structured/institutionalized setting and in ordinary or mundane daily activities. As the following discussion will show, the inception of colonialism on the African continent changed everything, including the practicality and relevance of African systems of education, the roles women played in education, and the importance of education in women's lives. Colonial rulers not only established their own form of education intended to help sustain the colonial enterprise, but they also effectively set the stage for African women's high illiteracy rates in contemporary times. The introduction of colonial education was in fact a double-edged sword for African women: on the one hand, it rendered their roles in the African system of education ineffective; while on the other hand, it denied them access to, and participation in, the new system of education.

FORMAL EDUCATION IN THE COLONIAL PERIOD

By all intent and purpose, colonial rulers did not introduce Western-style education to produce African intellectuals who might one day free the African continent of colonial rule. Rather, their educational system was created to produce a pool of Africans who not only would serve as clerks, aides, translators, and administrators, but who would also be fully acculturated into European culture and properly impressed by colonial rule. As the main lotus of their "civilizing" mission, the colonial education, now referred to a "formal education," was intentionally structured to counter, and if possible purge from African societies, all traces of African educational systems and the values they imparted to people. Colonial education granted to a limited extent, an opportunity for some Africans to gain influence and power and to adjust their socioeconomic positions in the new political order. This group of people, we should add, did not include African women for the most part. Colonial rulers did not see women as worthy of education because of their own gender notions about women, although interestingly, they shifted the blame for women's lack of access to education on African families.

As has been pointed out about the Belgian Congo, colonial authorities aimed their recruitment efforts at boys; yet they blamed parents for refusing to send their daughters to school. Admittedly, during the earlier days of colonization, parents fearing that their daughters would be converted to Christianity—a vital aspect of the school system—were apprehensive in sending their daughters. Exposing the girl-child to foreign education and religion was an immense dilemma for parents because there was a great chance that young girls emerging from this educational system would reject their prearranged marriages, leaving their parents no option other then the repayment of their bride price, which the groom's family generally pays in advance.[21] A similar situation occurred in the Ghana (Gold Coast) in the 1930s when midwifery education was introduced by the colonial government. At first, they completely ignored girls as the target group for midwifery education, which could only be explained by their own gender notions and changes that were taking place in Europe at the time.

During this time frame in Europe, male physicians were wrestling obstetric care from women, adding to the fact that Europeans believed the proper place for women was the home. The colonizers transferred this background into the colonies, and it influenced how they administered their rule. It was only after Ghanaian women refused to receive care from male midwives and at a hospital environment that the colonial administration changed it tactics to target girls.[22] In the case of the Belgian Congo, the result of the parental apprehension and colonial insistence on religious conversation as part of their educational system was that at the time of Congo's independence in 1960, the country had produced only one female—Sophie Kanza, daughter of the mayor of Leopoldville—high school graduate. Obviously, the position of Kanza's father in the colonial administration may have played an important role in her getting education beyond the primary and elementary levels, and it can be assumed that the country would have entered a new dawn of political sovereignty with no female high school graduate.

The Catholic missionaries who were in charge of the largest portion of education in the Belgian Congo came from a background where the education of women was not a priority, and there was no reason for them to feign interest in the education of girls in the colony. The argument has been made that the ideology of the missionaries was based on gender differences, male superiority, and the superiority of the white race. Few girls received education provided by nuns, but it was geared toward developing in girls the "qualities of docility and of sweetness"[23] and the ability to manage the home. Girls were instructed in how to become good mothers, good wives, and how to instill Christian morality and values crucial to their roles as wives and mothers. At best, girls could train to become house servants to European families, learn to make Belgian-style household products such as cheese, butter, pottery, and mates as well as the basics of European-style washing, cooking, and sewing.

For boys, the missionaries aimed to create religious assistants such as priests, pastors, and altar boys, as well as give them training in areas that would be useful to the colonial project. They learned European farming techniques and practices, woodworking, ironworking, and bricklaying and were expected to become colonial agents, craftsmen, and instructors in the colonial schools. Boys could also learn French, a useful asset for those who wanted to work in the colonial administration. Missionary education in the

Belgian Congo was thus differentiated based on sex. The Protestant missionaries, who were in the minority, educated both girls and boys together but gave them different forms of training. The Catholic missionaries, on their part, differentiated as well as segregated education for boys and girls. Girls received lessons in religion in girls' schools, and reading, writing, and geography were reserved for boys because these subjects "were considered hazardous to girls' mental health and likely to distract them from their domestic duties."[24]

The result of these measures was that educational inequity began to develop between girls and boys; and by 1906, girls accounted for only 15 percent of the 48,000 schoolchildren in the country. The gap continued to widen and by 1958, there were only 20,000 girls out of the 1.5 million schoolchildren at the primary level. And at the time of the Congo's independence in 1960, the numbers for girls had barely increased. The result was that the majority of Congolese women could not speak French—a basic requirement to function in the new social and economic structure. And after 80 years of imperial education, women accounted for only a few positions in the nursing and teaching professions and even fewer in many other sectors. With very slight variations, the educational history in the Belgian Congo was not any different from those that occurred in other places in colonized Africa. Everywhere, girls were ignored and where they were allowed as much educational access as boys, at least in the case of South Africa, their training was generally retrogressive and geared toward domesticity, which ultimately reduced their public roles and set the stage for women's high illiteracy levels in the postcolonial era.

The case of South Africa was more complex for girls because though in numerical terms, a lot more girls attended school at the primary level than did boys, they still had to contend with racial inequality. The numerical advantage girls had at the primary level, it has been argued, was primarily because the pastoral societies of South Africa depended on young boys for herding and hence reduced the number of boys parents were willing to allow to attend school. In addition, some missionaries felt girls were more amenable to the values and tenets of Christianity. They focused their educational efforts on girls rather than on boys. This is not to say that the missionaries in South Africa thought of women any better. They considered women inferior human beings needing constant guidance and only good for domestic responsibilities. Yet, the missionary focus on girls appeared to put them in a privileged position; however, it was only "a numerical illusion."

In reality, the numerical advantage girls had over boys did not extend beyond the primary school level. At the secondary and tertiary levels, girls were no longer a factor. Educational inequality existed for both black and white girls but was more pronounced among blacks. For whites, only

1 girl as compared with 2 boys received a bachelor's degree, 1 out of 5 got a master's, and only 1 in 10 got a doctorate. For blacks, the majority only reached halfway through their secondary education, and only 1 girl as compared with 2 boys completed her education. At the university level, only 3 percent earned the right to attend, which is not to say they actually did enroll.[25] In general, South Africa's educational policy did not mandate school attendance for Africans. Those who did not attend missionary boarding schools, where religion was additionally taught, received basic education in sewing and later advance training in "housewifery," which prepared them to be the wives of teachers and preachers in the emerging male African elite.[26] The resultant effect for black women was that by 1970, as many as 60 percent of women in rural areas and 23 percent of women in the cities had never received formal education. In other places such as in Freetown in Sierra Leone and on the Gold Coast, predominantly the children of the elite class were the ones who received education in the colonial era. Even here, the numbers were not terrific.

In many west and east African countries, very few girls had the opportunity to attend school; and when they did, the level of their educational attainment was restricted to the primary and secondary levels. A select few managed to obtain a bachelor's degree. One woman who was privileged enough to obtain a college degree was Oyinkan Morenike Abayomi of Nigeria, who received her degree in Britain in the 1920s. Following in the footsteps of other pioneering West African women, Abayomi began working to bring Nigerian women closer to the government by establishing the Nigerian Women's Party in 1944 (which collapsed as a result of stiff competition from the Abeokuta Women's Union and from other radical nationalist movements).[27] She also realized the importance of formal education in improving the conditions of women in the new socioeconomic order and thus focused on promoting the education of girls with the establishment of the Queen's College in 1927, which until the 1950s was the only secondary school in the country for girls.

In spite of zeal to improve the conditions of women, Abayomi could not escape the colonial views about the roles of women in society. As a result, Queen's College only provided girls with training in domestic duties including needlework, home management, and singing. And it was only upon the request of parents that mathematics and foreign language were offered, added to the fact that only girls from the elite class could afford to attend.[28] It appears that everywhere one looks, education during the colonial period was abysmal for girls and restricted women's active participation in the public sphere. Colonial governments left about the 94 percent of education in the hands of missionaries whose interest was on spreading Christianity and not on providing education to suit the economic needs of the African people. With the collapse of colonial rule beginning in the

Students line up for morning prayers at a school in Aba, Nigeria, 2001. (Courtesy of A. Olusegun Fayemi)

late 1950s, one would expect that a reversal of women's educational fortunes would occur, but that was not the outcome. Indeed, it was not until the late 1990s that many African countries, together with international and nongovernmental organizations, began to focus their attention on women's education in an effort to bridge the ever-widening educational gap between women and men and to engender more spaces for women's active participation in education.

FORMAL EDUCATION IN THE POSTCOLONIAL PERIOD

The end of colonial rule brought hopes and aspirations to the Africans. Indeed, many people could not be happier with the crumpling of the colonial political order that had stifled and in most cases eroded Africa's sociocultural, economic, religious, and political structures. With the emergence of sovereign African states, peoples' expectations and demands increased for the complete removal of all the remnants of colonialism, the rejection of all things foreign, the restoration of African sociocultural and political structures, as well as the eradication of diseases and poverty. Nationalism engendered not only political liberation but also the search for a platform that would allow Africans to develop and to compete on the international scene. The result was that by the 1960s, higher education had become a priority for many African governments. Many scholars had by then begun to link education to economic development.

To these scholars, education was an avenue for people to acquire skills, knowledge, expertise, and attitudinal change vital for socioeconomic and political development as well as the antecedent for national integration. Higher education was seen as the crucial step to creating a modern society by stimulating liberal political discourses and socialization, technological advancements, political integration, and economic and social cooperation. Some researchers have suggested that economic productivity increases when investments are made in higher education. As to exact returns, individuals and nations should expect from their educational investments, researchers do not agree, but they accept that educational capital is a vital part of any country's development process.[29] Frederick H. Harbison and Charles A. Myers have made the following argument:

> If a country is unable to develop its human resources, it cannot build anything else, whether it is a modern political system, a sense of national unity, or a prosperous economy. The building of modern nations depends upon the development of people and organization of human activity. Capital, natural resources, foreign aid, and international trade, of course, play important roles in economic growth, but none is more important than manpower.[30]

The United Nations Educational, Scientific and Cultural Organization (UNESCO) affirms the above view with their statement that higher education is traditionally where social and economic leaders and experts in all fields receive a significant part of their personal and professional training. Education, thus, has special responsibilities for ensuring that both women and men receive their skills and knowledge on an equal basis.[31] To a degree, the logic of the correlations between education and development made sense for in the early postcolonial era countries deemed as modernized had high levels of higher educational rates. With optimism and a will to change conditions on the continent, many African leaders accepted the logic of the reciprocity between education and development and began in the 1960s to focus their attention on strengthening their systems of formal education as the primary mode of attaining social and economic development and safeguarding their newly won political sovereignty. For instance, in 1961, during the Conference of Ministers of Education of Independent States in Africa in Addis Ababa, Ethiopia, the participants affirmed the importance of education in the development of the new African nations.

The ministers called for more resources to be allocated to education. Accordingly the Addis Ababa Conference was a watershed in the educational development on the continent. This was in the sense that for the first time, an international conference was held in Africa to discuss education for Africans, and by Africans, coupled with the fact that African leaders began to recognize that higher education was pivotal in the social, economic, and cultural transformation of African societies.[32] For African women, their access to education at the higher level was crucially important if they were to improve their statuses as individuals and work as equal partners in national decision making and in socioeconomic development for all. Stimulating economic and social growth through education may have been a laudable endeavor on the part of the new African governments if only they had been able to execute their educational policies to the fullest.

As the major financier of education and the largest employer of graduates, political instability and bad economic policies during the early postcolonial period crippled many governments. The result was that many governments neglected or substantially reduced investments into their educational systems not only at the higher level but also at the primary and secondary ones. For many Africans, especially women, who envisioned a change in their condition had their hopes dashed with the continuity of colonial policies, or they simply forgot about them with the lack of governments' will to act on the needs of people. Formal education as provided by African governments as well as postcolonial missionary education has not been able to meet the visions of the vast majority of African people, and the lack of educational opportunities for women continues to be a major problem in many countries. Different reasons have been given for women's lack of education and the high dropout and failure rate of girls in schools. Some of these reasons included parents channeling their few financial resources toward the education of their sons, rather than their daughters; and the failure of parents to provide school supplies for their daughters' education.

Furthermore, there is also the constant need for girls to help with childcare and other domestic responsibilities, the value parents place on their daughters to get into marriage at a young age, and the need for girls to spend longer periods learning traditional skills. Postcolonial governments' continuation of colonial educational policies also made many of the knowledge people acquired in schools redundant for the contemporary labor market. For example, Sierra Leone's continual focus on colonial subjects slanted too much to the classic liberal arts have resulted in little or no effective knowledge and skill development essential for economic development. That is, "neither the core curriculum, nor the electives made ample provision for instruction in a unified system of values—moral, civic, or patriotic—that were considered essential to a productive work force."[33]

Sierra Leone is not alone in the problem. Many researchers have equally suggested that across Africa, when women managed to reach higher levels of education, they typically clustered in disciplines that colonial educators delineated as the proper areas for women's education such as in domestic sciences, teaching, nursing, and in home economics. In the case of South Africa, it has been argued that women's lack of access to higher education, together with their overconcentration in "caretaker" careers, have been significant in their economic and social subordination.[34] Others see the major problem as emanating from the limited number of women in the mathematics and sciences. In other words, women will find it extremely difficult to achieve social, economic, and political equity without mathematical knowledge and skills.[35] Some have allocated some of the problem to the nature of education provided at the secondary school level, where girls are often either forced into subjects viewed as suitable for their mental capacity or discouraged from pursuing studies in the sciences.[36] While some women have managed to enter into the fields of medicine and law, their percentile representation in these fields has been under 20 percent for decades in many places on the continent.

By gendering areas appropriate for each sex and encouraging women to focus in these areas, Western education amplified the economic disparity between women and men. It limited women's exposure to the benefits attached to being educated in certain fields and restricted them to occupations that have few opportunities for improvement, have low pay, have high retrenchment risks, and are less prestigious than those held by educated males. In all fairness, some African governments upon gaining their independence did strive to improve the educational levels of girls and opportunities for women to pursue higher education. However, the need to conform to international economic trends and political instabilities made it particularly hard for these new governments to reconfigure their educational systems with different tools other than what colonialism had given them.

When Guinea attained its independence in 1958, Ahmed Sékou Touré focused a lot of his attention on increasing the educational rate of girls. By 1966, the proportion of girls in school had risen from one in four in 1959 to one in two. Although by the 1970s, education in the country had deteriorated, and the gains in girls' education had stalled; nonetheless, the country's adoption of local languages for primary education encouraged girls to stay in school, at least at the primary level. The overall figures for the rest of the continent during the late 1960s and the early 1980s were not very encouraging for girls. In Togo in 1980, boys had a 99 percent attendance rate at the primary level, while girls only had a 35 percent rate. Guinea Bissau had 83 percent for boys and 37 percent for girls. During this same period, about three-fourths of all African women were illiterate, and in some places, such as Congo, Tanzania, Lesotho, and Uganda, the figures were even higher.

Ghana and Nigeria were no exception. At the time of Ghana's independence, there were only about one-third of girls who had received primary school education, and the number hardly increased in the first few decades of postcolonial rule. In 1973, female students only accounted for 10 percent of the student population in Ghana's universities. As one of Nigeria's biggest cities in the 1960s, Kano had a population of about 1 million, yet in 1968, there were just about 50,000 children enrolled in primary schools of which only 27 percent were girls. In 1976, almost a decade later, the number of schoolchildren had tripled to 160,000; however, the enrollment of girls had dropped below 25 percent.[37] According 1969 United Nations data for primary education in Africa, girls, on average, constituted only 36 percent of the total enrollment. Their enrollment in secondary education was between 8 and 28 percent of the total student population in 25 African countries, and they represented between 1 and 10 percent at the university level in 1967.[38]

The above suggests a gloomy picture for girls' education during the early periods of decolonization, but in recent years, many African governments have come to realize the need to increase girls' education and to provide a more equitable environment for women to access economic opportunities based on their educational backgrounds. In other words, it is more politically advantageous for African governments to educate their female population—although a more educated population does not necessarily equate development—but donor countries and organizations are more likely to hold back financial aid from countries that refuse to educate half of their population. Thus, for the period between 1999 and 2008, the United Nations enrollment figures for children of school age indicates an increased by 18 percentage points in Africa, south of the Saharan. This increase, although not substantial enough, has come about as a result of new policies and measures some governments have put in place.

Some countries such as Burundi, Ghana, Kenya, Mozambique, Malawi, and Tanzania have abolished school fees at the primary level, and this has resulted in a surge in primary enrollment in these countries. In Tanzania, the enrollment rate at the primary level doubled to 99.6 percent in 2008 from the 1999 rates. Tanzanian's 99.6 percent increase in enrollment at the primary level was the result of the government embarking on an ambitious program of education reform, which included constructing 54,000 classrooms between 2002 and 2006 as well as hiring 18,000 additional teachers. In Malawi, the United Nations Population Fund (UNFPA) worked with some youth councils to repeal a law that allowed girls 16 years of age to get married and supported campaigns that kept girls in school. Malawi has also been providing free school supplies in an effort to promote girls' education in grades one to four. The World Food Program (WFP) has also been helping in some countries by providing meals to schoolchildren, which act as an incentive for parents to send their children, particularly the girl-child to school. Botswana's introduction and implementation of a readmission policy has helped to cut female dropout rates in half. Cameroon, for many decades, has been allocating one-fifth of its national budget to education in an effort to bring education closer to the people.[39]

The increase in enrollment, however, brought its own set of challenges regarding school infrastructure and teachers. To meet these challenges, Ghana, for example, recruited retired teachers as well as volunteers to satisfy the demand for teachers, especially in the rural areas.[40] In addition, Ghana launched in 2003 the Education Sector Strategic Plan under which the country aimed at a Gender Parity Index of one for all levels of education and training, even though the efforts toward promoting girls' education began in the 1990s. Under the Education Sector Strategic Plan, concrete measures were taken to ensure improvements in gender parity in enrollments. In some cases, both governmental and nongovernmental organizations provided direct financial assistance to parents for the education of girls. The government also established a ministry specifically responsible for promoting the education of girls and for ensuring that the educational disparity between girls and boys and between women and men is bridged.

Additional measures put into operation to improve girls' enrollment at the basic level included providing material support such as school uniforms, stationery, school bags, and food rations; district and national level scholarship program for girls; implementing gender differentiated capitation grants that provided higher levels of funding for female students; and ensuring that schools had separate sanitation facilities for female students. Others included encouraging the recruitment of female teachers to act as role models for girls; ensuring the security of the female students while in school; and sensitizing parents and communities on the importance of girls' education through the "Send Your Girl Child to School Campaign."[41] In Uganda, the government has been trying to address the educational disparity between girls and boys by introducing affirmative action policies, which sets the passing rate for girls below that of boys. Although many have argued that such policies reduce the quality of female graduates, some have suggested that the obstacles African women have had to deal with in formal education makes such affirmative actions necessary.[42]

The above efforts have started to show some results for African women in terms of the work opportunities, their contributions to society, and their status in their families and communities in general. The opportunity to access higher education has allowed some women to attain positions comparable to, or even better, than those most men hold. While some women in high governmental positions, especially those in political offices, face gender-based prejudices and differential treatment from the public and from their male colleagues, for most women in high positions, they do not encounter such injustices. In recent years, women's support associations and networks have taken matters into their own hands through mentorship programs, cooperation with one another, scholarship programs, and

Giggling schoolgirls make their way to school in Addas Ababa, Ethopia, 1997. (Courtesy of A. Olusegun Fayemi)

political agitation to improve women's access to education and their participation in the labor force. Some groups have begun to encourage female students to enter into fields such as the sciences and technology traditionally thought of as male-dominated domains.

Many of these associations have also been providing opportunities through conferences, seminars, and workshops for women who have experience in the science and technology fields to interact with girls and young women in the secondary and tertiary levels of education to encourage them to enter into mathematics, sciences, and technology fields. The mentorship programs allow younger women to benefit from the knowledge and experiences of women who have worked in these fields. For example, the Association of South African Women in Science and Engineering (SA WISE) is one of the few groups in Africa that provides mentoring services and support systems for women interested in pursuing careers in the sciences and engineering fields. As part of its mission statement, SA WISE has indicated that there is a critical shortage of people trained in the technological fields in Africa, evident by the scanty number of scientists and engineers on the continent.[43] In 1980, Africa had a combined number of

49 per 1 million population for both women and men involved in the sciences and engineering as compared to North America, which had 2,679 and Latin America, which had 251.

The organization points out that women's role in society is not only critical for development, but they are also the group with the greatest influence on the next generation by setting the standards for health and hygiene and by forming the majority of the agricultural labor force. Essentially, they envision women's education as a guarantee of the education of the next generation and women as the greatest resource a country could possibly have. Hence, when countries provide encouragement and opportunity for girls and women in the science and engineering fields, they are availing for themselves one of the most important resources for development. According to their constitution, full membership is open to all women who meet one or more of the following qualifications: women have worked or currently working in the science or engineering fields in South Africa; have a bachelor degree in technology; have a bachelor degree in science; have higher degrees in science and engineering; and have taught in the fields of science, biology, or mathematics in South Africa. Associate membership is open to undergraduate female students in science. Men who are in these fields are allowed membership if they wish to associate themselves with the objectives of the organization.

By bringing these various groups of women (and men) together, SA WISE hopes to raise the profile of women in these disciplines, highlight women's particular problems, lobby for women's career development, contribute to the development of science and engineering in South Africa, and provide leadership and role models for young people wishing to enter into these fields.[44] Another dimension to how women are helping to improve girls' education is through training to become teachers. Across the continent, women form the largest pool in the teaching field, and while some scholars have argued that women's overconcentration in this field is in itself a form of educational disparity, the critical roles women play in the teaching field cannot be emphasized enough. Many have come to realize that if more female teachers are employed into the teaching field, the learning environment could be "more girl-friendly and protective, and ones in which girls' perspectives are understood and their specific needs met."[45]

In particular, when it comes to providing education in refugee communities, female teachers could be a vital source of hope, example, encouragement, and protection for girls. Recognizing their roles, the International Rescue Committee (IRC) in 2002 opened an avenue for women in Guinea and Sierra Leone to play essential roles in the various refugee schools it supports in these countries. The program involves training female classroom assistants with the responsibility of safeguarding female students against sexual abuse and exploitation, to promote learning, and to help create a female-friendly environment in the schools for girls. As part of their responsibilities, the classroom assistants monitor the school attendance of girls; follow up on any absences by making home visits; help girls with their studies; support extracurricular health education; and social club activities for girls such as needlework, games, and sports. In addition, they independently maintain a logbook of students' grades, which on the one hand helps students stay on track and on the other hand, prevents teachers from exploiting girls for sex in exchange for higher grades.[46] Evidently, the presence of the classroom assistants in the schools has been an important step for girls already living in difficult circumstances to have an uninterrupted schooling schedule and to stay on track in their education.

In the period before Europeans imposed their imperial power on African societies, opportunities for women's education were plentiful. Women themselves played the essential role of transmitting the sociocultural, economic, religious, and political values necessary for the next generations to be productive members of society. Every society had its own forms of values and knowledge considered important to pass on as well as the specific structures through which such values and knowledge were transmitted. In some places, education passed on from one generation to the next through ordinary everyday activities; in others, there were elaborate structures in place for imparting knowledge; and yet still, some combined semistructured and structured systems to impart knowledge. Education during the precolonial period was also gendered, although not in terms of denying one sex access to a particular form of education because of their sex even when they needed that form of education. Rather, women had control and expertise over certain areas of knowledge while men also had their own sphere of influence. Educational opportunities and occupational roles for both women and men were in general comparable in many precolonial African societies.

With the formal introduction of colonial rule, education became a highly gendered realm with women at the worse end of the spectrum. Throughout the continent, women's education came to be characterized by low enrollment rates, lack of access to certain forms of knowledge, restriction to domestic training, and limited economic benefits. A combination of factors including colonial pejorative notions about African women, their prior gender notions about the role of women in society, African parents' reservations about exposing their daughters to foreigners, parents' expectation to marry off their daughters, and limited financial resources all accounted for women's low educational status. Furthermore, the capitalist market economy introduced by the colonial rulers accentuated the discrepancies in the income levels of women and men with the same level of education and led to both the differential treatment of women at the workplace and the subjugation of their work roles.

In contemporary times, the same sociocultural normative practices, gender ideologies, and economic factors of the colonial period, compounded by current political instabilities in many African nations continue to militate against African women's chances for successful educational pursuits. In some countries, education in general is in a deplorable state, and the rate of girls enrolled in school at all levels is abysmal. Fortunately, some countries since the 1960s have come to recognize that if Africa is to succeed in its race to catch up with the rest of the world in development, then women must have equal access to educational and job opportunities. These countries have been pushing to erase the parity between girls and boys in primary and secondary education and between women and men at the university level and in the labor force. In the end, if countries are to continue to improve the rates of women's education and women are to maintain the gains they have made over the years in education, then changes in how society perceives the value of women's education and their roles in society is necessary. When women's education is seen as valuable as that of men's, the need to push one sex forward over the other might, perhaps, cease to exist and African women will rightfully be able to participate in the various dimensions of Africa's development in the 21st century and beyond.

NOTES

1. Philomina E. Okeke, "Higher Education for Africa's Women: Prospects and Challenges," in Ali A. Abdi, Korbla P. Puplampu, and George J. Sefa Dei (eds.), *African Education and Globalization* (New York: Lexington Books, 2006), 80.

2. United Nations Educational, Scientific and Cultural Organization (UNESCO), "Educational Statistics," http://www.unesco.org/new/en/education/ (accessed on February 24, 2011).

3. Rowena Martineau, "Women and Education in South Africa: Factors Influencing Women's Educational Progress and their Entry into Traditionally Male-Dominated Fields," *Journal of Negro Education*, Vol. 66, No. 4, "Education in a New South Africa: The Crisis of Conflict, the Challenges of Change," Vol. 66 (1997): 383–395.

4. UNESCO Institute for Statistics, "Global Education Digest 2008: Comparing Education Statistics Across the World," http://www.uis.unesco.org/template/pdf/ged/2008/GED%202008_EN.pdf (accessed on February 25, 2011).

5. Lioba Moshi, "Foreword," in Marianne Bloch, Josephine A. Beoku-Betts, and B. Robert Tabachnick (eds.), *Women and Education in Sub-Saharan Africa* (Boulder, CO: Lynne Rienne Publishers, 1998), xi.

6. Ibid.

7. Karen Hyde, *Improving Women's Education in Sub-Saharan Africa: A Review of the Literature*, PHREE Background Paper Series (Washington, DC: World Bank Education and Employment Division, Population and Human Resources Department, 1989).

8. Bolanle Awe made this argument in her presentation at the University of Wisconsin–Madison Symposium on African Women and Education organized in 1988. Her discussion was cited in Lynda R. Day, "Rites and Reason: Pre-colonial Education and its Relevance to the Current Production and Transmission of Knowl-

edge," in Marianne Bloch, Josephine A. Beoku-Betts, and B. Robert Tabachnick (eds.), *Women and Education in Sub-Saharan Africa* (Boulder, CO: Lynne Rienne Publishers, 1998), 51.

9. Niara Sudarkasa, "Sex Roles, Education, and Development in Africa," *Anthropology and Education Quarterly,* Vol. 13, No. 3, "African Education and Social Stratification" (1982): 279–289.

10. Herbert Moore Phillips, *Basic Education: A World Challenge: Measures and Innovations for Children and Youth in Developing Countries* (New York: John Wiley & Sons, 1975), 24.

11. Benjamin G. Dennis, *The Gbandes, A People of the Liberian Hinterlands* (Chicago, IL: Nelson-Hall Co., 1972), 127–128.

12. Day, 49–69.

13. For a detailed discussion of reproductive instructions that officials of the Bundu society provide to girls, see Carol P. MacCormack (ed.), *The Ethnography of Fertility and Birth* (London: Academic Press, 1981).

14. MacCormack, "Biological Events and Cultural Control," *Signs: Journal of Women in Culture and Society,* Vol. 3, No. 1, "Women and National Development: The Complexities of Change" (1977): 93–100.

15. Caroline H. Bledsoe, *Women and Marriage in Kpelle Society* (Stanford, CT: Stanford University Press, 1980), 73–75.

16. Day, 49–69.

17. Ibid.

18. Clarice S. Davies, A. Gyorgy, and C. Kayser (eds.), *Women of Sierra Leone: Traditional Voices: Women in Traditional Vocations* (Freetown, Sierra Leone: Partners in Adult Education Women's Commission, 1992), 95.

19. MacCormack, "Health, Fertility, and Birth in Moyamba District, Sierra Leone," in MacCormack (ed.), *The Ethnography of Fertility and Birth* (London: Academic Press, 1981), 105–109.

20. Jomo Kenyatta, *Facing Mount Kenya* (New York: Vintage Books, 1938).

21. Catherine Coquery-Vidrovitch, *African Women: A Modern History*, trans. Beth Gillian Raps (Boulder, CO: Westview Press, 1997), 143.

22. Stephen K. Addae, *The Evolution of Modern Medicine in a Developing Country: Ghana, 1880–1960* (Durham, NC: Durham Academic Press, 1997).

23. Coquery-Vidrovitch, 143.

24. Ibid.

25. Ibid.

26. Martineau, 383–395.

27. Jane L. Parpart, "Women and the State in Africa," A Working Paper, http://pdf.usaid.gov/pdf_docs/PNAAX586.pdf (accessed on February 20, 2011).

28. Cheryl Johnson, "Grass Roots Organizing: Women in Anticolonial Activity in Southwestern Nigeria," *African Studies Review,* Vol. 25, No. 2/3 (1982): 137–157.

29. Theodore W. Schultz, *The Economic Value of Education* (New York: Columbia University Press, 1963); Schultz, "Capital Formation by Education," *Journal of Political Economy,* Vol. 67 (1960): 571–583; Edward F. Renshaw, "Estimating the Returns to Education," *Review of Economics and Statistics,* Vol. 42 (1960): 318–324.

30. Fredrick H. Harbison and Charles Andrew Myers, *Education, Manpower and Economic Growth* (New York: McGraw-Hill, 1964), V, 6.

31. UNESCO, *Thematic Debate: Women and Higher Education, Issues and Perspectives* (Paris: UNESCO Secretariat, 1998), 5.

32. Kingsley Banya and Juliet Elu, "The World Bank and Financing Higher Education in Sub-Saharan Africa," *Higher Education*, Vol. 42, No. 1 (2001): 1–34.

33. Fransis S. Nicol, "The Secondary School Curriculum and its Relevance to the Manpower Needs of Sierra Leone," (PhD diss., University of Maryland, 1991), 204.

34. Nicola Swainson, "Tertiary Education and Training Needs for Post-Apartheid South Africa," in Commonwealth Fund for Technical Cooperation (ed.), *Human Resources Development for a Post-Apartheid South Africa* (London: Commonwealth Secretariat, 1993).

35. Elizabeth Fennema, "Girls, Women, and Mathematics," in Fennema and Jane Ayer (eds.), *Women and Education: Equity or Equality* (Berkeley, CA: McCutchan, 1984), 137–164.

36. Jeniffer A. Thomson, "Women in Science," in Margaret Lessing (ed.), *South African Women Today* (Cape Town, South Africa: Maskew Millar Longman, 1994).

37. Ibid.

38. Elsie Boulding, *Handbook of International Data on Women* (New York: Sage Publications, 1976).

39. Dorothy L. Njeuma, "An Overview of Women's Education in Africa," in Jill Ker Conway and Susan C. Bourque (eds.), *The Politics of Women's Education: Perspectives from Asia, Africa, and Latin America* (Ann Arbor: The University of Michigan Press, 2000), 124.

40. United Nations, UN MDG Database, "The Millennium Development Goals Report 2010," www.mdgs.un.org (accessed on February 22, 2011).

41. United Nations Economic and Social Council, "Education Sector Strategic Plan (ESSP) Ghana, 2007," *ECOSOC Annual Ministerial Review*, 2007.

42. Rowena Martineau, "Women and Education in South Africa: Factors Influencing Women's Educational Progress and their Entry into Traditionally Male-Dominated Fields," *Journal of Negro Education*, Vol. 66, No. 4; "Education in a New South Africa: The Crises of Conflict, the Challenges of Change" (1997): 383–395.

43. South Africa Women in Science and Engineering (SA WISE), "SA WISE Constitution," http://web.uct.ac.za/org/sawise/about/constitution.html (accessed February 24, 2011).

44. Ibid.

45. Jackie Kirk and Rebecca Winthrop, "Female Classroom Assistants: Agents of Change in Refugee Classroom in West Africa?" in Mary Ann Maslak (ed.), *The Structure and Agency of Women's Education* (New York: State University of New York Press, 2008), 161–164.

46. Ibid.

SUGGESTED READING

Abdi, Ali A., Korbla P. Puplampu, and George J. Sefa Dei. *African Education and Globalization: Critical Perspectives.* New York: Lexington Books, 2006.

Bloch, Marianne, Josephine A. Beoku-Betts, and B. Robert Tabbachnick. *Women and Education in Sub-Saharan Africa: Power, Opportunities, and Constraints.* Boulder, CO: Lynne Rienner Publishers, 1998.

Forum for African Women Educationalists (FAWE). *Female Participation in African Universities: Issues of Concern and Possible Action.* Nairobi, Africa: FAWE, 2001.

Kwapong, Alexander A. and Barry Lesser (eds.). *Capacity Building and Human Resource Development in Africa.* Halifax, Nova Scotia: Lester Pearson Institute for International Development, 1989.

Mashak, Mary Ann (ed.). *The Structure and Agency of Women's Education.* New York: State University of New York Press, 2008.

Glossary

Akpeteshie: A distilled local gin in Ghana made from the juice of the palm tree. It is a very popular drink and has a number of nicknames including "kill me quick," "apio," "agbaa," and "ogbogblo," all indicating its power to intoxicate a person at a very fast rate.

Asaase Yaa: The Akan name for the earth goddess. She is the mother-goddess of the Akan people and responsible for the fertility of the land and the fertility of the people.

Asantehene: The title of the king of the Asante people of Ghana.

Ayeba: The second of the four manifestations of a female supreme deity among the Uzo people of Nigeria. She is also believed to be a creator god and referred to as the founder of the universe.

Bilateral: A kinship system that emphasizes neither the female line of descent nor the male line of descent. They are both given equal recognition. This kinship system is not very widespread on the African continent. It can be found in societies such as the Afikpo of eastern Nigeria and the Birifor of the Ghana-Ivory Coast border.

Bondo: A women's initiation society found among some groups in Liberia and Sierra Leone.

Bori Cult: A pre-Islamic spirit cult found in Hausa societies in East and West Africa and popular among Muslim women.

Boubous: A flowing garment worn by both women and men in many African countries.

Bragro: Literally means "celebrating menstruation." It is a puberty rite performed among the Akan of southern Ghana to celebrate the menstruation of a girl. It involves various activities including secluding the girl for a number of days to teach her womanhood and motherhood skills and preparing her for a public celebration during which time potential suitors will have the opportunity to examine her beauty and her childbearing capabilities.

Bundu: A system of collective solidarity among the Mende women of the Sierra Leonean hinterlands.

Clitoridectomy: The removal of the clitoris, and it is practiced in a number of African societies. It is also commonly referred to as female genital mutilation and female circumcision.

Conjugal: A family system based on sexual relations. In conjugal families, marriage serves as the key element that ties the family unit together. Because marriage holds the family together, any breakage in the marriage turns to break up the family structure. Even when the marriage remains intact, the family may still disintegrate when older children leave to establish their own families and households without strings of generational ties with one another.

Consanguineal: In consanguineal family structure, the group's relationship is based on their descent from a common ancestor. Therefore, it tends to endures across generations since individuals marrying in and their children maintain collective kin ties regardless of the existence of marriage. Consanguineal family system is widespread in many African societies.

Dipo: A puberty rite performed among the Krobo people of the Ga-Adangbe group of southern Ghana. It celebrates a girl's ability to avoid premarital sex after she comes of age and ushers her into womanhood. The celebration is normally done for a group of girls of the same age group. During the public celebration, boys of marriageable age get the chance to select their future wives from among the girls.

Ekpo Society: An exclusive male secret society among the Ibibio of southeastern Nigeria. This society is believed to have been started by women, which men later took over.

Ekwe: A title used to refer to wealthy Igbo (Nigeria) women.

Fufu: A local food in Ghana made from pounded yam or cassava mixed with cocoyam or plantain. It is very popular, particularly among the Akan people.

Igba ohu: A system of woman-to-woman marriage, which allows wealthy Igbo women (Ekwes) to take other women as their wives. The system requires the Ekwes to be completely responsible for the upkeep and the well-being of the women wives. In return, the women wives bear the children of the Ekwes and help them in their businesses.

Impango: A poem/praise song performed by women among the Tonga of Zambia. It requires skills even when the genres used for the song is universally known.

Indlovukati: The name given to the king's mother among the Swazi of southern Africa.

Jom-na'i: A title used by the Bororo Fulani people of Cameroon to refer to Bororo men who own substantial amounts of cattle. It means "master of the herd." It is not common to find Bororo women bearing this title.

Kirai: A praise epithet or nickname that Hausa women of northern Nigeria give to a person as a form of praise.

Lineage: A lineage was thus born consisting of individuals who recognized themselves as kin based on descent from a known common ancestor.

Lu: A traditional practice among the Kom people of Cameroon in which women would use public displays and demonstrating to shame social offenders into repentance. Kom women used it as part of their tactics to seize political power from men during the *Anlu* Rebellion of 1958–1961.

Mafo: The name given to the chief's mother among the Fon of the Republic of Benin and southwest Nigeria.

Malaya: A Usumbura (now called Bujumbura, Burundi) word referring to women prostitutes.

Marabout: A Muslim religious scholar or teacher.

Maroka: Hausa women and men singers or eulogists.

Matrilineal: In matrilineal societies, people trace their kinship ties through women. In these societies, descent is believed to have originated from a common ancestress. Children born into matrilineal societies belong to the mother's family, and inheritance is through the line of women.

Matrilocal: A residential arrangement that allows married women to maintain their residence with their maternal families. In this arrangement, a husband may live with his family, or he may live alone. He may go to his wife's residence to sleep and to eat, or his wife may come to sleep at his residence and bring him food.

Mawu-Lisa: A supreme deity among the Ewe people of the Republic of Benin. It is personified as both female and male. Mawu is the female part of the two personifications identified with the moon. She is believed to be a creator god, a mother, gentle and forgiving, and the eldest of the two. Lisa is the male part and identified with the sun. He is believed to possess all the opposite qualities of Mawu.

Molimo: An important festival among the Mbuti pygmies. It is believed women once controlled this festival.

Mukama: Means king among the Kitara people of Uganda.

Nana Buku: The female god among the people of Togo and central Benin. She is believed to be a creator god.

Ndahura: A female spirit among the Kitara of Uganda who manifests her powers through female mediums.

Nyabingi: A female deity in Kitara society (Uganda).

Obaa Hemaa/Ohemaa: The name given to queen mothers among the Akan of southern Ghana.

Obaa Payin: An Akua phrase used to refer to an elderly woman. Obaa means "woman," and payin means "older person."

Obi: The title of the king among the Igbo people of Nigeria.

Oginarau: The last of the four manifestations of a female supreme deity among the Uzo people of Nigeria. She is associated with the heavens and referred to as the one who dwells in the heavens.

Olokun: The Bini god of the sea. He and his pantheon of river deities are the most widely worshiped in Benin in West Africa.

Omu: An office that allowed a woman, acting as the official mother of the society, to control the affairs of women among the Igbo people of Nigeria. The woman occupying this office was also called Omu, and her political role was comparable to that of the Obi (king) in the governance of the people. During the period of colonial rule in Nigeria, the colonial government gradually abolished this office.

Oriki: Praise poetry Yoruba women use to honor a person.

Oyankopong: The Akan name for the supreme being.

Patrilineal: In patrilineal societies, people trace their kinship ties and descent through the male line. Children born into patrilineal societies belong to the father's family, and inheritance is through the male line.

Patrilocal: A residential arrangement in which a woman resides with her husband and his family and usually remains with them after the death of her husband. She may choose to marry another member of her late husband's family or just remain with them and her children.

Pepo: A pre-Islamic spirit cult found among the Swahili people of East Africa.

Polygyny: A system that allows a man to have more than one wife at a time. It is practiced widely across Africa, south of the Sahara.

Poro: A women's secret society found among the Senufo of Côte d'Ivoire.

Pressure-engraving: In pressure-engraving, the artist applies force or pressure instead of fire and heat to make imprints and decorations on the surface of an object.

Purdah: The seclusion and the veiling of Muslim women. It is practiced in many Islamic societies across the African continent.

Pyro-engraving: An artistic technique in which the artist uses fire or heat to make incised or raised patterns, characters, lines, and the like on the surface of an object.

Roko: Praise song practiced by both women and men among the Hausa of northern Nigeria.

Sande: A women's initiation society found among some groups in Liberia and Sierra Leone.

Sandobele: Among the Senufo of Côte d'Ivoire, female diviners are referred to as Sandobele.

Sandogo: A women's secret society found among the Senufo peoples of Sierra Leone.

Shaikh: An Islamic scholar.

Tariqas: Islamic brotherhoods. Muslim women have been noted to play significant roles within these organizations. These groups are generally organized around charismatic leaders, and they place great emphasis on mysticism and emotional elements of religion.

Temearu: The first of the four manifestations of a female supreme deity among the Uzo people of Nigeria. She is believed to be responsible for creation or for the making of all the peoples of the earth. She is referred to as a creator god.

Ucu: A string of white beads a Zulu girl gives to the man she has decided to marry. It forms part of the ukuqoma ceremony.

Ukwemula: A puberty rite performed among the Zulu people of South Africa to initiate a young girl of a marriageable age into womanhood.

Ukuqoma: Refers to a ceremony a Zulu girl goes through to choose officially her marriage partner. It involves the girl raising a white flag in the compound of her would-be husband and giving him a string of white beads.

Umakhweyana: A Zulu bow instrument that unmarried women use to communicate their feelings of love and longings for their future husbands.

Umbongo: A ceremony a Zulu boy holds to demonstrate his willingness to marry the girl who has chosen him during the ukuqoma ceremony. He uses the occasion to officially express his appreciation to the girl for selecting him.

Wa'karyabo: Praise song Hausa women of northern Nigeria use to praise a person, usually a person with a royal background.

Woyingi or Oyin: The third of the four manifestations of a female supreme deity among the Uzo people of Nigeria. She is believed to have given birth to all the people of the earth and referred to as our mother.

Zar Cult: A pre-Islamic spirit cult found in Muslim communities in Sudan and mostly patronized by Muslim women.

Zitengulo: Elegiac poetry. The zitengulo is a sad mourning song Tonga women of Zambia compose and perform as solos when death occurs in the family. It is a simple short composition done exclusively for a particular person. The women composing it base their songs on the life's work of the deceased, and the women work alone in coming up with the lyrics and melody to complete the song.

Bibliography

Abu, Katherine. "The Separateness of Spouses: Conjugal Resources in Ashanti Town." In Christine Oppong (ed.), *Female and Male in West Africa*. London: George Allen and Unwin, 1983.

Addae, Stephen K. *The Evolution of Modern Medicine in a Developing Country: Ghana, 1880–1960*. Durham, NC: Durham Academic Press, 1997.

Aidoo, Agnes A. "The Asante Queen Mother in Government and Politics in the Nineteenth Century." In Filomina Chioma Steady (ed.), *The Black Women Cross-Culturally*. Rochester, VT: Schenkman Books, 1985.

Amadiume, Ifi. *Male Daughters, Female Husbands: Gender and Sex in an African Society*. Atlantic Highlands, NJ: Zed Books, 1987.

Amadiume, Ifi. *Reinventing Africa: Matriarchy, Religion, and Culture*. London: Zed Books, 2001.

Ames, David W. "Igbo and Hausa Musicians: A Comparative Examination." *Ethnomusicology*. Vol. 17 (1973): 250–278.

Arhin, Kwame. "The Political and Military Roles of Akan Women." In Christine Oppong (ed.), *Female and Male in West Africa*. London: George Allen and Unwin, 1983.

Armstrong, Alice. *Women and Rape in Zimbabwe*. Roma, Lesotho: Institute of Southern African Studies, National University of Lesotho, 1990.

Aronson, Lisa. "African Women in the Visual Arts." *Signs, Journal of Women in Culture and Society*. Vol. 16 (1991): 550–574.

Aronson, Lisa. "Women in the Arts." In Margaret Jean Hay and Sharon Stichter (eds.), *African Women South of the Sahara*. New York: Longman Group, 1992.

Banya, Kingsley and Juliet Elu. "The World Bank and Financing Higher Education in Sub-Saharan Africa." *Higher Education*. Vol. 42 (2001): 1–34.

Barnes, Sandra T. "Gender and the Politics of Support and Protection in Pre-colonial West Africa." In Flora Edouwaye Kaplan (ed.), *Queens, Queen Mothers, Priest-*

esses, and Power: Case Studies in African Gender. New York: New York Academy of Sciences, 1997.

Bay, Edna G. "Servitude and Worldly Succession in the Palace of Dahomey." In Claire C. Robertson and Martin A. Klein (eds.), *Women and Slavery in Africa.* Madison, WI: Heinemann, 1997.

Beach, David N. "An Innocent Woman, Unjustly Accused? Charwe, Medium of the Nehanda Mhondoro Spirit, and the 1896–97 Central Shona Rising in Zimbabwe." *HA.* Vol. 25 (1998): 27–54.

Ben-Amos, Paula. "Artistic creativity in Benin Kingdom." *African Arts.* Vol. 19 (1986): 60–63, 83.

Berger, Iris and Francis White. *Women in Sub-Saharan Africa: Restoring Women to History.* Bloomington: Indiana University Press, 1999.

Bernard, Guy. *Ville Africaine: Famille Urbaine: Les Enseignants de Kinshasa.* Paris: Mouton, 1968.

Berns, Maria C. and Barbara Rubin Hudson. *The Essential Gourd: Art and History in Northeastern Nigeria.* Los Angeles: University of California, 1986.

Binford, Martha. "Julia: An East African Diviner." In Nancy A. Falk and Rita M. Gross (eds.), *Spoken Worlds: Women's Religious Lives in Non-Western Cultures.* San Francisco: Harper & Row Publisher, 1980.

Bledsoe, Caroline H. *Women and Marriage in Kpelle Society.* Stanford, CA: Stanford University Press, 1980.

Boone, Sylvia A. *Radiance from the Waters: Ideals of Feminine Beauty in Mende Art.* New Haven, CT: Yale University Press, 1986.

Bösch, P. *Les Banyamwazi: Peuple de l'Afrique Orientale.* Munster: Anthropos Bilbiothek, 1930.

Boserup, Ester. *Women's Role in Economic Development.* Oxford, UK: Earthscan, 1970.

Boulding, Elsie. *Handbook of International Data on Women.* New York: Sage Publications, 1976.

Bovin, M. "Muslim Women in the Periphery: the West African Sahel." In Bo Utas (ed.), *Women in Islamic Societies.* London: Scandinavian Institute of Asian Studies, 1983.

Boyd, Jean and Murray Last. "The Role of Women as Agents Religieux in Sokoto." *Canadian Journal of African Studies.* Vol. 19 (1985): 283–300.

Brooks, George E. Jr. "The Signares of Saint-Louis and Goree: Women Entrepreneurs in Eighteenth Century Senegal." In Nancy J. Hafkin and Edna G. Bay (eds.), *Women in Africa: Studies in Social and Economic Change.* Stanford, CA: Stanford University Press, 1976.

Bunger, Robert L. *Islamization among the Upper Pokomo.* Syracuse, NY: Program of Eastern African Studies, Syracuse University, 1973.

Burt, Eugene C. "Mural Painting in Western Kenya." *African Arts.* Vol. 16 (1983): 60–63.

Buxton, Jean. "The Significance of Bride-wealth and the Levirate among the Nilotic and Nilo-Hamitic Tribes of the Southern Sudan." In Isaac Schapera (ed.), *Studies in Kinship and Marriage.* Dedicated to Brenda Z. Seligman on her 80th Birthday. London: Royal Anthropological Institute of Great Britain and Ireland, 1963.

Chappel, T.J.H. "The death of a cult in Northern Nigeria." *African Arts.* Vol. 6 (1973): 70–74.

Charumbira, Ruramisai. "Nehanda and Gender Victimhood in the Central Mashonaland 1896–97 Rebellions: Revisiting the Evidence." *History in Africa.* Vol. 35 (2008): 103–131.

Christy, Carol A. *Sex Differences in Political Participation: Processes of Change in Four-teen Nations.* New York: Praeger, 1987.

Collins, Robert O. *Documents from the African Past.* Princeton, NJ: Markus Wiener Publishers, 2001.

Colson, Elizabeth. "Family Change in Contemporary Africa." *Annals of New York Acad-emy of Sciences.* Vol. 96 (1962): 641–647.

Colson, Elizabeth. "Family Change in Contemporary Africa." In John Middleton (ed.), *Black Africa: Its Peoples and their Cultures Today.* London: The Macmillan Company, 1970.

Comaroff, Jean and John L. Comaroff. *On Revelation and Revolution: Christianity, Co-lonialism and Consciousness in South Africa.* Chicago, IL: University of Chicago Press, 1991.

Copet-Rougier, Elizabeth. "Etude de la Transformation du Marriage chez les Mkako du Cameroun." In David Parkin and David Nyamwaya (eds.), *Transformations of African Marriage.* Manchester, UK: Manchester University Press, 1987.

Coquery-Vidrovitch, Catherine. *African Women: A Modern History.* Translated by Beth Gillian Raps. Boulder, CO: Westview Press, 1997.

Coulon, Christian. "Women, Islam and Baraka." In Donal B. Cruise O'Brien and Chris-tian Coulon (eds.), *Charisma and Brotherhood in African Islam.* Oxford: Clar-endon, 1988.

Courtney-Clarke, Margaret. *African Canvas: The Arts of West African Women.* New York: Rizzoli, 1990.

Crabtree, David. "Women Liberation and The Church." In Sarah Betley Doely (ed.), *Women Liberation and The Church: The New Demand for Freedom in the Life of Christian Church.* New York: Association Press, 1970.

Darish, Patricia. "Dressing for the Next Life: Raffia Textile Production and Use among the Kuba of Zaire." In Annett B. Weiner and Jane Scheneider (eds.), *Cloth and Human Experience.* Washington, DC: Smithsonian Inst. Press, 1997.

Davies, Clarice S., A. Gyorgy, and C. Kayser (eds.). *Women of Sierra Leone: Traditional Voices: Women in Traditional Vocations.* Freetown: Partners in Adult Education Women's Commission, 1992.

Day, Lynda R. "Rites and Reason: Pre-colonial Education and its Relevance to the Cur-rent Production and Transmission of Knowledge." In Marianne Bloch, Josephine A. Beoku-Betts, and B. Robert Tabachnick (eds.), *Women and Education in Sub-Saharan Africa.* Boulder, CO: Lynne Rienner Publishers, 1998.

Dennis, Benjamin G. *The Gbandes, A People of the Liberian Hinterlands:* Chicago, IL: Nelson-Hall Co., 1972.

Denzer, LaRay. "Gender and Decolonization: A Study of Three Women in West African Public Life." In Andrea Cornwall (ed.), *Readings in Gender in Africa.* Blooming-ton: Indiana University Press, 2005.

Dewey, William. "Shona Male and Female Artistry." *African Arts.* Vol. 19 (1986): 64–67.

Dinan, Claudia. "Pragmatists or Feminists? The Professional Single Woman in Accra, Ghana." *Cahiers d'Etudes Africaines.* Vol. 65 (1977): 155–176.

Diop, Adja Khady. "The Work of Senegalese Women." In Esi Sutherland-Addy and Ami-nata Diaw (eds.), *Women Writing Africa: West Africa and the Sahel.* New York: The Feminist Press at the City University of New York, 2005.

Doke, Clement Martyn and Benedict Wallet Vilakazi. *Zulu-English Dictionary.* Witwa-tersrand, South Africa: Witwatersrand University Press, 1948.

Dolphyne, Abena Florence. *The Emancipation of Women: An African Perspective*. Accra: Ghana Universities Press, 1991.

Douglas, Mary. "The Lele of the Kasai." In Cyril Daryll Forde (ed.), *African Worlds: Studies in the Cosmological Ideas and Social Values of African Peoples*. Piscataway, NJ: Transaction Publishers, 1999.

Dupire, Marguerite. "The Position of Women in a Pastorial Society." In Denise Paulme (ed.), *Women of Tropical Africa*. Berkeley: University of California Press, 1971.

Eades, Jeremy S. *The Yoruba Today*. Cambridge: Cambridge University Press, 1980.

Elkan, Walter. *An African Labor Force: Two Case Studies in East African Factory Employment*. Uganda: East African Institute of Social Research, 1956.

Ethhel, Albert. "Women of Burundi: A Study of Social Values." In Paulme (ed.), *Women of Tropical Africa*. Berkeley: University of California Press, 1971.

Etienne, Mona. "Contradictions, Constraints, and Choice: Widow Remarriage among the Baule of Ivory Coast." In Betty Potash (ed.), *Widows in African Societies*. Stanford, CA: Stanford University Press, 1986.

Etienne, Mona. "Women and Men, Cloth and Colonization: The Transformation of Production-Distribution Relations among the Baule (Ivory Coast)." In Mona Etienne and Eleanor Burke Leacock (eds.), *Women and Colonization: Anthropological Perspectives*. New York: Praeger, 1980.

Evans-Pritchard, Edward. *The Position of Women in Primitive Societies and Other Essays in Social Anthropology*. London: Faber and Faber, 1965.

Falola, Toyin. "Gender, Business, and Space Control: Yoruba Market Women and Power." In Bessie House-Midamba and Felix K. Ekechi (eds.), *African Market Women and Economic Power: The Role of Women in African Development*. Westport, CT: Greenwood Press, 1995.

Faulkner, Mark R. J. *Overtly Muslim, Covertly Boni: Competing Calls of Religious Allegiance on the Kenyan Coast*. Boston: Brill, 2006.

Fennema, Elizabeth. "Girls, Women, and Mathematics." In Fennema and Jane Ayer (eds.), *Women and Education: Equity or Equality*. Berkeley, CA: McCutchan, 1984.

Ferguson, Anne and Kimberly Ludwig. "Zambian Women in Politics: An Assessment of Changes Resulting from the 1991 Political Transition." *MSU Working Papers on Political Reform in Africa*. East Lansing: Michigan State University, 1995.

Field, Margaret J. *Search of Security: An Ethno-psychiatric Study of Rural Ghana*. Evanston, IL: Northwestern University Press, 1962.

Finnegan, Ruth H. *Oral Literature in Africa*. Oxford: The Oxford Library of African Literature, 1970.

Foster, Anne. "Development and Women's Political Leadership: The Missing Link in Sub-Saharan Africa." *Flecher Forum of World Affairs*. Vol. 17 (1993): 101–116.

Friedman, Stewart D. and Jeffrey Greenhaus. *Work and Family—Allies or Enemies? What Happens When Business Professionals Confront Life Choices*. New York: Oxford University Press, 2000.

Geary, Christraud. "Basketry in the Aghem-Fungom Area of the Cameroon Grassfields." *African Arts*. Vol. 20, No. 3 (1987): 42–53, 89–90.

Geisler, Gisela. *Women and the Remaking of Politics in Southern Africa: Negotiating Autonomy, Incorporation and Representation*. Uppsala, Sweden: Nordiska Africkainstitutet, 2004.

General Book LLC. *African Women in Politics: Simone Gbagbo, Djoueria Abdallah*. Memphis, TN: General Books, 2010.

Gessain, Monique. "Coniagui Women." In Paulme, (ed.), *Women of Tropical Africa*. Berkeley: University of California Press, 1971.

Glaze, Anita. "Dialectics of Gender: Senufo Masquerades." *African Arts*. Vol. 19 (1986): 37.

Glaze, Anita. "Woman Power and Art in a Senufo Village." *African Arts*. Vol. 8 (1975): 24–65.

Goetz, Anne Marie and Shireen Hassim. *No Shortcuts to Power: African Women in Politics and Policy Making*. New York: Zed Books, 2003.

Goody, Jack. "The Classification of Double Descent Systems." *Current Anthropology*. Vol. 2 (1961): 3–25.

Griaule, Marcel. *Jeux Dogons* (Dogon Games). Paris: Université. Institut d'ethnologie, 1938.

Guyer, Jane. "Beti Widow Inheritance and Marriage Law: A Social History." In Potash (ed.), *Widows in African Societies*. Stanford, CA: Stanford University Press, 1986.

Guyer, Jane. "Female Farming in Anthropology and African History." In Micaela di Leonardo (ed.), *Gender at the Crossroads of Knowledge: Feminist Anthropology in the Postmodern Era*. Berkeley and Los Angeles: University of California Press, 1991.

Guyer, Jane. "Women in the Rural Economy: Contemporary Variations." In Hay and Stichter (eds.), *African Women South of the Sahara*. New York: Longman Group Limited, 1995.

Hackett, Rosalind I. J. *Religion in Calabar: The Religious Life and History of a Nigerian Town*. Berlin: Mouton de Gruyter, 1989.

Hackett, Rosalind I. J. "Women in African Religions." In Arvind Sharma (ed.), *Religion and Women*. New York: State University of New York Press, 1994.

Hafkin, Nancy J. and Edna G. Bay (eds.). *Women in Africa: Studies in Social and Economic Change*. Stanford, CA: Stanford University Press, 1976.

Halpern, Diane F. and Fanny M. Cheung. *Women at the Top: Powerful Leaders Tell Us how to Combine Work and Family*. Malden, MA: Wiley-Blackwell, 2008.

Hanson, Holly. "Queen Mothers and Good Government in Buganda." In Jean Allman, Susan Geiger, and Nakanyike Musisi (eds.), *Women in Colonial Histories*. Bloomington: Indiana University Press, 2002), 221.

Harbison, Fredrick H. and Charles Andrew Myers. *Education, Manpower and Economic Growth*. New York: McGraw-Hill, 1964.

Harrell-Bond, Barbara. *Study of Marriage among the Professional Groups in Sierra Leone*. Unpublished Report to the Department of Social Anthropology, Edinburgh University, 1971.

Hay, Jean Margaret and Sharon Stichter (eds.). *African Women South of the Sahara*. New York: Longman Scientific and Technical, 1995.

Hoch-Smith, Judith and Anita Spring (eds.). *Women in Ritual and Symbolic Roles*. New York: Plenum Press, 1978.

Hoffer, Carol. "Mende and Sherbro Women in High Offices." *Canadian Journal of African Studies*.Vol. 6 (1972): 151–164.

Hogben, Sidney John and Anthony H. M. Kirk-Greene. *The Emirates of Northern Nigeria: A Preliminary Survey of their Historical Traditions*. Oxford: Oxford University Press, 1966.

Holden, Pat (ed.). *Women's Religious Experience*. London: Croom Helm, 1983.

Hoogensen, Gunhild and Bruce Solheim. *Women in Power: World Leaders since 1960*. Westport, CT: Praeger Publishers, 2006.

Hunt, Rose Nancy. "Domesticity and Colonialism in Belgian Africa: Usumbura's *Foyer Social, 1946–1960.*" *Signs, Journal of Women in Culture and Society.* Vol. 15 (1990): 447–474.

Hunter, Monica. "Effects of Contact with Europeans on the Status of Pondo Women." *Africa.* Vol. 6 (1933): 259–76.

Hyde, Karen. *Improving Women's Education in Sub-Saharan Africa: A Review of the Literature,* PHREE Background Paper Series. Washington, DC: World Bank Education and Employment Division, Population and Human Resources Department, 1989.

Imam Ayesha M. "Engendering African Social Sciences: An Introductory Essay." In Ayesha Imam M., Amina Mama, and Fatou Sow (eds.), *Engendering African Social Sciences.* Dakar, Senegal: CODESRIA, 1997.

International Feminist Collective. *Sammen er vi stærke–før den alternative kvindekonference 1980.* Copenhagen, 1981.

Inter-Parliamentary Union. *Women in National Parliaments.* Geneva: Inter-Parliamentary Union, 1999.

Jankowiak, William and Edward Fischer. "A Cross-Cultural Perspective on Romantic Love." *Ethnology.* Vol. 31 (1992): 149–155.

Jobs and Skills Program for Africa (JASPA). *African Employment Report 1990.* Addis Ababa: International Labor Organization, 1991.

Johnson, Cheryl. "Grass Roots Organizing: Women in Anticolonial Activity in Southwestern Nigeria." *African Studies Review.* Vol. 25 (1982): 137–157.

Johnson, Cheryl. "Women and Gender in the History of Sub-Saharan Africa." In Bonnie G. Smith (ed.), *Women in Global Perspective.* Vol. 3. Urbana: University of Illinois Press, 2005.

Jones, A. M. "African Music in Northern Rhodesia and Some Other Places." In Bronislaw Stefaniszyn (ed.), *The Material Culture of the Ambo of Northern Rhodesia.* United Kingdom: Manchester University Press, 1974.

Joseph, Rosemary M. F. "Zulu Women's Bow Songs: Ruminations on Love." *Bulletin of the School of Oriental and African Studies.* Vol. 50 (1987): 90–119.

Jules-Rosette, Bennetta. *The Messages of Tourist Art: An African Semiotic System in Comparative Perspective.* New York: Plenum, 1984.

Jules-Rosette, Bennetta. *The New Religions of Africa.* Norwood, NJ: Ablex Publishing, 1979.

Jules-Rosette, Bennetta. "Privilege Without Power: Women in African Cults and Churches." In Rosalyn Terborg-Penn, Sharon Harley, and Andrea Benton Rushing. *Women in Africa and the African Diaspora.* Washington, DC: Haword University Press, 1987.

Kasomo, Daniel. "The Role of Women in the Church in Africa." *International Journal of Sociology and Anthropology.* Vol. 2 (2010): 126–139.

Kayongo-Male, Diane and Philista Onyango. *The Sociology of the African Family.* New York: Longman Group, 1984.

Kenyatta, Jomo. *Facing Mount Kenya.* New York: Vintage Books, 1938.

Kiernan, Jim P. "The 'Problem of Evil' in the Context of Ancestral Intervention in the Affairs of the Living." *Man.* New Series. Vol. 17 (1982): 194–195.

Kilson, Marion. "Ambivalence and Power: Mediums in Ga Traditional Religion." *Journal of Religion in Africa.* Vol. 4 (1972): 171–177.

Kilson, Marion. "Women in African Traditional Religion." *Journal of Religion in Africa.* Vol. 8 (1976): 138–139.

King, Ursula. *Religion and Gender*. Cambridge, MA: Blackwell, 1995.

Kinsman, Margaret. "'Beast of Burden': the Subordination of Southern Tswana Women, ca. 1800–1840." *Journal of Southern African Studies*. Vol. 10 (1983): 39–54.

Kirge, Eileen Jensen and Jacob Daniel Krige. *The Realm of a Rain Queen*. London: Oxford University Press, 1943.

Kirk, Jackie and Rebecca Winthrop. "Female Classroom Assistants: Agents of Change in Refugee Classroom in West Africa?" In Mary Ann Maslak (ed.), *The Structure and Agency of Women's Education*. New York: State University of New York Press, 2008.

Konde, Emmanuel. *African Women and Politics: Knowledge, Gender, and Power in Male Dominated Cameroon*. New York: Mellen, 2005.

Koopman, Jeanne. "Women in the Rural Economy: Past, Present, and Future." In Margaret Jean Hay and Sharon Stichter (eds.), *African Women South of the Sahara*. New York: Longman Group Limited, 1995.

Kopf, Jennifer. "Repression of Muslim Women's Movements in Colonial East Africa." In Karen M. Morin and Jeanne Kay Guelke (eds.), *Women, Religion, and Space*. New York: Syracuse University Press, 2007.

Kopytoff, Igor (ed.). *The African Frontier: the Reproduction of Traditional African Societies*. Bloomington: Indiana University Press, 1989.

LaDuke, Betty. *Africa: Women's Art, Women's Lives*. Trenton, NJ: Africa World Press, 1997.

Lan, David. *Guns and Rain: Guerillas and Spirit Mediums in Zimbabwe*. London: James Currey, 1985.

Landberg, Pamela. "Widows and Divorced Women in Swahili Society." In Betty Potash (ed.), *Widows in African Society*. Stanford, CA: Stanford University Press, 1986.

LaPin, Deirdre. "Women in African Literature." In Margaret Jean Hay and Sharon Stichter (eds.), *African Women South of the Sahara*. New York: Longman Group, 1995.

Lebeuf, Annie M. D. "The Role of Women in the Political Organization of African Societies." In Denise Paulme (ed.), *Women of Tropical Africa*. Berkeley and Los Angeles: University of California Press, 1963.

Levin, Ruth. *Marriage in Langa Location*. Cape Town: Cape Town University, 1947.

Lewis, Ian M. "Spirit Possession and Deprivation Cults." *Man*. New Series. Vol. 1 (1966): 307–329.

Linton, Ralph. *The Study of Man: An Introduction*. New York: Prentice Hall, 1936.

Little, Kenneth L. *African Women in Town: An Aspect of Africa's Social Revolution*. Cambridge: Cambridge University Press, 1973.

Little, Kenneth and Anne Price. "Some Trends in Modern Marriage among West Africans." In Colin M. Turnbull (ed.), *Africa and Change*. New York: Knopf, 1973.

Longmore, Laura. *The Dispossessed: A Study of the Sex-Life of Bantu Women in Urban Areas in and around Johannesburg*. London: Cape, 1959.

MacCormack, Carol P. "Biological Events and Cultural Control." *Signs, Journal of Women in Culture and Society*. Vol. 3, Women and National Development: The Complexities of Change (1977): 93–100.

MacCormack, Carol P. "Control of Land, Labor, and Capital in Rural Southern Sierra Leone." In Edna G. Bay (ed.), *Women and Work in Africa*. Boulder, CO: Westview Press, 1982.

MacCormack, Carol P. *The Ethnography of Fertility and Birth*. London: Academic Press, 1981.

MacCormack, Carol P. "Health, Fertility, and Birth in Moyamba District, Sierra Leone." In MacCormack (ed.), *The Ethnography of Fertility and Birth*. London: Academic Press, 1981.

MacCormack, Carol P. "Sande: The Public Face of a Secret Society." In Bennetta Jules-Rosette (ed.), *The New Religions of Africa: Priest and Priestess in Contemporary Cults and Churches*. Norwood, NJ: Ablex, 1978.

Mack, Beverly B. "Metaphor Is a Bridge to Ultimate Reality: Metaphor in Hausa Women's Poetry." *Research in African Literatures*. Vol. 37 (2006): 43–60.

Mair, Lucy. *African Marriage and Social Change*. London: Frank Cass & Co. Ltd., 1969.

Mair, Lucy. "Freedom of Consent in African Marriage." *The Anti-Slavery Reporter and Aborigines' Friend*. Vol. 11 (1958): 63–65.

Mandala, Elias. "Capitalism, Kinship, and Gender in Lower Tchiri (Shire) Valley of Malawi, 1860–1960: An Alternative Theoretical Framework." *African Economic History*. Vol. 13 (1984): 137–169.

Marks, Shula and Richard Rathbone. "The History of the Family in Africa: Introduction." *The Journal of African History*. Vol. 24 (1983): 145–161.

Marris, Peter. *Family and Social Change in an African City*. Evanston, IL: 1962.

Martineau, Rowena. "Women and Education in South Africa: Factors Influencing Women's Educational Progress and their Entry into Traditionally Male-Dominated Fields." *Journal of Negro Education*. Vol. 66, "Education in a New South Africa: The Crisis of Conflict, the Challenges of Change." (1997): 383–395.

Matland, Richard E. "Women's Representation in National Legislatures: Developed and Developing Countries." *Legislative Studies Quarterly*. Vol. 23 (1998): 109–125.

Matthews, Thomas. "Mural Painting in South Africa." *African Arts*. Vol. 10 (1977): 28–33.

Mbiti, John S. "Flowers in the Garden: the Role of Women in African Religion." In Jacob K. Olupona (ed.), *African Traditional Religions in Contemporary Society*. New York: Paragon House, 1991.

McCall, Daniel. "Trade and the Role of Wife in a Modern West African Town." In Aidan William Southall (eds.), *Social Change in Modern Africa: Studies Presented and Discussed*. United Kingdom: Oxford University Press, 1963.

McHardy, Cécile. "Love in Africa." *Présence Africaine*. Vol. 68 (1968): 52–60.

McLuskie, Kathleen and Lynn Innes. "Women and African Literature." *Wasafiri*. Vol. 8 (1988): 3–7.

Media Monitoring Project. "Biased? Gender, Politics, and the Media." In Commission for Gender Equality (ed.), *Redefining Politics: South African Women and Democracy*. Braamfontein, South Africa: Commission for Gender Equality, 1999.

Meyerowitz, Eva L. *The Akan of Ghana*. London: Faber and Faber, 1958.

Middleton-Keirn, Susan. "Convivial Sisterhood: Spirit Medium-ship and Client-Core Network among Black South African Women." In Hoch Smith and Spring (eds.), *Women in Ritual and Symbolic Roles*. New York: Plenum Press, 1978.

Migraine-George, Thérèse. *African Women and Representation: From Performance to Politics*. Trenton, NJ: Africa World Press, 2008.

Moshi, Lioba. "Foreword." In Marianne Bloch, Josephine A. Beoku-Betts, and B. Robert Tabachnick (eds.), *Women and Education in Sub-Saharan Africa*. Boulder, CO: Lynne Rienne Publishers, 1998.

Mukonyora, Isabel. *Wandering a Gendered Wilderness: Suffering and Healing in an African Initiated Church*. New York: Peter Lang Publishing, 2007.

Muller, Jean-Claude. "Where to Live? Widows' Choices among the Rukuba." In Potash (ed.), *Widows in African Society*. Stanford, CA: Stanford University Press, 1986.

Murray, Kenneth C. "Pottery of the Ibo of Ohuhu-Ngwa." *Nigerian Field*. Vol. 37 (1972): 148–175.

Nadel, Siegfried Frederick. *A Black Byzantium: The Kingdom of Nupe in Nigeria*. London: Oxford University Press, 1942.

Nadel, Siegfried Frederick. "Witchcraft in Four African Societies: A Comparison." *American Anthropologist*. Vol. 54 (1952): 18–29.

Ngubane, Harriet. "The Consequences for Women of Marriage Payments in a Society with Patrilineal Descent." In David Parkin and David Nyamwaya (eds.), *Transformation of African Marriage*. Manchester, UK: Manchester University Press, 1987.

Nhlapo, T. R. "The Africa Family and Women's Right: Friends or Foes?" *Acta Juridica*. Vol. 135 (1991): 135–146.

Nicol, Fransis S. "The Secondary School Curriculum and its Relevance to the Manpower Needs of Sierra Leone." PhD Dissertation, University of Maryland, 1991.

Njeuma, Dorothy L. "An Overview of Women's Education in Africa." In Jill Ker Conway and Susan C. Bourque (eds.), *The Politics of Women's Education: Perspectives from Asia, Africa, and Latin America*. Ann Arbor: The University of Michigan Press, 2000.

Nketia, Kwabena J. H. *Funeral Dirges of the Akan People*. New York: Negro University Press, 1969.

Nnaemeka, Obioma. "From Orality to Writing: African Women Writers and the (Re) Inscription of Womanhood." *Research in African Literature*. Vol. 25 (1994): 137–157.

Nwapa, Flora. *Efuru*. London: Heinemann, 1966.

Nzomo, Maria. "The Gender Dimension of Democratization in Kenya: Some International Linkages." *Alternatives*. Vol. 18 (1993): 61–73.

O'Barr, Jean and Kathryn Firmin-Sellers. "African Women in Politics." In Margaret Jean Hay and Sharon Stichter (eds.), *African Women South of the Sahara*. New York: Longman Group, 1995.

Obiechina, Emmanuel N. *An African Popular Literature: A Study of Onitsha Market Pamphlets*. Cambridge: Cambridge University Press, 1973.

Oboler, Regina Smith. *Women, Power, and Economic Change: The Nandi of Kenya*. Stanford, CA: Stanford University Press, 1985.

Okeke, Philomina E. "Higher Education for Africa's Women: Prospects and Challenges." In Ali A. Abdi, Korbla P. Puplampu, and George J. Sefa Dei (eds.), *African Education and Globalization*. New York: Lexington Books, 2006.

Okonjo, Kamene. "Women's Political Participation in Nigeria." In Oppong (ed.), *Female and Male in West Africa*. London: George Allen and Unwin, 1983.

Oppong, Christine. *Marriage among a Matrilineal Elite: A Study of Ghanaian Civil Servants*. Cambridge: Cambridge University Press, 2008.

Ottenberg, Phoebe V. "The Changing Economic Position of Women among the Afikpo Ibo." In William Russell Bascom and Melville Jean Herskovits (eds.), *Continuity and Change in African Cultures*. Chicago, IL: University of Chicago Press, 1959.

Papanek, Hanna. "Family Status Production: The 'Work' and 'Non-Work' of Women." *Signs, Journal of Women in Culture and Society*. Vol. 4 (1979): 775–781.

Parpart, Jane L. "Women and the State in Africa." A Working Paper, http://pdf.usaid.gov/pdf_docs/PNAAX586.pdf (accessed on February 20, 2011).

Parrinder, Edward Geoffrey. *West African Religion*. London: Epworth Press, 1961.

Paulme, Denise. *Women of Tropical Africa*. Berkeley: University of California Press, 1971.

Philips, Anne. *Engendering Democracy*. University Park: Pennsylvania State University Press, 1991.

Philips, Arthur (ed.). *Survey of African Marriage and Family Life*. New York: Oxford University Press, 1953.

Phillips, Herbert Moore. *Basic Education: A World Challenge: Measures and Innovations for Children and Youth in Developing Countries*. New York: John Wiley & Sons, 1975.

Potash, Betty. "Female Farmers, Mother-in-law and Extension Agents: Development Planning and a Rural Luo Community." *Working Papers on Women in International Development*. Vol. 90 (1985).

Potash, Betty. *Widows in African Societies: Choices and Constraints*. Stanford, CA: Stanford University Press, 1989.

Potash, Betty. "Women in the Changing African Family." In Margaret Jean Hay and Sharon Sticher (eds.), *African Women South of the Sahara*. New York: Longman Publishing, 1995.

Quarcoo, A. K. and M. Johnson. "The Pottery Industry of the Shai People of Southern Ghana." *Baessler-Arch*. Vol. 16 (1968): 47–88.

Quimby, Lucy. "Islam, Sex Roles, and Modernization in Bobo-Dioulasso." In Bennetta Jules-Rosette (ed.), *The New Religions of Africa: Priests and Priestesses in Contemporary Cults and Churches*. Norwood, NJ: Ablex, 1979.

Radcliffe-Brown, Alfred R. and Daryll Forde. *African Systems of Kinship and Marriage*. New York: Oxford University Press, 1950.

Rançon, Dr. A. *Dans la Haute-Gambie, Voyage d'exploration Scientifique 1891–1892*. Annales de l'Institut Colonial de Marseille, Soc. D'Editions Scientifiques, 1894.

Rangeley, W. "Notes on Cewa Tribal Law." *Nyasaland Journal*. Vol. I (1948): 47.

Renshaw, Edward F. "Estimating the Returns to Education." *Review of Economics and Statistics*. Vol. 42 (1960): 318–324.

Richards, Audrey I. "Bemba Marriage and Present Economic Conditions." *Rhodes-Livingstone Paper*. No. 4 (1940): 35.

Roberts, Penelope A. "The State and the Regulation of Marriage: Sefwi Wiawso (Ghana), 1900–1940." In Haleh Afshar (ed.), *Women, State and Ideology: Studies from Africa and Asia*. New York: State University of New York Press, 1987.

Rosaldo, Renato. "Imperialist Nostalgia." *Representations*. Special Issue: Memory and Counter-Memory (1989): 107–122.

Rosenfeld, Chris Prouty. *Empress Taytu and Menilek II: Ethiopia, 1883–1910*. Trenton, NJ: Red Sea Press, 1986.

Rubin, Barbara. "Calabash Decoration in North East State, Nigeria." *African Arts*. Vol. 4 (1970): 20–25.

Schildkrout, Enid. "Age and Gender in Hausa Societies: Socio-economic Roles of Children in Urban Kano." In Jean Sybil La Fontaine (ed.), *Sex and Age as Principles of Social Organization*. New York: Academic Press, 1978.

Schildkrout, Enid. "Dependence and Autonomy: The Economic Activities of Secluded Hausa Women in Kano, Nigeria." In Edna G. Bay (ed.), *Women and Work in Africa*. Boulder, CO: Westview Press, 1982.

Schultz, Theodore W. "Capital Formation by Education." *Journal of Political Economy*. Vol. 67 (1960).

Schultz, Theodore W. *The Economic Value of Education*. New York: Columbia University Press, 1963.

Schwartz, Nancy L. "World Without End: the Meanings and Movements in the History Narratives and 'Tongue-Speech' of Legio of African Church Mission among the Luo of Kenya." PhD Dissertations, Princeton University, 1989.

Shanklin, Eugenia. "*Anlu* Remembered: The Kom Women's Rebellion of 1958–1961." *Dialectical Anthropology*. Vol. 15 (1990): 159–181.

Shapera, Isaac. *Handbook of Tswana Law and Custom*. London: Oxford University Press, 1938.

Shaw, Rosalind. "Gender and the Structuring of Reality in Temne Divination: An Interactive Study." *Africa*. Vol. 55 (1985): 289.

Shostak, Marjorie. *Nisa: The Life and Words of a !Kung Woman*. Cambridge, MA: Harvard University Press, 1981.

Sifuniso, Monde. "Zambian Women in Parliament." In Mbuyu Nalumango and Monde Sifuniso (eds.), *Woman Power in Politics*. Lusaka, Zambia: Zambia Women Writers Association, 1998.

Simons, Harold J. *African Women: Their Legal Status in South Africa*. London: C. Hurst, 1968.

Smith, Daniel Jordan. "Romance, Parenthood, and Gender in a Modern African Society." *Ethnology*. Vol. 40 (2001): 129–151.

Smith, Edwin William (ed.), *African Ideas of God: A Symposium*. London: Edinburgh House Press, 1950.

Smith, Fred T. "Gurensi Basketry and Pottery," *African Arts*, Vol. 12 (1978): 78–81.

Smith, Fred T. "Gurensi Wall Decoration." *African Arts*. Vol. 11 (1978): 36–41.

Smith, M. G. "The Social Functions and Meaning of Hausa Praise-Singing." *Journal of the International African Institute*. Vol. 27 (1957): 26–45.

South Africa Women in Science and Engineering (SA WISE). "SA WISE Constitution." http://web.uct.ac.za/org/sawise/about/constitution.html (accessed February 24, 2011).

Spindel, Carol. "Kpeenbele Senufo Potters." *African Arts*. Vol. 22 (1989): 66–73.

Spring, Anita. "Epidemiology of Spirit Possession among the Luvale of Zambia." In Hoch-Smith and Spring (eds.), *Women in Ritual and Symbolic Roles*. New York: Plenum Press, 1978.

Staudt, Kathleen. "Class Stratification and its Implication for Women's Politics." In Claire Robertson and Iris Berger (eds.), *Women and Class in Africa*. New York: Africana Publishing, 1986.

Stewart, Charles C. and Elizabeth K. Stewart. *Islam and Social Order in Mauritania: A Case Study from the Nineteenth Century*. Oxford: Clarendon Press, 1973.

Stichter, Sharon B. "The Middle-Class Family in Kenya: Changes in Gender Relations." In Sharon B. Stichter and Jane L. Parpart (eds.), *Patriarchy and Class: African Women in the Home and the Workforce*. Boulder, CO: Westview Press, 1988.

Strobel, Margaret. *Muslim Women in Mombasa, 1890–1975*. New Haven, CT: Yale University Press, 1979.

Strobel, Margaret. "Women in Religious and Secular Ideology." In Margaret Jean Hay and Sharon Stichter (eds.), *African Women South of the Sahara*. New York: Longman Publishing, 1995.

Sudarkasa, Niara. "Sex Roles, Education, and Development in Africa." *Anthropology and Education Quarterly*. Vol. 13, African Education and Social Stratification (1982): 279–289.

Sudarkasa, Niara. "Women and Migration in Contemporary West Africa." In Wellesley Editorial Committee (ed.), *Women and National Development: the Complexities of Change.* Chicago, IL: University of Chicago Press, 1977.

Swainson, Nicola. "Tertiary Education and Training Needs for Post-Apartheid South Africa." In Commonwealth Fund for Technical Cooperation (ed.), *Human Resources Development for a Post-Apartheid South Africa.* London: Commonwealth Secretariat, 1993.

Thomson, Jeniffer A. "Women in Science." In Margaret Lessing (ed.), *South African Women Today.* Cape Town: Maskew Millar Longman, 1994.

Uchendu, Victor C. "Concubinage among the Ngwa Igbo of Southern Nigeria." *Africa.* Vol. 35 (1965): 187–197.

Ufomata, Titi. "Linguistic Images, Socialization, and Gender in Education." *Africa Development.* Vol. 23 (1998): 61–75.

United Nations. *World's Women: Trends and Statistics, 1970–1990.* New York: United Nations, 1991.

United Nations Development Program (UNDP). *Human Development Report.* New York: Oxford University Press, 2000.

United Nations Educational, Scientific and Cultural Organization (UNESCO). "Educational Statistics." http://www.unesco.org/new/en/education/ (accessed on February 24, 2011).

United Nations Educational, Scientific and Cultural Organization (UNESCO). "Education Sector Strategic Plan (ESSP) Ghana, 2007." *ECOSOC Annual Ministerial Review.*

United Nations Educational, Scientific and Cultural Organization (UNESCO). "Global Education Digest 2008: Comparing Education Statistics Across the World." http://www.uis.unesco.org/template/pdf/ged/2008/GED%202008_EN.pdf (accessed on February 25, 2011).

United Nations Educational, Scientific and Cultural Organization (UNESCO). *Thematic Debate: Women and Higher Education, Issues and Perspectives.* Paris: UNESCO Secretariat, 1998.

United Nations Educational, Scientific and Cultural Organization (UNESCO). UN MDG Database. "The Millennium Development Goals Report 2010." www.mdgs.un.org (accessed on February 22, 2011).

Vellenga, Dorothy D. *Tropical Africa.* Berkeley: University of California Press, 1963.

Vellenga, Dorothy D. "Who is a Wife? Legal Expressions of Heterosexual Conflict in Ghana." In Oppong (ed.), *Female and Male in West Africa.* London: George Allen and Unwin, 1983.

Vidal, Claudine. "Guerre des sexes à Abijan: Masculin, Feminin, CFA." *Cahiers d'Etudes Africaines.* Vol. 8 (1977): 121–153.

Wachege, P. N. *African Women's Liberation: A Man's Perspective.* Kenya: Kiambu, 1992.

Wagner, Günter. *The Bantu of North Kavirondo.* London: Oxford University Press, 1949.

Weinbaum, Batya. "The Other Side of the Paycheck." In Zillah R. Eisenstein (ed.), *Capitalist Patriarchy and the Case for Socialist Feminism.* New York: Monthly Review Press, 1979.

White, Frances E. "Women in West and West-Central Africa." In Iris Berger and E. Francis White (eds.), *Women in Sub-Saharan Africa: Restoring Women to History.* Bloomington: Indiana University Press, 1999.

Whyte, Susan Reynolds. "Men, Women and Misfortune in Bunyole." In Pat Holden (ed.), *Women's Religious Experience*. London: Croom Helm, 1983.

Willis, John Ralph (ed.). *Studies in West African Islamic History: The Cultivators of Islam*. London: Frank Cass, 1979.

Wilson, Peter J. "Status Ambiguity and Spirit Possession." *Man*. New Series. (1967): 67–78.

Wolff, Norma. "A Hausa Aluminum Spoon Industry." *African Arts*. Vol. 19 (1986): 40–44.

Zahan, Dominique. *The Religion, Spirituality, and Thought of Traditional Africa*. Chicago, IL: University of Chicago Press, 1979.

Zuesse, Evan. *Ritual Cosmos: The Ritual Sanctification of Life in African Religions*. Athens: Ohio University Press, 1979.

Index

About the Authors

NANA AKUA AMPONSAH is a doctoral candidate at the history department at the University of Texas at Austin. Amponsah completed her bachelor's degree in history at the Oklahoma Panhandle State University and her master's degree in history at the Fort Hays State University in Kansas. Her research interest is in the history of African women, gender relations, and reproductive health. She focuses particularly on the changing conceptions of African womanhood and motherhood, and the sociocultural and health dialogues surrounding women and gender in their historical contexts in colonial and postcolonial Ghana. She has published in her research area and is currently working on a coedited volume on *Women, Gender, and Sexualities in Africa*. She has just completed work on a book on the *Role of African Women in History*.

TOYIN FALOLA is a Distinguished Teaching Professor and the Frances Higginbotham Nalle Centennial Professor in History at the University of Texas at Austin. He is the author of numerous books and the series editor of *Culture and Customs of Africa* by Greenwood Press. His memoir, *A Mouth Sweeter Than Salt*, captures his childhood and received various awards. He has an honorary doctorate from Monmouth University in New Jersey.